ENGLISH ESSAY WRITING HANDBOOK

EMMANUEL TATAH MENTAN

authorHOUSE®

AuthorHouse™
1663 Liberty Drive
Bloomington, IN 47403
www.authorhouse.com
Phone: 1 (800) 839-8640

Published by AuthorHouse 01/21/2019

ISBN: 978-1-5462-7578-7 (sc)
ISBN: 978-1-5462-7579-4 (e)

Contents

Acknowledgements

I would like to express my gratitude to the many people who saw me through this book; to all those who provided support, talked things over, read, wrote, offered comments, allowed me to quote their remarks and assisted in the editing, proofreading and design. I am thinking particularly about the numerous authors whose works were of tremendous help to putting together this handbook for readers and writers.

Guidebooks on Style

These books—and many others—show how to use language correctly and appropriately for academic purposes. Find the approach that works for you.

- Matthew Clark. *A Matter of Style*. PE 1421. C595 2002. Teaches style through a close reading of good prose, past and present. Looks at word order, rhythm, metaphor, and more.
- Claire Kehrwald Cook. *Line by Line*. PE1441 C66 1985. How to improve your writing by becoming a more skilful and perceptive editor of your own prose.
- Patricia T. O'Connor. *Woe is I: The Grammarphobe's Guide to Better English in Plain English*, 3rd ed. PE1112 O28 2010. A sensible, jargon-free primer on grammar, punctuation, and usage.
- Ben Yagoda. *When You Catch an Adjective, Kill It*. PE1199 Y34 2006. This enjoyable tour through the nine parts of speech covers the history of the language while offering helpful advice on usage.
- William Zinsser. *On Writing Well: An Informal Guide to Writing Nonfiction*. PE1429 Z5 2006. This lively book discusses good

style in various situations—university, work, journalism. Sit down and browse through it for pleasure.

Books on Specific Subjects

This good collection of books gave advice on the special demands of writing in certain subject areas. Most include good examples of student papers.

- Sylvan Barnet. *A Short Guide to Writing about Art*, 10th ed. N7476 B37 2011
- Timothy Corrigan. *A Short Guide to Writing about Film*, 8th ed. PN1995 C5977 2012
- Roseann Giarrusso et al. *A Guide to Writing Sociology Papers*, 6th ed. HM569 G95 2007
- Andrea A. Gilpin and Patricia Patchet-Golubev. *A Guide to Writing in the Sciences*. T11 G55 2000.
- Richard Marius. *A Short Guide to Writing about History*, 8th ed. D13 M294 2012
- Aloysius Martinich. *Philosophical Writing: An Introduction*, 3rd ed. B52.7 M37 2005
- Margot Northey and Lorne Tepperman. *Making Sense: A Student's Guide to Research and Writing: Social Sciences*, 5th ed. H91 N67 2012
- Jan A. Pechenik. *A Short Guide to Writing about Biology*, 8th ed. QH304 P43 2013
- Edgar V. Roberts. *Writing about Literature*, 13th ed. PE1408 R593 2012
- Christopher Thaiss and James F. Sanford. *Writing for Psychology*. BF76.7 T53 2000

Documentation

These manuals offered authoritative guides on the four main referencing systems used at U of T. Use the one suited to your discipline.

For briefer coverage, see the basic handbooks listed above under **Basic Books**.

- *MLA Handbook for Writers of Research Papers*, 7th ed. PE1478 M57 2009. The *MLA Handbook* explains the formats for acknowledging sources in the humanities, including ways to refer to non-print sources (films, paintings, e-mail, etc.).
- *Publication Manual of the American Psychological Association*, 6th ed. BF76.7 A46 2010. This handbook sets out the parenthetical author-date format most used in the social sciences. Also offers good advice on style in the social sciences, and on using numbers, tables, and illustrations.
- Kate L. Turabian. *A Manual for Writers of Term Papers, Theses, and Dissertations: Chicago Style for Students and Researchers*, 8th ed. LB2369 T8 2013. This manual has long been the most useable guide on the traditional system of providing endnotes or footnotes still preferred in history and a few other disciplines.
- *Scientific Style and Format: The CSE Manual for Authors, Editors, and Publishers*, 7th ed. T11 S386 2006. A thorough manual on scientific writing. Includes guidelines for the three main conventions of scientific referencing: citation-sequence, name-year, and citation-name.

English as a Second Language

These books provide indispensable support for second-language learners seeking to expand their range as speakers and writers.

- *Collins Cobuild English Usage*, 3rd ed. PE1460 C63 2012. This manual includes many practical tips. Look up troublesome phrases or idioms; review the way specific words are used.
- *Longman Dictionary of Contemporary English*. PE1628 L64 2009 [shelved in DICTIONARIES]. This dictionary packs a lot of useful information about each word and illustrates its definitions with well-chosen example sentences. Comes with a DVD-ROM that provides pop-up definitions and reads sentences

aloud to you. Oxford and Collins Cobuild also produce fine advanced learner dictionaries.

- Janet Lane and Ellen Lange. *Writing Clearly: An Editing Guide.* PE1128 L3375 1999. A good self-help guide that will help you master sentence structure and grammar.
- Betty Schrampfer Azar. *Understanding and Using English Grammar,* 3rd ed. PE1128 A97 1999. More elementary yet also more exhaustive than Lane and Lange's Writing Clearly. Lots on verbs and parts of speech. Comes with a two-volume companion workbook that includes answers to exercises.

These books were invaluable to this handbook. To these authors, I owe a huge debt of gratitude.

Preface

Objectives for writing this book on Essay Writing

An essay does more than inform or persuade a reader. The process of writing an essay teaches a student or its writer how to research a topic and organize his or her thoughts into an introduction, a body and a conclusion. Essay writing objectives apply to expository and persuasive essays on a variety of topics.

Thesis Development

Every essay should clearly state a thesis -- the main idea of the essay. A mere overview of a topic that does not take a stand one way or the other is not a thesis. This handbook demonstrates that the main idea of any essay should be obvious to the reader.

Organizational Patterns

The essay should be well organized and should not stray from the main topic. The essay should start by introducing the reader to the main points that the writer will cover in the essay. It should use transitions from general to specific to present the information. The essay should end with a conclusion that sums up the main points and restates the thesis.

Content Details

The writer should provide detailed information about the thesis, supported by reputable, authoritative research references. He should make the writer's strongest points first, including just one main point in each paragraph. He should anticipate and rebut the opponent's arguments against the thesis and discuss plausible alternatives to that thesis.

Style Points

The writer should use a consistent, academic voice. The essay should conform to assigned style guidelines and should be free of misspellings and grammatical errors. The writer should cite all references in proper format, and each reference must support the material for which he'/she cited it.

How to write a better English Literature essay

The major objective of this handbook is to answer the question: How can one write a good English Literature essay? Although to an extent this depends on the particular subject you're writing about, and on the nature of the question your essay is attempting to answer, there are a few general guidelines for how to write a convincing essay – just as there are a few guidelines for writing well in any field. We at *Interesting Literature* call them 'guidelines' because we hesitate to use the word 'rules', which seems too programmatic. And as the writing habits of successful authors demonstrate, there is no *one* way to become a good writer – of essays, novels, poems, or whatever it is you're setting out to write. The French writer Colette liked to begin her writing day by picking the fleas off her cat. Edith Sitwell, by all accounts, liked to lie in an open coffin before she began her day's writing. Friedrich von Schiller kept rotten apples in his desk, claiming he needed the scent of their decay to help him write. (For most student essay – writers, such an aroma is probably allowed to arise in the writing-room more organically, over time.)

We will address our suggestions for successful essay-writing to the average student of English Literature, whether at university or school level. There are many ways to approach the task of essay-writing, and these are just a few pointers for how to write a better English essay – and some of these pointers may also work for other disciplines and subjects, too.

Of course, these guidelines are designed to be of interest to the non-essay-writer too – people who have an interest in the craft of writing in general. If this describes you, we hope you enjoy the list as well. Remember, though, everyone can find writing difficult: as Thomas Mann memorably put it, 'A writer is someone for whom writing is more difficult than it is for other people.' Nora Ephron was briefer: 'I think the hardest thing about writing is writing.' So, the guidelines for successful essay-writing are as follows:

1. Planning is important, but don't spend too long perfecting a structure that might end up changing. This may seem like odd advice to kick off with, but the truth is that different approaches work for different students and essayists. You need to find out which method works best for you. It's not a bad idea, regardless of whether you're a big planner or not, to sketch out perhaps a few points on a sheet of paper before you start, but don't be surprised if you end up moving away from it slightly – or considerably – when you start to write. Often the most extensively planned essays are the most mechanistic and dull in execution, precisely because the writer has drawn up a plan and refused to deviate from it. What *is* a more valuable skill is to be able to sense when your argument may be starting to go off-topic, or your point is getting out of hand, *as you write*. (For help on this, see point 5 below.) We might even say that when it comes to knowing how to write a good English Literature essay, *practising* is more important than planning.

2. Make room for close analysis of the text, or texts. Whilst it's true that some first-class or A-grade essays will be impressive without containing any close reading as such, most of the highest-scoring and most sophisticated essays tend to zoom in on the text and examine its language and imagery closely in the course of the argument. (Close reading of literary texts arises from theology and the analysis of Holy Scripture, but really became a 'thing' in literary criticism in the early twentieth century, when T. S. Eliot, F. R. Leavis, William Empson, and other influential essayists started to subject the poem or novel to close scrutiny.) Close reading has two distinct advantages: it increases the specificity of your argument (so you can't be so easily accused of generalizing a point), and it improves your chances of pointing up something about the text which none of the other essays your marker is reading will have said. For instance, take *In Memoriam* (1850), which is a long Victorian poem by the poet Alfred, Lord Tennyson about his grief following the death of his close friend, Arthur Hallam, in the early 1830s. When answering a question about the representation of religious faith in Tennyson's poem *In Memoriam* (1850), how might you write a particularly brilliant essay about this theme? Anyone can make a general point about the poet's crisis of faith; but to look closely at the language used gives you the chance to show *how* the poet portrays this.

For instance, consider this stanza, which conveys the poet's doubt:
I falter where I firmly trod,
And falling with my weight of cares,
Upon the great world's altar-stairs
That slope thro' darkness up to God.

A solid and perfectly competent essay might cite this stanza in support of the claim that Tennyson is finding it increasingly difficult to have faith in God (following the untimely and senseless death of his friend, Arthur Hallam). But there are several ways of then doing something more with it. For instance, you might get close to the poem's imagery, and show how Tennyson conveys this idea, through the image of the 'altar-stairs' associated with religious worship and the idea of the stairs leading 'thro' darkness' towards God. In other words, Tennyson sees faith as a matter of groping through the darkness, trusting in God without having evidence that he is there. If you like, it's a matter of 'blind faith'. That would be a *good* reading. Now, here's how to make a good English essay on this subject even better: one might look at how the word 'falter' – which encapsulates Tennyson's stumbling faith – disperses into 'falling' and 'altar' in the succeeding lines. The word 'falter', we might say, itself falters or falls apart. That is doing more than just interpreting the words: it's being a highly careful reader of the poetry and showing how attentive to the language of the poetry you can be – all the while answering the question, about how the poem portrays the idea of faith. So, read and then reread the text you're writing about – and be sensitive to such nuances of language and style. The best way to *become* attuned to such nuances is revealed in point 5. We might summarize this point as follows: when it comes to knowing how to write a persuasive English Literature essay, it's one thing to have a broad and overarching argument, but don't be afraid to use the *microscope* as well as the telescope.

3. Provide several pieces of evidence where possible. Many essays have a point to make and make it, tacking on a single piece of evidence from the text (or from beyond the text, e.g. a critical, historical, or biographical source) in the hope that this will be enough to make the point convincing. 'State, quote, explain' is the Holy Trinity of the Paragraph for many. What's wrong with it? For one thing, this approach is too formulaic and basic for many arguments. Is one quotation enough to support a point? It's often a matter of degree, and although one piece of evidence is better than none, two or three pieces will be even more persuasive. After all, in a court of law a single eyewitness account won't be enough to convict the accused of the crime, and even a confession from the accused would carry more weight if it comes supported by other, objective evidence (e.g. DNA, fingerprints, and so on).

Let's go back to the example about Tennyson's faith in his poem *In Memoriam* mentioned above. Perhaps you don't find the end of the poem convincing – when the poet claims to have rediscovered his Christian faith and to have overcome his grief at the loss of his friend. You can find examples from the end of the poem to suggest your reading of the poet's insincerity may have validity, but looking at sources beyond the poem – e.g. a good edition of the text, which will contain biographical and critical information – may help you to find a clinching piece of evidence to support your reading. And, sure enough, Tennyson is reported to have said of *In Memoriam*: 'It's too hopeful, this poem, more than I am myself.' And there we have it: much more convincing than simply positing your reading of the poem with a few ambiguous quotations from the poem itself.

Of course, this rule also works in reverse: if you want to argue, for instance, that T. S. Eliot's *The Waste Land* is overwhelmingly inspired by the poet's unhappy marriage to his first wife, then using a decent biographical source makes sense – but if you didn't show evidence for this idea from the poem itself (see point 2), all you've got is a vague, general link between the poet's life and his work. Show *how* the poet's marriage is reflected in the work, e.g. through men and women's relationships throughout the poem being shown as empty, soulless, and unhappy. In other words, when setting out to write a good English essay about any text, don't be afraid to *pile on* the evidence – though be sensible, a handful of quotations or examples should be more than enough to make your point convincing.

4. Avoid tentative or speculative phrasing. Many essays tend to suffer from the above problem of a lack of evidence, so the point fails to convince. This has a knock-on effect: often the student making the point doesn't sound especially convinced by it either. This leaks out in the telling use of, and reliance on, certain *uncertain* phrases: 'Tennyson might have' or 'perhaps Harper Lee wrote this to portray' or 'it can be argued that'. An English university professor used to write in the margins of an essay which used this last phrase, 'What *can't* be argued?' This is a fair criticism: anything can be argued (badly), but it depends on what evidence you can bring to bear on it (point 3) as to whether it will be a persuasive argument. (Arguing that the plays of Shakespeare were written by a Martian who came down to Earth and ingratiated himself with the world of Elizabethan theatre is a theory that *can* be argued, though few would take it seriously. We wish we could say 'none', but that's a story for another day.)

Many essay-writers, because they're aware that texts are often open-ended and invite multiple interpretations (as almost all great works of literature invariably do), think that writing 'it can be argued' acknowledges the text's rich layering of meaning and is therefore valid. Whilst this is certainly a fact – texts are open-ended and can be read in wildly different ways – the phrase 'it can be argued' is best used sparingly if at all. It should be taken as true that your interpretation is, at bottom, probably unprovable. What would it mean to 'prove' a reading as correct, anyway? Because you found evidence that the author intended the same thing as you've argued of their text? Tennyson wrote in a letter, 'I wrote *In Memoriam* because…'? But the author might have lied about it (e.g. in an attempt to dissuade people from looking too much into their private life), or they might have changed their mind (to go back to the example of *The Waste Land*: T. S. Eliot championed the idea of poetic impersonality in an essay of 1919, but years later he described *The Waste Land* as 'only the relief of a personal and wholly insignificant grouse against life' – hardly impersonal, then). Texts – and their writers – can often be contradictory, or cagey about their meaning. But we as critics have to act responsibly when writing about literary texts in any good English essay or exam answer. We need to argue honestly, and sincerely – and not use what Wikipedia calls 'weasel words' or hedging expressions.

So, if nothing is utterly provable, all that remains is to make the strongest possible case you can with the evidence available. You do this, not only through marshalling the evidence in an effective way, but by writing in a confident voice when making your case. Fundamentally, 'There is evidence to suggest that' says more or less the same thing as 'It can be argued', but it foregrounds the *evidence* rather than the argument, so is preferable as a phrase. This point might be summarized by saying: the best way to write a good English Literature essay is to be honest about the reading you're putting forward, so you can be confident in your interpretation and use clear, bold language. ('Bold' is good, but don't get too cocky, of course...)

5. Read the work of other critics. This might be viewed as the Holy Grail of good essay-writing tips, since it is perhaps the single most effective way to improve your own writing. Even if you're writing an essay as part of school coursework rather than a university degree, and don't need to research other critics for your essay, it's worth finding a good writer of literary criticism and reading their work. Why is this worth doing?

Published criticism has at least one thing in its favor, at least if it's published by an academic press or has appeared in an academic journal, and that is that it's most probably been peer-reviewed, meaning that other academics have read it, closely studied its argument, checked it for errors or inaccuracies, and helped to ensure that it is expressed in a fluent, clear, and effective way. If you're serious about finding out how to write a better English essay, then you need to study how successful writers in the genre do it. And essay-writing is a genre, the same as novel-writing or poetry. But why will reading criticism help you? Because the critics you read can *show* you how to do all of the above: how to present a close reading of a poem, how to advance an argument that is not speculative or tentative yet not over-confident, how to use evidence from the text to make your argument more persuasive. And, the more you read of other critics – a page a night, say, over a few months – the better you'll get. It's like textual osmosis: a little bit of their style will rub off on you, and every writer learns by the examples of other writers. As T. S. Eliot himself said, 'The poem which is absolutely original is absolutely bad.' Don't get precious about your own distinctive writing style and become afraid you'll lose it. You can't *gain* a truly original style before you've looked at other people's and worked out what you like and what you can 'steal' for your own ends.

We say 'steal', but this is not the same as saying that plagiarism is okay, of course. But consider this example. You read an accessible book on Shakespeare's language and the author makes a point about rhymes in Shakespeare. When you're working on your essay on the poetry of Christina Rossetti, you notice a similar use of rhyme, and remember the point made by the Shakespeare critic. This is not plagiarizing a point but applying it independently to another writer. It shows independent interpretive skills and an ability to understand and apply what you have read. This is another of the advantages of reading critics, so this would be our final piece of advice for learning how to write a good English essay: find a critic whose style you like, and study their craft.

If you're looking for suggestions, we can recommend a few favorites: Christopher Ricks, whose *The Force of Poetry* is a tour de force; Jonathan Bate, whose *The Genius of Shakespeare*, although written for a general rather than academic audience, is written by a leading Shakespeare scholar and academic; and Helen Gardner, whose *The Art of T. S. Eliot*, whilst dated (it came out in 1949), is a wonderfully lucid and articulate analysis of Eliot's poetry. James Wood's *How Fiction Works* is also a fine example of lucid prose and how to close-read literary texts. Doubtless readers of *Interesting Literature* will have their own favorites to suggest in the comments, so do check those out, as these are just three personal favorites. What's your favorite work of literary scholarship/criticism? Suggestions please.

Much of all this may strike you as common sense, but even the most commonsensical advice can go out of your mind when you have a piece of coursework to write, or an exam to revise for. We hope these suggestions help to remind you of some of the key tenets of good essay-writing practice – though remember, these aren't so much commandments as recommendations. No one can 'tell' you how to write a good English Literature essay as such. And remember, be interesting – find the things in the poems or plays or novels which really ignite your enthusiasm. As John Mortimer said, 'The only rule I have found to have any validity in writing is not to bore yourself.'

CHAPTER ONE

INTRODUCTION AND SUMMARY

The essay is a commonly assigned form of writing that every student will encounter while in academia. Therefore, it is wise for the student to become capable and comfortable with this type of writing early on in his or her training.

An essay can have many purposes, but the basic structure is the same no matter what. You may be writing an essay to argue for a particular point of view or to explain the steps necessary to complete a task.

Essays can be a rewarding and challenging type of writing and are often assigned either to be done in class, which requires previous planning and practice (and a bit of creativity) on the part of the student, or as homework, which likewise demands a certain amount of preparation. Many poorly crafted essays have been produced on account of a lack of preparation and confidence. However, students can avoid the discomfort often associated with essay writing by understanding some common genres within essay writing.

Before delving into its various genres, let's begin with a basic definition of the essay.

What is an essay?

Though the word *essay* has come to be understood as a type of writing in Modern English, its origins provide us with some useful insights. The word comes into the English language through the French influence on Middle English; tracing it back further, we find that the French form of the word comes from the Latin verb *exigere*, which means "to examine, test, or (literally) to drive out." Through the excavation of this ancient word, we are able to unearth the essence of the academic essay: to encourage students to test or examine their ideas concerning a particular topic.

Essays are shorter pieces of writing that often require the student to hone a number of skills such as close reading, analysis, comparison and contrast, persuasion, conciseness, clarity, and exposition. As is evidenced by this list of attributes, there is much to be gained by the student who strives to succeed at essay writing.

The purpose of an essay is to encourage students to develop ideas and concepts in their writing with the direction of little more than their own thoughts (it may be helpful to view the essay as the converse of a research paper). Therefore, essays are (by nature) concise and require clarity in purpose and direction. This means that there is no room for the student's thoughts to wander or stray from his or her purpose; the writing must be deliberate and interesting.

Teaching Essay Writing

Teaching essay writing is a very common assignment that is requested by teachers or professors. Teaching essays vary in nature and type. When writing, you make a persuasive statement and prove the point in your work. Examples of teaching essays include: child development paper, innovation teaching essay, language teaching essay, love essay, etc.

In order to write a professional composition, you have to conduct a substantial research on the topic, back your statement with samples and/ or calculations or prepare proof by acquiring first-hand information. Sufficiently important for your teaching essay is the attention catcher at the beginning, which can include a quote of a famous person/scholar or a very interesting statement that you will be further covered in your work.

One of the main goals of your teaching essay is the introduction of the reader to a new idea or topic. It has to be constructed in a manner that motivates the person to experiment and agree with your position. Persuasive approach that you use has to be carefully chosen in order to assure that the reader feels the positive change your proposal brings.

Before writing this kind of paper you have to organize the structure of your work, where you will answer basic questions such as what, when, why, etc. This is necessary because the purpose of your teaching essay is the introduction of something new by means of showing the theory and practice of your point. This will make your teaching essay look professional and constructive. Work on teaching essay involves your critical and creative thinking because one of the steps engages your analysis and persuasion.

There are various kinds of teaching essays that you can be asked to write in school or university. Child teaching essay includes covering such aspects as age, techniques and methods of teaching the child something new. Your teaching essay can be based on widely used norms of child development and care. In the innovation paper you will provide instructions on the usage of innovative tool, describe in details its benefits and reasons why this product is better that others. While writing a critical thinking teaching essay, you have to keep in mind and cover all aspects necessary for the improvement of thinking and ways of its implementation.

If you experience difficulties writing your own teaching essay or book reports of any kind, Innovative Writing Assistance Agency will be glad to help. If you order a teaching essay from our company, we will not provide you with the work that is already in the database. Though many companies propose you essay writing service, example writing is a key feature of our company. If you need a new paper that has not been used before, our professional writers will be willing to perform the job for you.

Discover the Basic Principles of an Essay

Topic

It is obvious, that the very first thing your students should think of before writing an essay is its topic. Remember, that an essay is not only about writing skills, but it demonstrates the ability of your students to research as well. So, you task is to teach them to research. That is why try to reject the chosen topics if they are too easy for a student, and you see that it will not take much time to write such a essay.

An essay is not an essay without any research. Explain to your students that it is always better for them to choose a topic they understand well and have an opportunity to make a research on. <u>Good research capability</u> is important for every student to get, that is why do not forget practicing different research tactics with them: tell in details about the methods they can use to find all the information needed, how to use this info wisely, and what are the best ways to distinguish the important facts.

Purpose

Informative and well-styles essays are impossible to write without a purpose. An essay can not be just a piece of writing about general things everybody knows and understands perfectly. So, teach your students that they should not be in a hurry to write their essays at once they've chosen the topic. Make them <u>decide upon the purpose of an essay.</u>

When a student perfectly understands what he writes an essay for, it will be much easier for him to draw the outline and start writing.

Examples

The process of teaching is impossible without examples. For your students to understand what a good piece of writing actually is, just give them some examples of excellent essays. It may be an essay of your former student for example. When they see a sample, your students will have an idea what a good essay should look like.

Use samples to tell students about each element their essays should include. They will perfectly understand what the good introduction is, what an informative body of an essay should look like, and how to make an appropriate conclusion. Moreover, your students will also have an opportunity to see how sentences are built, and what grammar constructions are used in an essay.

Outline

The last thing to do before starting to write an essay is to make its outline. Choose some topic and make a list of points your students would need to mention if they wrote an essay on it. Such a technique will give them a better understanding of what and essay is, and <u>how it should be written</u>.

Make sure that all students perfectly understand the fact they should follow an essay outline, because it will be much easier for them to write this piece of paper. Make it clear to them that every point of the outline should start from a new paragraph. Moreover, the smaller these paragraphs are – the more attractive an essay will look for its readers. It is not very comfortable to read very long paragraphs, as it will be more difficult to get the point in such a way. Eventually, it will be easier for students themselves to compose shorter paragraphs of an essay.

Introduction

Finally, it is time to start writing an essay. And here comes its most important part that is called an introduction. As a rule, students find it very difficult to write this part of their essay, as they do not know how to start a piece of writing in order to attract readers' attention and tell them shortly about what this essay is about.

It is clear, that an essay will not be good without a proper and attractive beginning, so, your task is to explain this moment to your students. Tell them, that no one will continue reading their essays if they do not make it eye-catchy and clear for a potential reader. Moreover, an essay introduction should be intriguing a bit.

Depending on the topic of an essay, students can start it with a story from their personal experience. This is a good way to grab an attention. Discuss this option with your students, listen to their suggestions. Discussions will help them learn the material better.

Conclusion

We have already mentioned the outline of an essay, that will help your students write the body of their essay right. Now it is high time for a conclusion, which is not less important than an introduction by the way. It is a real art to finish your <u>writing</u> in a way your reader would feel good and satisfied with everything he has read.

Tell your students how to conclude their essays appropriately.

Explain, that it is not good to abrupt a piece of writing. And do not forget to mention, that a conclusion of their essay should contain a summary if all points they discussed in the body!

To summarize everything mentioned above, we can say that the importance of essay writing skills should not be underestimated. Such skills will help students express their thoughts clearly and write really good and even professional essays and other kinds of paper work during their further study at colleges or universities. Be sure, they will thank you for teaching such a necessary information to them.

Tatah Mentan, Minnesota,January 11, 2018

CHAPTER TWO

WE LEARN BY DOING

Essay writing is hard work, and you only get better at it by doing it and by learning from your mistakes. Here are some common ones:

- the use of the 's (**apostrophe s**) and s (**possessive or genitive s**): its=of it ('the cat chased **its** tail') it's=it is ('**it's** a hard life'). When in doubt ask yourself whether you are shortening from 'it is' or not. In any case, the shortened form is not good practice in written language ('I should not have done that', would be better than 'I shouldn't have done that'; 'It is a hard life' better than 'It's a hard life').
- the **plural s** can also be a problem: Americans= more than one American, but Americans'= of the Americans ('Americans' image abroad tends to be filtered through the media').
- But, when the word ends in a **vowel,** you do need an apostrophe even in the singular: America's destiny= the destiny of America; Joe's self-perception=the self-perception of Joe; Joe Smith and Joe Brown make two Joes; hence ...the two Joes' self-perception...

When **writing about literature**, the most important rule is to write about it **in the present tense**, because literature, as an art form, has no past, no history. To us, as readers, it is always present. When you write about fiction in the past tense, it sounds naive, as if you assume these people are real.

Punctuation exists to **clarify** your writing and to give it a **rhythm for ease of reading**. It is generally better to aim for relatively short sentences, by being more **straightforward** and keeping it **simple**. There are good books on essay writing in the library.

Structure your essay in a logical way. You can do this with the **conventional order** of introduction-argument-conclusion/summary of argument. The **introduction is of crucial importance, since this is where you state what the central problem/question of your essay is and how you are going to go about answering or exploring it.** Ultimately this is what your essay will be judged by: whether you succeed in doing what you say you are going to do.

- Always make sure your **paragraphs** bear a clear relation to each other, by linking them explicitly. You can do this in several ways: 'having explored the reasons why .....we can now turn our attention to...' or 'Two aspects need to be discussed in this context. The first is.... Secondly...' and so on. This is called **'signposting'**, because phrases such as these guide the reader through your argument. If you find this too boring, then adopt a less explicit mode of signposting: 'We can usefully compare Eliot's use of the tradition [which you have just discussed] with H.D.'s....[your next point]'; or you can say simply 'By contrast, ...' or 'What follows from this is...'

Nothing helps as much in learning to write well as looking at writers whom you admire. In a very concrete sense then, **good writing depends on good reading** (of other people's work, and your own). But here are some tips:

- **Use full sentences**, which means: sentences including an active verb in the main part. 'Thus proving she is right' is not a full sentence, because 'Thus proving' belongs to a statement made in the preceding sentence. 'In doing this, she proves she is right' is a proper sentence, because the main statement here is active: 'she proves.'
- **It is not forbidden to use 'I'** in an academic essay, but neither is it good form to do so constantly. The 'I' should be used when you are stating **your intention, giving an opinion,** or when you want to **pose a question** (preferably not a rhetorical one). Whenever you are conveying knowledge (whether common or specialist) avoid 'I', and write objectively.

- Try and **avoid the passive voice** ('It can thus **be seen** that ...') and use active verbs instead—it makes your writing more lively: 'We can see that...' is more direct. But perhaps you don't need phrases such as these at all; perhaps you only need what you would say after 'it can thus be seen that': '...in Invisible Man Ellison presents a social history of African-Americans.'
- Other things to **avoid** are: **generalizations** of most kinds (be strict with yourself about whether you are conveying information or merely warming up, and whether you really know what you are talking about; **vagueness** (like 'of most kinds', or 'in various ways', which carries no informational content at all, it just suggests that it does) ; **moral judgments** (it is not our job, as scholars, to judge but to understand); and **existential statements** ('We all know that life presents us with challenges, and that they are there to be overcome'—but pronouncing on the meaning of life is not what academic essays are for).
- **Be as precise and specific as you can**; work from what **you** know or find useful in other people's work, and do not feel that somehow everything you say has to be couched in very complicated language. Part of what you learn at University is how to use a professional vocabulary, but don't overdo it: clarity, always, is key.
- Use **gender-neutral language**, whatever material you are dealing with. When you mean 'men' say 'men', when you mean 'men and women' use 'people'; when you mean 'humankind' use that, not 'man' or 'mankind'. Other forms you can use are s/he (instead of 'he' as a universal pronoun), but most people like to avoid this awkwardness altogether and use the plural form: 'they'.

And finally: edit your work before you submit it. A fresh eye (your own after a few days' break or someone else's) can do wonders for your writing, because whilst you are writing your essay or straight after you often cannot see your own mistakes or confusions. This requires a bit of planning, but once you get used to including the editing stage in your essay writing schedule, you will see that your work will really benefit from it.

Other Guides and Style Manuals The most useful guide for beginners is Kate L Turabian, *Manual for Writers of Term Papers, Theses and Dissertations*, 6th ed., rev. (Chicago, 1996); while a somewhat more professionally-directed work is A S Maney & R L Smallwood, *Style Book: Notes for Authors, Editors and Writers of Theses*, 5th ed., rev. (London, 1996). Both these works are available in British paperbacks. In the USA and for American readers, the standard tends to be set by *The Chicago Manual of Style: for Authors, Editors and Copywriters*, 14th ed., rev. (Chicago, 1993). This work too is currently available in the UK. A very good way of learning-by-doing is to choose a scholarly text and use this as a model.

Choosing an Essay Topic: Read the essay question and thoroughly understand it

If you don't have a thorough understanding of what the essay question is asking you to do, you put yourself at risk of going in the wrong direction with your research. So take the question, read it several times and pull out the key things it's asking you to do. The instructions in the question are likely to have some bearing on the nature of your research. If the question says "Compare", for example, this will set you up for a particular kind of research, during which you'll be looking specifically for points of comparison; if the question asks you to "Discuss", your research focus may be more on finding different points of view and formulating your own.

Begin with a brainstorm

Start your research time by brainstorming what you already know. Doing this means that you can be clear about exactly what you're already aware of, and you can identify the gaps in your knowledge so that you don't end up wasting time by reading books that will tell you what you already know. This gives your research more of a direction and allows you to be more specific in your efforts to find out certain things. It's also a gentle way of introducing yourself to the task and putting yourself in the right frame of mind for learning about the topic at hand.

Achieve a basic understanding before delving deeper

If the topic is new to you and your brainstorm has yielded few ideas, you'll need to acquire a basic understanding of the topic before you begin delving deeper into your research. If you don't, and you start by your research by jumping straight in at the deep end, as it were, you'll struggle to grasp the topic. This also means that you may end up being too swayed by a certain source, as you haven't the knowledge to question it properly. You need sufficient background knowledge to be able to take a critical approach to each of the sources you read. So, start from the very beginning. It's ok to use Wikipedia or other online resources to give you an introduction to a topic, though bear in mind that these can't be wholly relied upon. If you've covered the topic in class already, re-read the notes you made so that you can refresh your mind before you start further investigation.

Working through your reading list

If you've been given a reading list to work from, be organised in how you work through each of the items on it. Try to get hold of as many of the books on it as you can before you start, so that you have them all easily to hand, and can refer back to things you've read and compare them with other perspectives. Plan the order in which you're going to work through them and try to allocate a specific amount of time to each of them; this ensures that you allow enough time to do each of them justice and that focus yourself on making the most of your time with each one. It's a good idea to go for the more general resources before honing in on the finer points mentioned in more specialised literature. Think of an upside-down pyramid and how it starts off wide at the top and becomes gradually narrower; this is the sort of framework you should apply to your research.

Ask a librarian

Library computer databases can be confusing things, and can add an extra layer of stress and complexity to your research if you're not used to using them. The librarian is there for a reason, so don't be afraid to go and ask if you're not sure where to find a particular book on your reading list. If you're in need of somewhere to start, they should be able to point you in the direction of the relevant section of the library so that you can also browse for books that may yield useful information.

Use the index

If you haven't been given specific pages to read in the books on your reading list, make use of the index (and/or table of contents) of each book to help you find relevant material. It sounds obvious, but some students don't think to do this and battle their way through heaps of irrelevant chapters before finding something that will be useful for their essay.

Taking notes

As you work through your reading, take notes as you go along rather than hoping you'll remember everything you've read. Don't indiscriminately write down everything – only the bits that will be useful in answering the essay question you've been set. If you write down too much, you risk writing an essay that's full of irrelevant material and getting lower grades as a result. Be concise, and summarize arguments in your own words when you make notes (this helps you learn it better, too, because you actually have to think about how best to summarize it). You may want to make use of small index cards to force you to be brief with what you write about each point or topic. We've covered effective note-taking extensively in another article, which you can read **here**. Note-taking is a major part of the research process, so don't neglect it. Your notes don't just come in useful in the short-term, for completing your essay, but they should also be helpful when it comes to revision time, so try to keep them organized.

Research every side of the argument

Never rely too heavily on one resource without referring to other possible opinions; it's bad academic practice. You need to be able to give a balanced argument in an essay, and that means researching a range of perspectives on whatever problem you're tackling. Keep a note of the different arguments, along with the evidence in support of or against each one, ready to be deployed into an essay structure that works logically through each one. If you see a scholar's name cropping up again and again in what you read, it's worth investigating more about them even if you haven't specifically been told to do so. Context is vital in academia at any level, so influential figures are always worth knowing about.

Keep a dictionary by your side

You could completely misunderstand a point you read if you don't know what one important word in the sentence means. For that reason, it's a good idea to keep a dictionary by your side at all times as you conduct your research. Not only does this help you fully understand what you're reading, but you also learn new words that you might be able to use in your forthcoming essay or **a future one**. Growing your vocabulary is never a waste of time!

Start formulating your own opinion

As you work through reading these different points of view, think carefully about what you've read and note your own response to different opinions. Get into the **habit** of questioning sources and make sure you're not just repeating someone else's opinion without challenging it. Does an opinion make sense? Does it have plenty of evidence to back it up? What are the counter-arguments, and on balance, which sways you more? Demonstrating your own intelligent thinking will set your essay apart from those of your peers, so think about these things as you conduct your research.

Be careful with web-based research

Although, as we've said already, it's fine to use Wikipedia and other online resources to give you a bit of an introduction to a topic you haven't covered before, be very careful when using the internet for researching an essay. Don't take Wikipedia as gospel; don't forget, *anybody* can edit it! We wouldn't advise using the internet as the basis of your essay research – it's simply not academically rigorous enough, and you don't know how out of date a particular resource might be. Even if your Sixth Form teachers may not question where you picked up an idea you've discussed in your essays, it's still not a good habit to get into and you're unlikely to get away with it at a good university. That said, there are still reliable **academic resources** available via the internet; these can be found in dedicated sites that are essentially online libraries, such as JSTOR. These are likely to be a little too advanced if you're still in Sixth Form, but you'll almost certainly come across them once you get to university.

Look out for footnotes

In an academic publication, whether that's a book or a journal article, footnotes are a great place to look for further ideas for publications that might yield useful information. Plenty can be hidden away in footnotes, and if a writer is disparaging or supporting the ideas of another academic, you could look up the text in question so that you can include their opinion too, and whether or not you agree with them, for extra brownie points.

Don't save doing all your own references until last

If you're still in Sixth Form, you might not yet be required to include academic references in your essays, but for the sake of a thorough guide to essay research that will be useful to you in the future, we're going to include this point anyway (it will definitely come in useful when you get to university, so you may as well start thinking about it now!). As you read through various books and find points you think you're going to want to make in your essays, make sure you note down where you found these points as you go along (author's first and last name, the publication title, publisher, publication date and page number). When you get to university you will be expected to identify your sources very precisely, so it's a good habit to get into. Unfortunately, many students forget to do this and then have a difficult time of going back through their essay adding footnotes and trying to remember where they found a particular point. You'll save yourself a great deal of time and effort if you simply note down your academic references as you go along. If you are including footnotes, don't forget to add each publication to a main bibliography, to be included at the end of your essay, at the same time.

Putting in the background work required to write a good essay can seem an arduous task at times, but it's a fundamental step that can't simply be skipped. The more effort you put in at this stage, the better your essay will be and the easier it will be to write. Use the tips in this article and you'll be well on your way to an essay that impresses!

Getting Started

Before we can get our students writing, they need to have something to write about. For some students, this is a huge problem. They may talk all day (often when they shouldn't), but when it comes time to write, they draw blanks. In a desperate attempt to fill in those blanks, we may give them writing prompts. I have done it myself. But I think there are better ways of dealing with students blanking out-what I call "writer's blank"-than simply handing them topics. As my editor mentioned to me in an e-mail, quoting John Dewey, there's a world of difference between "having to say something and having something to say."

The Problem with Prompts

Real writers write for real reasons about things that are important to them. They write because they want to change things, influence people, or express themselves. If we are constantly flooding our students with writing prompts like "Describe a special day/friend/teacher" and "Persuade your administration to take your point of view about gum/homework/vending machines/dress code", we are not teaching them to do what real writers do.

Many of the standardized topics we throw at students aren't bad, but when it is all we give them, they often give up on generating their own topics. Worse yet, they may forget how to come up with their own topics. Worst of all, they may disassociate writing from real-life relevance altogether.

When I ask students to come up with their own topics, I can tell how "far gone" they are by their responses: The student who has not yet been crushed under the weight of standardized-test-like prompts will say, "I can write about my own topic! Great!" The student who is partially crushed by generic prompts will say, "I don't know if I can think of anything!"

The student who has been completely smushed under the weight of Persuade the Principal to Take Your Point of View About Improving Cafeteria Food will say, "Please, please just give me a topic! I can't think of anything! I have nothing to say! Nothing interests me!" When you hear students saying things like this, the situation is critical.

But there is a cure to the ennui of the writing-blanked. It is to start, bit by bit, to have students delve into their own lives and the world around them for topics. This will make them better, more engaged writers, but more importantly, writing has the power to make any of us better, more engaged human

Tapping Into Students' Lives

Many of my students over the years have been writing-blanked. Some years it felt as if most of them were. I've had students tell me that nothing interests them, that they can't remember anything important that has ever happened to them, that they don't have anything that makes them angry. I never seemed to be able to reach some of these students. For whatever reason, they didn't want to tap into their own lives for material, or they simply didn't want to think about their own lives.

But for the most part, I've had success with getting students to realize they have plenty to say. What follows are some of the strategies I have used to get them to this realization.

Why Write?

Too often, I think, we tell students that they need to know how to do things because they will need those skills at some "later" time. You'll need to know this in high school. You'll need to know this for college. And, of course, the ever-popular "You will need to know this because it will be on the test." What about "You need to know this for real life?"

When I survey my students early in the year, most of them say they have received plenty of the "you'll need it for the test" advice, but very little, if any, of the "you'll need it to live your life" advice. I try to remedy this situation.

At the beginning of the school year I usually start with an activity called Why Write? I write at the top of my board, "Why Write?" Students form groups, and I tell them it is each group's job to brainstorm as many real-life reasons to write as they possibly can. Every time I do this activity, I find we have trained them well, for when I ask for examples, many of them first call out, "For the state test!" and "So we can do well in high school." I quickly point out to them that these are academic reasons, not "real- life" purposes. I also point out that our definition of writing is "putting words together to create meaning." This means that typing things without using a pen counts as writing. Signing your name on a check does not

(At this juncture, many students like to point out to me that I do much of my writing for school, so I must not live in the real world. I inform them that not having to live in the real world is one of the many fringe benefits of a career in teaching. They never know whether to take me seriously.)

Once they get the hang of it, though, when we've hit on five or six examples, and hands are reaching in the air for more, I tell them to work in their groups for ten minutes-which often turns out be 20-25 minutes-to come up with more real-life reasons to write. I walk around to encourage them and drop an occasional hint. When time is up, I rotate around the room, one suggestion per group, till we run out of suggestions or time, whichever comes first. Usually we run out of time rather than reasons.

Examples of Real-Life Reasons to Write

résumés
job applications and cover letters
love letters
eulogies
thank-you notes
scripts for videos at work
editorials/letters to the editor
letters of complaint
business letters
flyers and brochures
advertisements
instructions
directions
e-mails
letters (business and friendly)
excuses
insurance narratives
toasts/speeches/tributes

Our lists are never the same, and never complete, but that's not the point. The point is that there are many, many real-life reasons to write that have nothing to do with school. Students keep this list at the front of their language arts notebooks, and we refer to it throughout the year. I tell them to remind me of it if I start talking about The Test too much.

Students need to know that they have plenty of opportunities to write outside the realm of tests. They also need to know that their writing, if it's done well, can affect and influence other people, and possibly even change the world around them. But once we have emphasized how many real-life reasons there are to write, we must once again delve into the question of what to write about.

Most students have special interests, but they often don't think of them as topics for writing. Often, they are also unaware of how the things they are interested in are connected to each other-hence, the idea of an Enthusiasm Map. It is a kind of stream-of consciousness way of brainstorming topics to write about. I model it for students on the board or overhead before I have them do it. They usually dive in with, well, enthusiasm. This is completely nonlinear. Students may follow one category all the way down to a very specific topic, or they may list several categories around their name from the start, and then develop them. Encourage them to look for connections between seemingly dissimilar enthusiasms. On my map, for example, I have connections between Cartooning and Movies,Group Games and Teaching, and "Peanuts" and Theology. The challenge is for them to come up with everything they can possibly think of that interests them, and then to see how their different interests relate.

When students know their enthusiasms, they can write about them all in different ways. They can explain why they like something, describe how to do something, persuade other people to like it, compare something they like to something else they like or hate, or write a narrative about it. They can even defend their enthusiasms when they come under attack. I once wrote a whole op-ed piece about the demise of traditional, hand-drawn animation in favor of computer animation, a phenomenon I heartily protest. I ask my students to update their map periodically since they may be developing new interests. As a class, we delve into this list whenever they need an expository topic. Have students start by writing their name at the center of a blank piece of paper that is turned sideways. Then have them draw lines out to major categories and then subcategories of interests.

Spheres of Interest

List Another way of looking at potential topics is to ask students to think about their spheres of interest and influence. I ask them to imagine themselves at the center of concentric circles: immediately outside themselves are their own personal interests and everyday lives, beyond that circle is the local community and the school they attend. For many younger students, fifth or sixth graders, for instance, that is as far as their sphere of reference extends. Beyond the local community and school, there are state issues (like standardized testing), then national issues (like presidential elections and the issues that come with them), then world issues (climate change, terrorism), and finally universal/metaphysical issues (science topics like black holes and string theory, as well as religious or philosophical questions). As students get older, their spheres of interest should begin to extend outward, not just as writers, but as people. Writing can help students begin to extend those circles outward. I'll put the following list on the board, and ask students to add examples of issues that could be added as potential writing topics

Spheres of interest: Issues that interest me, bug me . . .
Personal: cartoons, football . . .
Home: TV usage, chores, which way the toilet paper should face . . .
School: gum, homework . . .
Local: litter, nowhere to skateboard . . .
State: standardized tests, severe weather . . .
Country: Internet dangers for teens, presidential election, capital punishment . . .
World: climate change, terrorism, war, poverty . . .
Universe/metaphysical: religious issues, philosophical issues, science issues like string
theory, cloning, black holes . . .

One thing we note when working on this list is that some issues can fall into more than one sphere and some (perhaps the best ones to write about) can be both national and personal. If the military and war are national issues, they are also personal issues if you have a sibling deployed overseas. I will sometimes assign an essay to come from a specific "sphere" so that we can discuss how the "size" of the topic influences how you write about that topic. Writing about the school flip-flop policy requires a different kind of thinking than writing a paper about the war on terror.

Ongoing Topics List

As the year progresses, I ask students to begin looking for topics everywhere. At my household (where our children are unfortunate enough to have two English teachers for parents), if we find ourselves complaining about some injustice in society, some ludicrous behavior or attitude that we've observed, some moronic policy we see being enacted by local or national government, we will find ourselves saying, "Sounds like a 'My Word.'" We usually don't actually write a "My Word" due to lack of time, but we frequently find ourselves having opinions and wanting to express them. I try to encourage my students to do the same.

I ask students to set aside a page at the front of their notebooks (the fronts of their notebooks are very crowded) and keep an ongoing list of possible writing topics-this in addition to things that they may already have thought of on their various maps. It sometimes helps to remind them to add to this list on a regular basis, at the start of class every Monday or Friday, for example. Just make it a habit. My ideal is for students to have so many topics to choose from that they won't get to them all and can take some to high school with them. I also keep a list like this myself, and I sometimes share it with them.

Issues Bulletin Board

A class-wide strategy for keeping "big issues" in the forefront of students' minds is to create an issues bulletin board where you tack interesting articles, editorials, and printed Internet stories about various issues. It creates a centralized place for students to go and find provocative things to write about.

Flash Nonfiction

In some ways, you are continually "setting the stage" for student writers. In my classroom I try to duplicate, as closely as possible, the conditions that real writers work under. But even grownup writers spend time honing their craft, reading books about how to improve as writers, and even doing exercises from some of those books. I have read Julia Cameron's The Artist's Way and The Right to Write, both of which give specific journaling exercises, as well as writing books by Peter Elbow and William Zinsser that have suggestions for specific writing activities that are not polished pieces in and of themselves, but may help writers hone the skills they will use on those polished pieces later.

If there is one common thread throughout all of the arts, it is the idea of discipline and practice improving your skills as an artist. Musicians have finger exercises; singers do vocal warms-ups; visual artists have sketchbooks. As a cartoonist, I have a sketch pad where I jot down ideas for strips or series of strips as well as doodles. I assign myself little exercises: try drawing the same character's face with as many different expressions as possible, or try drawing a character doing some new action, or from a different angle. These sketches and initial ideas never make it into the newspaper like my finished comic strips, but they contribute to the quality of those finished strips.

When I teach middle schoolers writing, I try to think about it as I would an art class or a cartooning class-I want polished final works of art, but to get to those, I need to assign smaller sketches to develop various techniques involved in the bigger piece.

I have heard these exercises called many things: Show-me Sentences, Detail Paragraphs, Quick Writes, and just plain Journals. I tend to avoid calling them journals, simply because I think a journal is very personal-a free-form account and reflection on one's own life. These exercises are more focused and teacher-generated. I had thought of calling them "Writing Sketches," but that lacked something-probably alliteration. The name that seems to have stuck in my classroom is Flash Nonfiction. They are quick, focused writing assignments, for use either at the beginning of class or as homework.

Usually, I explain the Flash Nonfiction assignment and give students about five to ten minutes to complete it, depending on the length. When they finish, I ask them to pair up and share with each other. I usually give them something to focus on as they read each other's writing, which helps keep them on task. For example, I may ask them to pick out the best detail, find the most vivid verbs, or make one suggestion for a place that needs more detail. The sharing usually only takes about four minutes. Time permitting, I ask for volunteers to share either some whole exercises, or maybe just one good detail from their papers (which means that more people can share).

Assigning Flash Nonfiction as homework has its advantages as well. You can start class with the pair/share activity, but only students with the homework done get to participate. You can be done with the pair/share and group discussion in anywhere from six to ten minutes and then be on to the rest of the class.

A Different Kind of Practice

If you've been thinking these writing exercises sound like good ways to practice writing to a prompt for the state writing test, you are correct. But there's a difference here: some teachers teach using nothing but state test-style prompts, and all the teaching is geared toward test performance. The purpose of writing exercises I provide throughout this book is first and foremost to hone their real-world writing skills; the test is incidental. If you focus on writing exercises mainly as a way to better test scores rather than to better writers, you defeat both purposes, and neither test scores nor writers themselves are likely to improve.

How to Write an Essay

Step 1: Ask the Right Questions

It is time to start thinking about literature as having meaning outside of the story itself. It is time to interact with a text in a more personal and worldly way. It is time to write an essay that does more than summarize. To get started, answer these questions based on the text you are studying:

1. What theme **subjects** does the text discuss? Note, we›re not talking about *plot* here. We're talking about *themes*. This means things like love, power, revenge, growing up, death, freedom, war, etc. *Make a list.*
2. Which theme subject from #1 do I like, understand, and feel comfortable analyzing with this book? *Pick one or two.*

Step 2: Ask Some More Questions, Brainstorm Answers

I like to tell my students that if they spend the most time in the *planning* stages of writing an essay (thinking, brainstorming, and organizing) then the rough draft will practically write itself. The best brainstorming is, again, sparked by asking and answering the right questions. The following questions, if answered using as much information from the book--and your brain--as possible, will lead you to a great **theme statement** which will be turned in to your essay›s **thesis statement**. Insert the theme subject(s) you chose in step one into the blank and answer these questions using evidence from the plot of the book:

1. What are all the **causes** of [theme subject] in this story?
2. What are all the **effects** of [theme subject] in this story?
3. If you chose two subjects to work with, how do these two subjects interrelate?
4. Based on the ideas generated in questions 1-3, what do you believe the author is trying to teach us, or say generally, about [theme subject] through this book?*
5. Craft ideas in #4 using some key words and narrow down your answer to **one sentence.**

Question #4, above, is the most important question to answer well. If you can narrow down a *universal idea* based on the plot of the book, you have effectively written a **theme statement**. But this is tricky. First, this idea needs to be somewhat broad. It must be applicable beyond the story (as in, a lesson, thought, or truth that applies to life) so it cannot contain direct references to plot details. However, this idea also needs to be specific enough that it isn't something that could be said about absolutely any book on the planet. Finally, it must be proven using examples from the story. Confused?

Example

Let's go back to *Romeo and Juliet* for a second, and see how steps one and two are illustrated in the following example.

Step One:

1. What **subjects** are discussed and dealt with in *Romeo and Juliet*?
   ...love...relationships...fighting...suicide...defiance...family...death... grudges...
2. Which of the above subjects do I want to discuss?
   ...fighting and family...

Step Two:

1. What are the **causes** of fighting in the story?
   ...Capulets and Montagues hate each other from a long time family feud, a grudge that has never been settled
   ...many characters fight over petty insults...
   ...Montagues and Capulets fight out of a long time hatred of one another
2. What are the **effects** of fighting in the story?
   ...decree from the Prince to harshly punish all public fights...
   ...Romeo and Juliet must hide their love for one another and marry in secret...
   ...Tybalt kills Mercutio...Romeo kills Tybalt...Romeo is banished... Juliet fakes her death...Romeo kills Paris then himself...Juliet kills herself when she sees Romeo is dead...
   ...LOTS of people die
3. How are **family** and **fighting** related?

...two families who have a long time grudge against one another fight out of hatred

4. Based on the above ideas, what do you think Shakespeare is trying to say about **fighting** and **family** through this play?
   ...it is a bad thing...lots of people will get hurt or die...
5. Narrow down ideas using more effective vocabulary.
   ...Fighting between families almost always leads to destruction.

That final sentence in #5 is your **theme statement**. With a couple more steps, this theme statement can become a great **thesis statement** and an excellent essay.

CHAPTER THREE

THESIS STATEMENT

What is a Thesis Statement?

A thesis statement is a statement in an essay that the writer plans to support, discuss or prove. Not all of these statements can be empirically proven, but many of them represent an argument. It should also stand out as an indicator of the clear direction in which the writer will take the essay. It should be strongly worded, impossible to miss, and in shorter essays of a few pages, it should show up in the first paragraph or introduction.

Most essays live or die by the strength of their thesis statements and by their ability to keep focused on their thesis. If the writer hasn't clearly indicated the focus or argument, it will often be difficult for him to stay focused on the issue he plans to discuss, argue or explain. Even if the essay is about how to build the perfect peanut butter sandwich, the writer will significantly improve the quality of the essay by letting readers know that this is what the subject is.

To create a good thesis statement, a writer can ask himself a single question: What is the main focus of my essay? Sometimes, when a person must write on a topic that is already assigned, the answer is already provided. If a writing prompt is in the form of a question, the writer can simply restate the question into a statement, then set about creating a body of paragraphs that support that statement.

When the writer concludes the essay, he may want to briefly restate the thesis statement and refer to how he's supported it. It should be clear by the end of the essay that he has stayed focused on the topic, and done all he could to write a clear paper. At the end of the peanut butter sandwich essay, the writer might tell the audience that he has fulfilled his task.

This statement is just as valuable when writing a speech. Most experts will teach that the three key elements of a speech are for the speaker to tell the audience what he is going to tell them, tell them, and then tell them what he told them. A short essay should work much in the same manner. The thesis equals telling the audience, the body is the exploration of the thesis, and the conclusion restates what the writer told the audience. With these ideas in mind, a writer can focus on writing a terrific thesis for each work that will help him clearly organize and present his thoughts for both written and spoken material.

What is the importance of a Thesis Statement?

Starting college can be extremely scary with all of the new concepts being thrown at you. It is a whole new way of living and the work can be very different. Writing is crucial to many college classes. Unlike high school level writing, college level writing can be a bit more thorough. Professors tend to look for key elements in your essays. One of the most essential parts to any essay is the thesis statement. Learning how to form a thesis statement is very important. A thesis statement is an imperative trait to form a strong essay. Normally one or two sentences, a thesis unifies and provides direction for a piece of writing.

There are two main reasons why thesis statements are so important for an essay.

- First, the writer develops a thesis to create a focus on an essay's main idea. It is important for the writer to be able to write the main idea in a few sentences to create a clear idea for the paper. Not only does the thesis guide the reader, but also the writer. The thesis provides direction to help the writer keep their paper organized.
- Second, having a well-crafted thesis statement helps the reader understand the main idea of the essay. The thesis statement sets the reader up for the rest of the essay. Usually at the end of the introduction paragraph, the thesis leads into the body paragraph, which provides evidence and ideas to back up the

thesis. The thesis statement is important because it tells the audience what they will be reading about.

Because thesis statements are essential in any essay, it is important for writers to understand what makes up a solid thesis. As the basis of an essay, a thesis must support three things: audience, purpose, and content. This basically just means answer who, why, and what in your thesis. Who are you writing this thesis for? Be sure to identify the audience to clarify who your paper is for. Why are you writing this thesis? Establish a purpose to ensure that the reader knows the direction of your paper. What will be included in this thesis? Determine the key points of your essay and include them in your thesis.

What is the Importance of Writing an Effective Thesis Statement?

One thing all well-written essays have in common is a clear focus on a central idea. The thesis is the central idea of your essay -- all other ideas support the thesis to form a cohesive unit. The thesis statement provides your essay with the structure it needs to stay focused on the topic and answer your audience's questions.

What are the Qualities of an Effective Thesis Statement?

An effective thesis statement performs several functions at once. It makes an assertion or claim that your audience can agree with or oppose, as well as answers the questions "how," "why" and "so what?" It predicts the content that will follow in the body of the essay, and sometimes even lists the paragraph topics as a kind of road map for the reader. All topic sentences in the body paragraphs should refer back to the thesis statement so that your essay does not lose focus. Ideally, your thesis statement should be as short and specific as possible. A clear, concise, and assertive thesis statement ensures that your reader fully understands your interpretation of the topic.

Why should one write a thesis statement?

Writing in college often takes the form of persuasion—convincing others that you have an interesting, logical point of view on the subject you are studying. Persuasion is a skill you practice regularly in your daily life. You persuade your roommate to clean up, your parents to let you borrow the car, your friend to vote for your favorite candidate or policy. In college, course assignments often ask you to make a persuasive case in writing. You are asked to convince your reader of your point of view. This form of persuasion, often called academic argument, follows a predictable pattern in writing. After a brief introduction of your topic, you state your point of view on the topic directly and often in one sentence. This sentence is the thesis statement, and it serves as a summary of the argument you'll make in the rest of your paper.

A thesis statement is the sentence that states the main idea of a writing assignment and helps control the ideas within the paper. It is not merely a topic. It often reflects an opinion or judgment that a writer has made about a reading or personal experience. For instance: Tocqueville believed that the domestic role most women held in America was the role that gave them the most power, an idea that many would hotly dispute today.

A thesis statement therefore:

- tells the reader how you will interpret the significance of the subject matter under discussion.
- is a road map for the paper; in other words, it tells the reader what to expect from the rest of the paper.
- directly answers the question asked of you. A thesis is an interpretation of a question or subject, not the subject itself. The subject, or topic, of an essay might be World War II or Moby Dick; a thesis must then offer a way to understand the war or the novel.
- makes a claim that others might dispute.
- is usually a single sentence near the beginning of your paper (most often, at the end of the first paragraph) that presents

your argument to the reader. The rest of the paper, the body of the essay, gathers and organizes evidence that will persuade the reader of the logic of your interpretation.

If your assignment asks you to take a position or develop a claim about a subject, you may need to convey that position or claim in a thesis statement near the beginning of your draft. The assignment may not explicitly state that you need a thesis statement because your instructor may assume you will include one. When in doubt, ask your instructor if the assignment requires a thesis statement. When an assignment asks you to analyze, to interpret, to compare and contrast, to demonstrate cause and effect, or to take a stand on an issue, it is likely that you are being asked to develop a thesis and to support it persuasively.

How can one craft a Thesis Statement?

A thesis is the result of a lengthy thinking process. Formulating a thesis is not the first thing you do after reading an essay assignment. Before you develop an argument on any topic, you have to collect and organize evidence, look for possible relationships between known facts (such as surprising contrasts or similarities), and think about the significance of these relationships. Once you do this thinking, you will probably have a "working thesis" that presents a basic or main idea and an argument that you think you can support with evidence. Both the argument and your thesis are likely to need adjustment along the way. Writers use all kinds of techniques to stimulate their thinking and to help them clarify relationships or comprehend the broader significance of a topic and arrive at a thesis statement.

What Makes a Strong Thesis Statement?

- A strong thesis statement gives *direction* to the paper and limits what you need to write about. It also functions to inform your readers of what you will discuss in the body of the paper. All paragraphs of the essay should explain, support, or argue with your thesis.

- A strong thesis statement requires *proof*; it is not merely a statement of fact. You should support your thesis statement with detailed supporting evidence will interest your readers and motivate them to continue reading the paper.
- Sometimes it is useful to mention your supporting points in your thesis. An example of this could be: John Updike's *Trust Me* is a valuable novel for a college syllabus because it allows the reader to become familiar with his writing and provides themes that are easily connected to other works. In the body of your paper, you could write a paragraph or two about each supporting idea. If you write a thesis statement like this it will often help you to keep control of your ideas.

Where Does the Thesis Statement Go?

A good practice is to put the thesis statement at the end of your introduction so you can use it to lead into the body of your paper. This allows you, as the writer, to lead up to the thesis statement instead of diving directly into the topic. If you place the thesis statement at the beginning, your reader may forget or be confused about the main idea by the time he/she reaches the end of the introduction. Remember, a good introduction conceptualizes and anticipates the thesis statement.

Tips for Writing/Drafting Thesis Statements

- *Know the topic.* The topic should be something you know or can learn about. It is difficult to write a thesis statement, let alone a paper, on a topic that you know nothing about. Reflecting on personal experience and/or researching will help you know more information about your topic.
- *Limit your topic.* Based on what you know and the required length of your final paper, limit your topic to a specific area. A

broad scope will generally require a longer paper, while a narrow scope will be sufficiently proven by a shorter paper.

- *Brainstorm.* If you are having trouble beginning your paper or writing your thesis, take a piece of paper and write down everything that comes to mind about your topic. Did you discover any new ideas or connections? Can you separate any of the things you jotted down into categories? Do you notice any themes? Think about using ideas generated during this process to shape your thesis statement and your paper.

How can you know if your Thesis Statement is strong?

If there's time, run it by your instructor or make an appointment at the Writing Center to get some feedback. Even if you do not have time to get advice elsewhere, you can do some thesis evaluation of your own. When reviewing your first draft and its working thesis, ask yourself the following:

- Do I answer the question? Re-reading the question prompt after constructing a working thesis can help you fix an argument that misses the focus of the question.
- Have I taken a position that others might challenge or oppose? If your thesis simply states facts that no one would, or even could, disagree with, it's possible that you are simply providing a summary, rather than making an argument.
- Is my thesis statement specific enough? Thesis statements that are too vague often do not have a strong argument. If your thesis contains words like "good" or "successful," see if you could be more specific: why is something "good"; what specifically makes something "successful"?
- Does my thesis pass the "So what?" test? If a reader's first response is likely to be "So what?" then you need to clarify, to forge a relationship, or to connect to a larger issue.
- Does my essay support my thesis specifically and without wandering? If your thesis and the body of your essay do not seem to go together, one of them has to change. It's okay to

change your working thesis to reflect things you have figured out in the course of writing your paper. Remember, always reassess and revise your writing as necessary.

- Does my thesis pass the "how and why?" test? If a reader's first response is "how?" or "why?" your thesis may be too open-ended and lack guidance for the reader. See what you can add to give the reader a better take on your position right from the beginning.

A strong thesis statement will therefore help you to accomplish the same thing. It gives readers an idea of the most important points of an essay, shows the highlights, and makes them want to read more.

A well-constructed thesis serves as a lighthouse for your readers, offering them a guiding light in the stormy sea of claims and evidence that make up your argumentative essay.

It will also help keep you, the writer, from getting lost in a convoluted and directionless argument.

Most importantly, a good thesis statement makes a statement. After all, it's called a thesis *statement* for a reason!

"This is an interesting statement!" you want your reader to think, "Let's see if this author can convince me."

This blog post will dissect the components of a good thesis statement and will give you 10 thesis statement examples that you can use to inspire your next argumentative essay.

Dissecting the Thesis Statement

Before I give you a blanket list of thesis statement examples, let's run through what makes for a *good* thesis statement. I've distilled it down to four main components.

Anatomy of an Argumentative
Thesis Statement

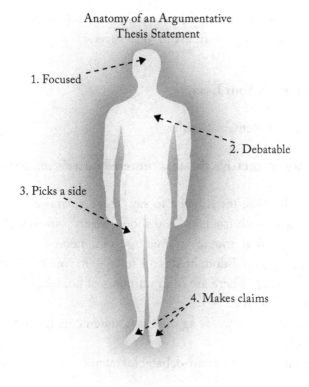

1. Focused

2. Debatable

3. Picks a side

4. Makes claims

1. A good argumentative thesis is focused and not too broad.

It's important to stay focused! Don't try to argue an overly broad topic in your essay, or you're going to feel confused and unsure about your direction and purpose.

✗ Don't write, "Eating fast food is bad and should be avoided."

This statement is too general and would be nearly impossible for you to defend. It leaves a lot of big questions to answer. Is all fast food bad? Why is it bad? Who should avoid it? Why should anyone care?

✔ Do write, "Americans should eliminate the regular consumption of fast food because the fast food diet leads to preventable and expensive health issues, such as diabetes, obesity, and heart disease."

In this example, I've narrowed my argument to the health consequences related to a diet of fast food. I've also chosen to focus on Americans rather than everyone in the universe. (Because, as we all know, inhabitants of the faraway planet Doublepatty 5 require the starches and fats inherent in fast food to survive).

Are you stuck On Your Essay?

Try the Thesis Statement Builder

2. A good argumentative thesis is centered on a *debatable* topic.

Back in the '80s, teens loved to say *"that's debatable"* about claims they didn't agree with (such as "you should clean your room" and "you shouldn't go to that movie"). This age-old, neon-colored, bangle-wearing, peg-legged wisdom holds true today—in your thesis statement.

✘Don't write, "There are high numbers of homeless people living in Berkeley, California."

No one can argue for *or* against this statement. It's not debatable. It's just a fact.

An argument over this non-debatable statement would go something like this:

"There are lots of homeless people in Berkeley."

"Yes, there sure are a bunch of them out there."

"Yup."

As you can see, that's not much of an argument.

✔Do write, "Homeless people in Lagos should be given access to services, such as regular food donations, public restrooms, and camping facilities, because it would improve life for all inhabitants of the city."

Now *that's debatable.*

Opponents could easily argue that homeless people in Lagos already receive adequate services (*"just look at all those luxurious sidewalks!"*), or perhaps that they shouldn't be entitled to services at all (*"get a job, ya lazy loafers!"*).

3. A good argumentative thesis picks a side.

I went into a lot of detail about the importance of picking sides in my post <u>The Secrets of a Strong Argumentative Essay</u>. Picking a side is pretty much the whole point of an argumentative essay.

Just as you can't root for both the Green Eagles of Nigeria and the Black Statrs of Ghana, you can't argue both sides of a topic in your thesis statement.

✗Don't write, "Secondhand smoke is bad and can cause heart disease and cancer; therefore, smoking should be outlawed in public places, but outlawing smoking is unfair to smokers so maybe non-smokers can just hold their breath or wear masks around smokers instead."

A wishy-washy statement like this will make your reader scratch his head in puzzlement. Are you for smoking laws or against them? Eagles or Black Stars? Black Stars or Eagles?

Pick a side, and stick with it!

Then stick up for it.

✔Do write, "Secondhand smoke is just as harmful as smoking and leads to a higher prevalence of cancer and heart disease. What's worse, people who inhale secondhand smoke are doing so without consent. For this reason, smoking in any public place should be banned."

4. A good thesis makes claims that will be supported later in the paper.

As I explained in my blog post <u>How to Create a Powerful Argumentative Essay Outline</u>, Your claims make up a critical part of building the roadmap to your argument.

It's important to first include a summary of your claims in your thesis statement. During the course of your essay, you will back each of your claims with well-researched evidence.

✗Don't write, "Humans should relocate to Mars."

This statement doesn't include any supporting claims. Why should humans move to Mars? What are the benefits of moving to a planet without oxygen or trees?

✔Do write, "It is too late to save earth; therefore, humans should immediately set a date for their relocation to Mars where, with proper planning, they can avoid issues of famine, war, and global warming."

This statement includes some thought-provoking claims. The reader will wonder how the author plans to defend them. (*"Famine, war, and global warming can be easily avoided on Mars? Go on…"*)

Now that you understand the four main components of a good thesis statement, let me give you more thesis statement examples.

10 Examples of Thesis Statements

Stuck On Your Essay?

Try the Thesis Statement Builder

Finally, I've come up with 10 debatable, supportable, and focused thesis statements for you to learn from. Feel free to copy these and customize them for use in your own argumentative essays.

There are a couple of things to be aware of about the following examples:

1. I have not done the research needed to support these claims. So some of the claims may not be useable once you dig into them.
2. Be careful not to use these thesis statements word-for-word; I wouldn't want you to get in trouble if your teacher did a copy/find Google maneuver on you!

#1. Why Vaccinations Should Be Mandatory

Inspired by this sample essay on vaccinations.

Today, nearly 40% of American parents refuse to vaccinate their children due to a variety of unfounded fears. Vaccinations against diseases such as polio, rubella, and mumps, should be mandatory, without exception, for all children of the U.S. who wish to attend school. These vaccinations are critical to the control and eradication of deadly infectious diseases.

#2. Government Surveillance Is Harmful

Inspired by this sample essay on government surveillance.

Government surveillance programs do more harm than good

because they invade civil liberties, lead innocent people to suffer unfair punishments, and ultimately fail to protect the citizens that they are designed to safeguard. For these reasons, programs such as PRISM operated by the NSA should be discontinued.

#3 Financial Compensation for Organ Donors

Inspired by this sample essay on organ donation.

People who sign up for organ donation freely give their hearts and other organs, but this free system limits the number of available donors and makes it difficult for recipients to access lifesaving transplants. Thus, organ donors should be financially compensated to produce more available organs and, at the same time, to decrease profitable, illegal organ harvesting activities in the black market.

#4. Our School Is Too Dependent on Technology

Inspired by this sample essay on technology dependence.

Our school's dependence on technology has caused students to lose the ability to think independently. This dependence has caused a greater prevalence of mood disorders, memory loss, and loneliness. Educators should combat these issues by requiring students to participate in regular technology detoxes.

#5 School Officials' Should Fight Cyberbullying

Inspired by this sample essay on cyberbullying.

Bullying has extended far beyond school and into cyberspace. Even though these acts of aggression take place outside of school boundaries, school officials should have the authority to discipline students who engage in cyberbullying without fear of reprisal. Doing so will help improve the online behavior of students and decrease incidences of cyberbully-related suicide attempts.

#6 The U.S. Media Should Update the Depiction of Traditional Families

Inspired by this sample essay on families.

The U.S. media depicts the traditional family as being comprised of a mother, father, and children; however, this notion of the traditional family is outdated and can be harmful to children who look to this as the gold standard. The U.S. media should, therefore, expand and redefine the definition of the traditional American family to include divorced and remarried parents, extended families living together, and families with same-gender parents. This will increase the overall sense of happiness and well-being among children whose families don't necessarily fit the mold.

#7 Student Loans Should Be Forgiven

Inspired by this <u>sample essay on student loans</u>.

Crippling student debt is stifling the growth of the U.S. economy because it inhibits graduates from being able to spend money on consumer goods and home purchases. To alleviate this, lenders should be required to forgive student loans in cases where students are unable to repay their debts. Doing so would benefit the growth of the economy by increasing tax revenues, unfreezing credit markets, and creating jobs.

#8 Marijuana Should Be Legalized

Inspired by this <u>sample essay on legalizing marijuana</u>.

Marijuana has numerous medical applications, such as treating symptoms of epilepsy, cancer, and glaucoma. Legalizing the use of marijuana in the U.S. will greatly benefit the medical sector by giving physicians access to this lifesaving drug.

#9 Foreign Aid to Africa Does Not Work

Inspired by this <u>sample essay on foreign aid to Africa</u>.

Sending foreign aid to African countries is doing more harm than good, and it should be discontinued; the practice has caused African countries to become vulnerable to inflation, currency fluctuations, corruption, and civil unrest.

#10 China's One-Child Policy Should Be Reversed

Inspired by this <u>sample essay on China's one-child policy</u>.

China's one-child policy was intended to help control population growth. Instead, it has led to unintended and negative consequences, such as a diminishing labor force, an aging population, the neglect of basic human rights, and an unbalanced gender population. To improve China's situation, the policy should be reversed.

Any one of these thesis statement examples will get you started on the road to writing an awesome argumentative essay.

More examples for deeper mastery

Suppose you are taking a course on 19th-century America, and the instructor hands out the following essay assignment: Compare and contrast the reasons why the North and South fought the Civil War. You turn on the computer and type out the following:

The North and South fought the Civil War for many reasons, some of which were the same and some different.

This weak thesis restates the question without providing any additional information. It does not tell the reader where you are heading. A reader of this weak thesis might think "What reasons? How are they the same? How are they different?" Ask yourself these same questions and begin to compare Northern and Southern attitudes (perhaps you first think "The South believed slavery was right, and the North thought slavery was wrong"). Now, push your comparison toward an interpretation—why did one side think slavery was right and the other side think it was wrong? You look again at the evidence, and you decide that you are going to argue that the North believed slavery was immoral while the South believed it upheld the Southern way of life. You write:

While both sides fought the Civil War over the issue of slavery, the North fought for moral reasons while the South fought to preserve its own institutions.

Now you have a working thesis! Included in this working thesis is a reason for the war and some idea of how the two sides disagreed over this reason. As you write the essay, you will probably begin to characterize these differences more precisely, and your working thesis may start to seem too vague. Maybe you decide that both sides fought for moral reasons, and that they just focused on different moral issues. You end up revising the working thesis into a final thesis that really captures the argument in your paper:

While both Northerners and Southerners believed they fought against tyranny and oppression, Northerners focused on the oppression of slaves while Southerners defended their own right to self-government.

Compare this to the original weak thesis. This final thesis presents a way of interpreting evidence that illuminates the significance of the question. *Keep in mind that this is one of many possible interpretations of the Civil War—it is not the one and only right answer to the question.* There isn't one right answer; there are only strong and weak thesis statements and strong and weak uses of evidence.

Let's look at another example. Suppose your literature professor hands out the following assignment in a class on the American novel: Write an analysis of some aspect of Mark Twain's novel Huckleberry Finn. "This will be easy," you think. "I loved Huckleberry Finn!" You grab a pad of paper and write:

Mark Twain's Huckleberry Finn is a great American novel.

Why is this thesis weak? Think about what the reader would expect from the essay that follows: most likely a general, appreciative summary of Twain's novel. But the question did not ask you to summarize; it asked you to analyze. Your professor is probably not interested in your opinion of the novel; instead, she wants you to think about why it's such a great novel—what do Huck's adventures tell us about life, about America, about coming of age, about race, etc.? First, the question asks you to pick an aspect of the novel that you think is important to its structure or meaning—for example, the role of storytelling, the contrasting scenes between the shore and the river, or the relationships between adults and children.

Now you write:

In Huckleberry Finn, Mark Twain develops a contrast between life on the river and life on the shore.

Here's a working thesis with potential: you have highlighted an important aspect of the novel for investigation. However, it's still not clear what your analysis will reveal. Your reader is intrigued but is still thinking, "So what? What's the point of this contrast? What does it signify?" Perhaps you are not sure yet, either. That's fine—begin to work on comparing scenes from the book and see what you discover. Free write, make lists, jot down Huck's actions and reactions. Eventually you will be able to clarify for yourself, and then for the reader, why this contrast matters. After examining the evidence and considering your own insights, you write:

Through its contrasting river and shore scenes, Twain's Huckleberry Finn suggests that to find the true expression of American democratic ideals, one must leave "civilized" society and go back to nature.

This final thesis statement presents an interpretation of a literary work based on an analysis of its content. Of course, for the essay itself to be successful, you must now present evidence from the novel that will convince the reader of your interpretation.

Works consulted

I consulted these works while writing the original version of this handout. This is not a comprehensive list of resources on the handout's topic, and I encourage you to do your own research to find the latest publications on this topic. Please do not use this list as a model for the format of your own reference list, as it may not match the citation style you are using.

Anson, Chris M., and Robert A. Schwegler. The Longman Handbook for Writers and Readers. 6th ed. New York: Longman, 2010.

Ruszkiewicz, John J., et al. The Scott, Foresman Handbook for Writers. 9th ed. New York: Longman, 2010.

Lunsford, Andrea A. The St. Martin's Handbook. 7th ed. Boston: Bedford/St. Martin's, 2011.

Ramage, John D., John C. Bean, and June Johnson. The Allyn & Bacon Guide to Writing. 7th ed. New York: Longman, 2014.

CHAPTER FOUR

NARRATIVE ESSAYS

What is a narrative essay?

A narrative essay is a format in which the author tells, or narrates, a story. They are non-fictional and deal with the author's personal development. Unlike other forms of writing, using the first person is acceptable in narrative essays. Narrative essays are different from short stories, which are fictional; the author is free to change the plot, add characters or rewrite the ending of a short story to better fit a narrative arc. With a narrative essay, the author must pull a cohesive narrative arc from her memory of true events. Narrative essays must include a thesis statement and the essay is used to support this. Short stories do not require a thesis statement.

Narrative essays often overlap with other forms of writing. Non-fiction narrative essays are considered a form of creative non-fiction, a genre that combines the truth-telling aspects of journalism with literary styles found in traditional fiction. Memoirs are similar to narrative essays. An organized collection of non-fiction narrative essays constitutes a memoir, but a single non-fiction narrative essay cannot be considered such. An autobiography is distinct from both a memoir and a narrative essay because it chronicles the events of a person's entire lifetime, rather than focusing on specific experiences.

Narrative Essay: Telling a Story

In a narrative essay, the writer tells a story about a real-life experience. While telling a story may sound easy to do, the narrative essay challenges students to think and write about themselves. When writing a narrative essay, writers should try to involve the reader by making the story as vivid as possible. The fact that narrative essays are usually written in the first person helps engage the reader. "I" sentences give readers a feeling of being part of the story. A well-crafted narrative essay will also build towards drawing a conclusion or making a personal statement.

Tips on Writing a Narrative Essay

In a narrative essay, the writer tells a story about a real-life experience. Everyone enjoys a good story—especially one that captures the imagination. However, the narrative essay goes further. In it, the writer places a personal experience within the context of a larger theme, such as a lesson learned. When writing a narrative essay, the writer wants not only to tell a good story, but also convey why the story has meaning.

The Five-Step Writing Process for Narrative Essays

At Time4Learning, we are great believers in the writing process. The writing process empowers students to write with better results by giving them proven steps to follow. Here, we examine how to write a narrative essay using the five-step writing process. Students should find these suggestions helpful:

1. Prewriting for the Narrative Essay

The prewriting phase in narrative essay writing is particularly important. In the prewriting phase, students think about their life experiences in the context of the assignment's theme, for example 'write about achieving a goal.' When selecting an experience to write about, keep in mind that even a small incident (or goal, in this case) can make a good essay topic if it has significance for the writer. If writers feel an emotional connection to their topic, their narrative essay will be more effective.

Once a topic is chosen, students should spend time sorting through their memories, and recalling details, including the year, season, setting, people, and objects involved. Think about the sequence of events and remember, no detail is too small. Often it's the small details that communicate big ideas. Creating an outline of the story's narrative flow is very helpful.

2. Drafting a Narrative Essay

When creating the initial draft of a narrative essay, follow the outline, but focus on making the story come alive, using the following techniques:

- Personal narrative essays are most naturally written in the first person, and using "I" gives the story an immediacy that engages the reader.
- In telling the story, don't gloss over the details. Readers have no prior knowledge of the story, and many times a skipped detail will skew their understanding.
- Use vivid descriptions and words that illustrate. In narrative writing, the writer's job is to involve the reader, rather than simply inform. Take a look at this sentence: "Losing the game felt like the bottom of my world dropped out." It conveys so much more about the significance of the writer's experience than simply saying, "I was disappointed that we lost the game."
- While narrative essays are non-fiction, elements of fiction should not be ignored. True stories also benefit from the writer's ability to use plot-building techniques.

3. Revising a Narrative Essay

In the revision phase, students review, modify, and reorganize their work with the goal of making it the best it can be. In revising a narrative essay, students should reread their work with these considerations in mind:

- Does the essay unfold in an easy-to-understand progression of events? Do the transitions make sense or confuse the reader?
- Does the essay involve the reader in the experience? Could there be more detail, or is there extraneous detail that distracts the reader's attention?
- Is the word choice descriptive, or merely informative?
- Has the larger message of the essay been conveyed effectively? Has a connection been made between the experience and its meaning to the writer? Will the reader be able to identify with the conclusion made?

In structuring a narrative essay, it's the writer's choice when to reveal the significance of the experience. Some writers make this connection to theme in the opening paragraph. Others like to focus on the experience and reveal its significance at the end. Writers should experiment which way works best for the essay. Clueing in the reader upfront helps their understanding, but saving the revelation to the end can leave the reader with more to think about.

4. Editing a Narrative Essay

At this point in the writing process, writers proofread and correct errors in grammar and mechanics, and edit to improve style and clarity. Having a friend read the essay is a good idea at this point, and allows the writer to see their work from a fresh perspective.

5. Publishing a Narrative Essay

Due to its personal nature, sharing a narrative essay with the rest of the class can be both exciting and a bit scary. Remember, there isn't a writer on earth who isn't sensitive about his or her own work. The important thing is to learn from the experience and use the feedback to make the next essay even better.

Time 4 Writing Teaches Narrative Essay Writing

Some techniques commonly used to this end include sensory descriptions, such as what the author has smelled, heard and saw; morals or messages, such as what the author has learned; and clear, visual language rather than abstract language.

The best narrative essays will draw the reader in with action and sequential events, often around a central theme such as rite of passage, family, conflict, success or failure.

These essays are often written from a first person perspective, with the aim of forging an intimate connection of empathy with the reader.

Examples of Narrative Essays

1. Personal narrative essay on love and relationships

Sometimes I really do impress myself with my ability to be amazed by life. It seems like some things have never happened to me or I am an alien from some other distant planet. "Human beings" surprise me, make me cry, make me laugh and make me happy. One Saturday morning, my "alien being" went out the house in desperate search of deserted paths, beautiful trees, the smell of grass, the sounds of the sleepy city, and something that would make me smile.

Autumn was already in the air and I was thinking about how cruel was the world and how impossible it is to be happy in it. It is not that I was broken hearted. But I thought that my patience has come to its end. I looked at the blue sky and sat on a bench. I was sitting there and thinking about how I want to be another person. Eventually, I realized that my main problem was that I felt that I could not overcome all the "love" obstacles that life made me face. I recalled everything I have read in books about love as well as everything that I have experienced myself. In the books everything seemed to be much smoother and easier. My main thought was "how people can possibly spend their whole life together?" A small rain started and made me feel even more stupid. I was alone in the park, early in the morning, without anyone to be here with me and ready to push away the relationship that was very dear believing that I do not have strength to overcome the obstacles.

The autumn wind made me wake up from my dreams. I took a deep breath and took a look around. Suddenly, I saw two people approaching me. As there was no one else in the park they caught my attention. As they were getting closer I heard them laughing. First, this laugh made me feel irritated as if they had broken my unity with this park and disturbed my thoughts. But all of a sudden I noticed the age of these people – they were old. I could not clearly identify the age. But, the woman looked as old as my grandmother. She had grey hair, blue eyes with a smile in them, and a smile on her face. She seemed so peaceful, she was in harmony with herself. Her sweater matched her eyes and made her look very fresh. And all the time she was looking at HIM.

Jim, I think we should change the park. It's the same every Saturday. You know how much I love being around people. Why don't you ever listen to me? Why do I have to say the same things every time? Isn't it just easy to do what I ask you to?

Sus! Hug me. That was all he said.

He looked at her, smiled, gave her a hug at this very moment. I stopped seeing an old man, but a strong man that knows his wife and how grouchy she can be and nevertheless he loves her! I thought about those many things they have "survived" together, so many hardships that made them cry, about all the problems that they are experiencing right now and the probability of that fact that one of them will outlive the other one. And the one that will outlive will think of their life together was the most beautiful and happy period of life.

They left. And I was sitting on my bench shocked and feeling some new special feelings in my heart. This feeling was hope! This old couple with all the grouching and tons of mistakes behind their backs made me feel that at the end it is happiness that matters. Eventually, all people will get old and die. And what makes the difference is the person you have dedicated your life to. And I made a wish – to wake up one day, being old and to be proud of being together with the person I love, to feel proud of having had enough forces to overcome all the obstacles and fighting for happiness. I looked at the sky again. The cloud seemed to have the shape of infinity. I thought that it was a sign. It was a sign that only such dedication could make life infinitely deep and pure. Finally, I knew what to do and I was so glad I went to that park early Saturday morning. We can survive in this world even if we are aliens as long as we have one more alien to share the life with.

2. Natural Disaster Narrative Essay

After midday the notorious winds would rise, whipping up the snow that still remained at the very top even in the height of summer, blinding unwary travelers, disorientating them, causing them to lose their way. A night spent lost on the open field meant exposure and inevitable death.

Outside a blizzard was raging, as it had been for seven days and seven nights. I was well used to storms but this one was particularly strong. The snow piled higher and higher, gradually rising above my window, above my door. On it went without abating, getting thicker and thicker, heavier and heavier. Suddenly the awful truth dawned on me. I was buried alive.

The memory is indelibly etched on her mind:

1 was plunged into total blackness and cold. I couldn't light my fire because the snow had broken the pipe of my wood stove, which jutted out of the cave, so there was no way of keeping warm or cooking. I didn't dare light candles either because I thought they would use up oxygen. When I looked out of the window it was nothing but a sheet of ice. When I opened the door it was just blackness. It was completely dark.

As the days wore on with no rescue in sight and no relief in the weather, I entombed in her cold, dark cave, faced the very real possibility that I was going to die. With my stove pipe broken, her window and door completely sealed with snow, I was convinced I was going to be asphyxiated.

I really thought I was going to die. I had a lot of time to think about it. It was interesting. I wasn't worried. I figured OK, if I'm going to die, I'm going to die. I was not afraid. I thought it would be fascinating to see what would happen.

I did not get the chance to see what death would be like. As I sat in the cave meditating, preparing to make the transition, I heard her voice once more. It said one word:

'Dig!' I opened the door to the cave, which opened inwards, and using one of the lids from tins began to dig my way out.

I dug up and up, piling the snow back into her cave which made the place even colder and wetter. I dug for an hour or more, not knowing which way I was going, for I was in total darkness and was disorientated, crawling along on my stomach, tunneling my way through the cold blackness to where I hoped the outside and oxygen lay. Suddenly I came out into the open air and was free. The relief was enormous.

To see light and breathe fresh air again was wonderful. However, the blizzard was still raging so I had to crawl back inside the cave again! Once I was there I realized that the air inside was not stale but fresh. I knew then that caves could 'breathe', that snow 'breathes' and I was not going to die.

However, the tunnel that I had made quickly filled up with snow again. All in all I had to dig myself out three times. When the blizzard finally abated, I stood outside almost blinded by the light and looked around. An extraordinary sight met my eyes. Everything, including the trees, was totally buried in snow. It was a featureless white landscape. A helicopter flew overhead, bringing supplies to the devastated area, and someone inside waved.

3. Childhood Memories Essay

It is obvious that all of our childhood memories are not accidental. When you are a child every scent, every sound, every move, every toy, the first day of school, the first kiss, the first step makes a difference. Everything together makes what is the personality of a man. All these are pieces of one whole entity. I was sitting and thinking –which of the memories I have is the brightest and most emotional for me. Is it the day when I stayed home alone for the first time? Is it the day when I was so disappointed with the Christmas gift I got? Or maybe when I broke grandma's favorite vase and put it back together with glue? I was thinking about good memories and bad memories, moments of tears and moments of innocent joy.

From one memory to another my heart started to feel strange and I felt really strange – like I was completely in another dimension which exists only in my head. And then. BANG! I got it so clear that I started shivering. I was about 6 years. My mom's best friend left to another town and asked my mom to stay at her place with me for two days in order to look after her two sons. One was a little older than I was, and the second boy appeared to be super grown-up for he was already fourteen. I always enjoyed staying at their place – a lot of toys, a lot of space, video games – everything a child needs to free the most sincere smile.

I remember the second day we were supposed to have the com-back party for my mom's friend at here place. I woke up. Mom went to work and reminded me to be nice and clean by the time she will come back with the guests. I stayed with Tony, the older of the boys and suddenly somebody called him and though he was not permitted to leave me alone – he left. He said he will not be long. But it took him forever. I realized that I was alone. I could not come out of the house. So I opened the window and thought that I was joking. And I was so desperate, so lonely, so betrayed at that moment. I pulled the curtain so strongly that I fell on the floor. And there I was standing – one little criminal! I was desperate to escape and knowing that I would be punished for destroying the curtain that was not even ours.

But, then something changed. I stopped wining, looked around and realized that I was in a safe place, that mom would come back and kiss me no matter what I had done. This was a moment of pure happiness, not the happiness of getting a new toy, or a dog, or going to the party of my best friend. It was the moment of clarity for me. It was the first time in my life when I realized that I was happy to have my mom and that I was safe. My eyes saw the world in different shades that moment. And by the way, I was not punished for the curtain. I felt asleep on my mom's knees.

4. Fighting Procrastination.

Essay Questions:
Why does procrastination take the best time of the life of any person?
Why do people tend to postpone everything for tomorrow?
What is the most effective way to stop procrastinating?

Thesis Statement:

Procrastination "hides" in almost every aspect of our everyday life and it is so hard to overcome it. I do not think I would be able to realize that I had this problem and cope with it until one situation happened to me.

Procrastination essay
"…Only Robinson Crusoe had everything done by Friday"
Unknown author

Introduction: Procrastination takes the best time of the life of any person. There are always hundreds reasons to wait and to postpone something that seems to be extremely unpleasant to do. Procrastination "hides" in almost every aspect of our everyday life and it is so hard to overcome it. I do not think I would be able to realize that I had this problem and cope with it until one situation happened to me. Procrastination takes the best time of the life of any person. There are always hundreds reasons to wait and to postpone something that seems to be extremely unpleasant to do. Procrastination "hides" in almost every aspect of our everyday life and it is so hard to overcome it. I do not think I would be able to realize that I had this problem and cope with it until one situation happened to me.

So, I woke up in the morning and realized that I did not do it again. It seemed that I was almost ready to do it but once more something else grabbed my attention. It was a trap with no way out. I felt terrible! I felt pain all the time and there was nothing I could do about it except doing IT. I remembered the words of Scarlet O'Hara: "I will think about it tomorrow", and thought that she was not right about that completely. The problem was that I was thinking about it all the time. I brushed my teeth thinking about it, had breakfast thinking about it. I prepared for my classes and was still thinking about it. I thought about it 24/7 and it was getting altogether scary. It got even funny when I thought that the whole thing would have taken only 1/10 of the time I spent thinking about it.

I desperately needed to do something to find a way to cope with it! And again I did nothing. Then I thought: "If I do it I will buy myself the biggest chocolate I will find in the nearest supermarket." I smiled imagining how I bite it and feeling how tasty it is. It seemed to be the best reward for me after all. In my imagination I played over and over again the scene of how I will do it until I understood that the best way to complete something was to begin it. I clenched my fists, collected all my will power against the force of the habit to procrastinate. I put on my favorite clothes, nicely brushed my hair, looked at the mirror and said: "I cannot lose that chocolate."

I laughed trying to imagine how I looked at the moment for other people. Crazy? The whole situation converted into a real adventure for me. I sneaked out of the house as a spy feeling like a have a special task to complete and I cannot fail it. I called it "Operation: chocolate" in my head. I walked to the place like I knew a special secret but could not put it into words. I recalled the two weeks I spent thinking about my problem and with every step my walk became more firm and confident. I almost start running because I was afraid to stop and turn back.

Conclusion: I came up to the door, took a deep breath and came in. Eventually, it was not that hard… to enter the dentist's office and after all to happily run out from it in a hurry to get myself a big chocolate converted something I was afraid of into something that became a real adventure. I have no reasons to procrastinate until I have my imagination working. If I need a reward – I can always invent it. I am not Robinson Crusoe and I do not need Friday to remember a special secret – once I begin nothing can stop me!

5. The Most Significant Person In My Life: The pain of loss…

Now I can say with certainty that I had never understood others suffering from unbearable loss of a dear person. For my part it used to be pity, compassion. When this happened to me, when my dear mother died, I started to understand all those people who lost someone they loved. There are perhaps no proper words to describe this pain, at least none used on this planet. This intolerable pain which tears you apart, which is like a stone on your heart, and which make tears run down your face with each recollection of the dear person who passed away. Time is unlikely to alleviate this hurt, no matter what others claim.

Every morning I still wake up thinking that she is there drinking her tea in the room, watching her favorite programs. Then suddenly the truth comes rushing up to me and I realize that it is just a dream hanging around me still, and a cold despair fall upon me. Despite my apparent tranquility and surface brightness, I feel empty inside. My mother's death was a really sobering experience I've passed through. It was the most devastating loss in my life.

The memory of my mother will follow me wherever I go, and however far tinting my dreams with a gentle scent of rosemary and the shimmering silver of her laugh. My mother had a serene charisma and a soothing aura around her. She was there to show me my first butterfly and my first rain. She was there when I made my first steps. She taught me to smile and laugh.

Moreover, my mother listened to all my fears and apprehensions with a gentle patience which can only be admired. She covered my winters of self-doubt and self-hate with such warm and tender blankets of caring love. Her eyes were so soft, wandering, and full of comprehension when they focused on other people. My mother's greatest desire was only to cherish, protect, and lavish affection and care to her family. When I had really bad times, she washed me with her healing sympathy and distracted me with her brilliant humor. My mother was the only person I could really rely on.

Every time I heard about my friends' conflicts or quarrels with their mothers, I was immensely surprised because I have never had conflicts or quarrels with my mother. I have always had feelings of love, tenderness, kindness toward her. In childhood I wanted to become as strong, calm and wise as my mom was. I couldn't figure out how she tolerated patiently my endless "why's" and "how's". She always had ready answers for all my questions. Now, after eighteen years of life experience I can also answer many questions, but I still can't put my thoughts into words so clearly. In all my actions I was free to make my own decisions. My mother almost never forbid me anything. Now I understand that it was my mother who taught me how to distinguish right from wrong, and she did it unobtrusively and without reprimanding.

No one has ever loved me the way she did. My mother was my sole support system, whenever something exciting happened or there was a crisis in my life, she was the first person I turned to. She understood me better than anyone else I knew. I miss our talks, her support, advices, and care.

When my family and I found out she had cancer, I was really distraught. It was a life changing moment. I tried to do my best to support my mother as soon as I got to know that she was incurably ill. I started doing more around the house (washing dishes, cooking for my mom etc., so that she could rest). Apart from that, I tried to find out as much as possible about breast cancer, still hoping that something could be done to make her healthy again. Till the day she finally passed away I had a hope that everything would turn out to be fine.

This feeling of emptiness and helplessness without the closest person never leaves you. Mother cannot be substituted by anyone, probably like deceased children cannot be substituted by anyone for their parents.

I regard myself a lucky person that I had a chance to tell my mother everything that was on my heart, to tell her how much I loved her. I can only imagine the unbearable pain of people who lose someone dear to them all of a sudden and feel that there are so many things they never said to them. Luckily, I had some time to thank my mother for sharing with me qualities that made her so special for others – the ability to forgive, honesty, devotion, kindness, generosity, cheerfulness, sensitivity, patience, dependability, delicacy. Sometimes a couple of soothing words said by her could cheer me up even in the most unlucky days. My mother's character was the basis on which my own character is built. I thanked her for her loving help and protection, for giving me everything I needed - and even a bit more - to grow up. With gentle hands, with calming words full of wisdom, with a lot of warm and loving hugs she mended my broken toys and broken heart all over again. I thanked her also for giving me enough confidence to face the hardships of this crazy world with a smile.

I remember all those times when I wasn't as nice as I should have been. I remember all those times when I didn't put her feelings before my own. I know that my mother forgave me for my misbehavior but for some reason when she passed away I remembered all the lost moments. Now, when she is no longer with me it leaves a space that no one else can fill because the bond between mother and child can never be broken.

When my mom passed away, just a little past a year ago, my whole life changed, my grades started slipping, I started skipping classes, I dropped all extra-curricular activities (soccer, basketball). As I stayed back another year in high school, I started to become depressed. I felt like there was a missing hole in my life. She was the dearest person in my life. I want to do something to keep the warmth and memory of my mom. It is good that there are photos and video records so that I can hear her voice again and see her smooth smile.

These days I try hard not to think about the past and focus on my future. Although my pain is still as immense as on the day of my mom's death, now I clearly see what I have to do to go on living. I mustn't stay on my own, with all my depressive thoughts. I will have to take up any activity - start yoga, read books, play computer games, do sports. It is also worth using my time and energy for helping other people. Helping others will give a meaning to my life, and I will have less time to plunge into the abyss of despair.

CHAPTER FIVE

DESCRIPTIVE ESSAYS

What is a Descriptive Essay?

A descriptive essay is one that describes something, defines something or paints a picture. There is a thesis but it isn't necessarily argumentative. A cousin of the narrative essay, a descriptive essay paints a picture with words. A writer might describe a person, place, object, or even memory of special significance. However, this type of essay is not description for description's sake. The descriptive essay strives to communicate a deeper meaning through the description. In a descriptive essay, the writer should show, not tell, through the use of colorful words and sensory details. The best descriptive essays appeal to the reader's emotions, with a result that is highly evocative.

Writers use the descriptive essay to create a vivid picture of a person, place, or thing. Unlike a narrative essay, which reveals meaning through a personal story, the purpose of a descriptive essay is to reveal the meaning of a subject through detailed, sensory observation. The descriptive essay employs the power of language and all the human senses to bring a subject to life for the reader.

If readers come away from a descriptive essay with the feeling that they have really met a person, gone to a particular place, or held a certain object, the writer has done a good job. If readers also feel an emotional connection and deep appreciation for the subject's significance, the writer has done a great job.

The Five-Step Writing Process for Descriptive Essays

Professional writers know one thing: Writing takes work. Understanding and following the proven steps of the writing process helps all writers, including students. Here are descriptive essay writing tips for each phase of the writing process:

1. Prewriting for the Descriptive Essay

In the prewriting phase of descriptive essay writing, students should take time to think about who or what they want to describe and why. Do they want to write about a person of significance in their lives, or an object or place that holds meaning? The topic doesn't have to be famous or unusual. The person could be a grandparent, the object, a favorite toy, and the place, a tree house.

Once a topic is chosen, students should spend time thinking about the qualities they want to describe. Brainstorm about all the details associated with the topic. Even when not writing about a place, reflect on the surroundings. Where is the object located? Where does the person live? Consider not just physical characteristics, but also what memories, feelings, and ideas the subject evokes. Memory and emotion play an important role in conveying the subject's significance. Plan the focus of each paragraph and create an outline that puts these details into a logical sequence.

2. Drafting a Descriptive Essay

When creating the initial draft of a descriptive essay, follow the outline, but remember, the goal is to give the reader a rich experience of the subject. Keep in mind, the most important watchword of writing a descriptive essay is **show,** don't tell. One of the best ways to show is to involve all of the senses—not just sight, but also hearing, touch, smell, and taste. Write so the reader will see the sunset, hear the song, smell the flowers, taste the pie, or feel the touch of a hand.

Don't Tell…Show!

Use descriptive and figurative language, as well as concrete images to describe the subject. Similes and metaphors work well. Here are some examples:

<u>Telling</u>

The house was old.

<u>Showing</u>

The house frowned with a wrinkled brow, and inside it creaked with each step, releasing a scent of neglected laundry.

He was smart.

If you had to pick a study buddy, you would pick this guy.

The clock had been in our family for years.

The clock stood by our family, faithfully marking the minutes and hours of our lives.

Enjoy the process of describing the subject—it can be a rewarding experience. A descriptive essay doesn't rely on facts and examples, but on the writer's ability to create a mental picture for the reader.

3. Revising a Descriptive Essay

In the revision phase, students review, modify, and reorganize their work with the goal of making it the best it can be. In revising a descriptive essay, students should reread their work with these considerations in mind:

- Does the essay unfold in a way that helps the reader fully appreciate the subject? Do any paragraphs confuse more than describe?
- Does the word choice and figurative language involve the five senses and convey emotion and meaning?
- Are there enough details to give the reader a complete picture?
- Has a connection been made between the description and its meaning to the writer? Will the reader be able to identify with the conclusion made?

Always keep the reader in mind from opening to concluding paragraph. A descriptive essay must be precise in its detail, yet not get ahead of itself. It's better to go from the general to the specific.

Otherwise, the reader will have trouble building the image in their mind's eye. For example, don't describe a glossy coat of fur before telling the reader the essay is about a dog!

4. Editing a Descriptive Essay

At this point in the writing process, writers proofread and correct errors in grammar and mechanics. It's also the time to improve style and clarity. Watch out for clichés and loading up on adjectives and adverbs. Having a friend read the essay helps writers see trouble spots and edit with a fresh perspective.

5. Publishing a Descriptive Essay

Sharing a descriptive essay with the rest of the class can be both exciting and a bit scary. Remember, there isn't a writer on earth who isn't sensitive about his or her own work. The important thing is to learn from the experience and take whatever feedback is given to make the next essay even better.

Examples of Descriptive Essays

Being created human; opposed to merely animal

It was the seventeenth-century philosophical paradigm that was mainly concentrated on separation of subject and object, as well as mind and body. Consequently, mind was perceived as a certain space to generate representations which differed from worldly objects. To this end, Descartes perceived human mind as a thinking thing, which significantly differed from other substantial things within the world existence. At that, since that time there is a serious philosophical debate over materiality and mentality, which greatly influence our existence. For instance, modern cognitive psychology attempts to reveal the evolution of the modern mind by defending the existence of discrete and objective entity, which is literally a mind. This substance can be therefore observed by us via the consequences of its functioning. (Thomas and Harrison, 2004).

Considering a person as a mental subject, John Locke claimed that consciousness predetermines personal identity (Charles, 2001). In due sense, Locke placed a difference between the so-called 'human hood' and 'personhood' based on consciousness. Thus, Locke stressed on the rationality of thinking predominantly based on consciousness. To this end, Locke emphasizes that reflexive consciousness unifies a person over time and at a time.

To him, to understand personal identity, one should understand that consciousness is more inclusive compared to memory, and is simultaneously essential and indispensable part of thinking. In due context, Locke states that "when we see, hear, smell, taste, feel, meditate, or will any thing, we know that we do so" (as cited in Martin, 2000, p.15). Thus, Locke compares consciousness with reflexive awareness. At that Locke's view of consciousness coincides with Descartes' perception of 'self-reflexive nature of consciousness'.

Further, Locke accounts for personal identity. In his reasoning, he states that every person is able to persist through change of substance. Secondly, a person should be responsible for own thoughts and deeds. At that, the main thing for a person is to remain accountable for the previous thoughts and deeds. Exactly this essential feature, according to Locke, distinguishes a person from a human. At that, persons acquire reflexive consciousness.

Therefore, Locke's main distinction lies between humans and persons due to identity, survival and accountability reasons. At that Locke relates human and personal identity to the resurrection, which is the doctrine of Christianity. In addition, Locke's idea of person corresponds with his perception of 'self'. At that, he states that a person "is thinking intelligent being that has reason and reflection, and can consider it self as it self, the same thinking thing in different times and places" (as cited in Martin, 2000, p.18).

In his Treatise of Human Nature (1739). Section IV, David Hume provides his considerations regarding personal identity. Overall, Hume states that 'self' or 'person' cannot be regarded as a single impression. Conversely, these subjects encompass various impressions and ideas.

David Hume thought that most of human beliefs are not reasonable. At that, clear reasoning ability is overwhelmed by human insights and feelings. At that, Hume stated that reason cannot be accountable for happenings around us. At that, we cannot judge about a person on the basis of reason. Therefore, due to Hume's radical thoughts, he is now known as a sceptical and anti-rationalist philosopher.

Among other philosophers the empirical approach has been most radically defended by David Hume. This has mainly predetermined the Anglo-Saxon philosophy of mind. At that, empiricists deny any independent status to the self. They particularly claim that there is no such thing as a self, neither any referent for the term I. At that, many empiricists tend to reduce the notion of 'self' to a series of perceptions or to some experiential by-product of one's states of mind. Moreover, many of them deny the existence of a self and describe it as linguistic illusion. However, empiricists agree that there is no self apart from, within, or above the person.

Due to these reasons, the empiricist approach has been criticized for its sceptical consequences. If the self is mere fiction, then we are left with a catalogue of more or less typical features of the individual. However, is it possible to isolate features that can serve as absolutely certain criterion for personal identity (Glas, 2006).

Conclusion

The philosophical discussion about personal identity has primarily been concentrated on qualitative identity-on the qualities (features, characteristics) that are necessary and/or sufficient for calling a person a person. These qualities refer to what human beings share. To know what it is to be a person, is an issue that cannot be separated from the question about whom this question is raised. The search for criteria for personhood by analytic philosophers is executed from a third person perspective (i.e., from a perspective that describes persons as objects or as facts in the world); however, personhood is not a quality or feature belonging to a neutral bearer or owner of that quality or feature. In human beings the relationship between owner and feature is itself a defining feature.

A person is a neutral bearer of functions, roles, attitudes, and inclinations. The person relates to these functions and roles in an instrumental way. At that, self-knowledge is gained in a subject-object relationship in which the person occupies the position of subject, and the functions and roles occupy the position of object. Current theorizing, for instance, in cognitive-behavioural theory underscores this instrumental view, which itself is part of a much larger, technical worldview (Glas, 2006).

References

Glas, G. (2006). PERSON, PERSONALITY, SELF, AND IDENTITY: A PHILOSOPHICALLY INFORMED CONCEPTUAL ANALYSIS. Journal of Personality Disorders. New York: Vol. 20, Iss. 2; pg. 126, 13 pgs

Martin, R. (2000). Locke's psychology of personal identity Journal of the History of Philosophy. Baltimore: Vol. 38, Iss. 1; pg. 41, 21 pgs

Thomas, J., Harrison, R. (2004) Archaeology's Place in Modernity/ Archaeology on Trial: Response to Julian Thomas. Modernism/ Modernity. Baltimore: Jan 2004. Vol. 11, Iss. 1; pg. 17, 20 pgs.

2. Pancreatitis diagnosis, treatments, symptoms

What is pancreatitis?

Pancreatitis is accompanied by the inflammation of the pancreas. The pancreas is a large gland. This gland is located behind the stomach and close to the duodenum—the first part of the small intestine. The pancreas is known for secretes digestive juices, or enzymes. These go through into the duodenum. The channel through which the digestive juices actually go is called the pancreatic duct.

Pancreatic enzymes are known for joining with bile. The liquid is produced in the liver. Then the liquid is stored in the gallbladder. The liquid is used for food dejecting. The pancreas is known for releasing the hormones insulin and glucagons. These are released into the bloodstream. The hormones are used to help the body regulate the glucose. The glucose is usually being taken from food and is used for energy production.

As usually, the digestive enzymes are being secreted by the pancreas. These do not become active until they reach the small intestine. In the case, the pancreas is inflamed, the enzymes inside it are known for attacking and damaging the tissues that produce enzymes.

Pancreatitis is divided into two groups: acute and chronic. The form can be characterized as rather serious and usually leads to a number of serious complications. One of these is bleeding, infection, and permanent tissue damage. The whole disorder can be characterized as acute and chronic. There are many signs and symptoms for each of the disease. Each of the diseases has its signs and symptoms. Also, there are a number of lab and other diagnostic tests that are used for diagnosis, interventions and treatments of the disease.

The gallbladder and the ducts are usually used to carry bile and other digestive enzymes. These are carried from the liver, gallbladder, and pancreas to the small intestine are called the biliary system.

What is acute pancreatitis? Acute pancreatitis is inflammation of the pancreas. The inflammation occurs suddenly and usually resolves in a few days with special treatment. Acute pancreatitis can be regarded as a life-threatening illness that is accompanied by severe complications. The disease takes away about 210,000 people in the United States. These are admitted to the hospital with acute pancreatitis. Usually pancreatitis is caused by the presence of gallstones—small, pebble-like substances made of hardened bile. These cause the inflammation in the pancreas. The inflammation is usually happens when the gallstones pass through the common bile duct.

Pancreatitis is often cased by chronic and heavy use of alcohol. This is one of the most widespread reasons of Pancreatitis. As for the acute pancreatitis, this one usually occurs within hours. Sometimes pancreatitis inflames as long as 2 days after consuming alcohol. Other causes of acute pancreatitis can be grouped in the following manner:

1. abdominal trauma
2. medications
3. infections
4. tumors
5. genetic abnormalities of the pancreas

Symptoms

Acute pancreatitis usually have the following symptoms:

1. Gradual or sudden pain in the upper abdomen. This pain sometimes extends through the back. The pain takes different forms. In many cases, the pain may be mild, then the feeling gets worse at the end of the eating.
2. The pain can be categorized as mild at first and worse after eating. But the pain can be described as severe at the beginning. After that it goes into constant and last for several days. It means that a person with acute pancreatitis is usually exposed to such symptoms are bad look and ill feeling.

A person that looks and feels very ill often needs immediate medical attention.

Other symptoms may include:

- a swollen and tender abdomen
- nausea and vomiting
- fever
- a rapid pulse

Severe acute pancreatitis is often associated with dehydration and low blood pressure. As a result of effect of these factors heart, lungs, or kidneys can fail. In case bleeding occurs in the pancreas, shock and even death may follow as the final outcome.

Diagnosis While asking about a person's medical history a person has to conduct a thorough physical examination. Under such circumstances the doctor is posed to order a blood test to assist in the diagnosis. During acute pancreatitis, the blood is reported to contain at least three times the normal amount of amylase and lipase. As for the digestive enzymes, these are often formed in the pancreas. Changes that occur in the body usually occur with such body chemicals as glucose, calcium, magnesium, sodium, potassium, and bicarbonate. The improvement of person's condition leads to the fact that the chemicals that exist in human body return to the normal level. In many cases pancreatitis is often difficult to diagnose because of the deep location of the pancreas. Under such circumstances, the doctors are posed to order a number of the following tests:

Abdominal ultrasound. Sound waves are sent toward the pancreas. These are used for a handheld device such as a technician glides over the abdomen. As for the sound waves, these are reported to bounce off the pancreas, gallbladder, liver, and other organs. The echoes make electrical impulses. These are in charge of creating a picture. The picture is called a sonogram. This is presented on a video monitor. In case the gallstones are causing inflammation, the sound waves are posed to bounce off them, thus showing their real location.

Computerized tomography (CT) scan. The CT scan can be regarded as a noninvasive x ray. This device produces three-dimensional pictures of parts of the body. Under such circumstances, a person has to lie on a table that slides into a donut-shaped machine. The test is posed to show the gallstones as well as the damage that is being caused by the gallstones to the pancreas.

Endoscopic ultrasound (EUS). The first stage is spraying a solution to numb the patient's throat. For this objective the doctor inserts an endoscope. The endoscope has a thin, flexible, lighted tube. This is inserted down the throat, through the stomach, and into the small intestine. The second step is turning on an ultrasound attachment. The scope is helpful in producing the sound waves. These are used to create visual images of the pancreas and bile ducts.

Magnetic resonance cholangiopancreatography (MRCP). MRCP is based on the use of magnetic resonance imaging. As for a noninvasive test, this is often used to produce cross-section images of parts of the body. The effect is the following - after being lightly sedated, the patient has to lie on a cylinder-like tube for the test. The second task is fulfilled by the technician, who injects dye into the patient's veins. This dye helps show the pancreas, gallbladder, and pancreatic and bile ducts.

Treatment Treatment for acute pancreatitis is based on the requirement that a few days' stay in the hospital can help for intravenous (IV) fluids, antibiotics, and medication. This is often used to relieve pain. When placed under such circumstances, a person is not able neither eat nor drink.

In the case of the patient's vomiting, a tube may be placed through the nose and into the stomach. This step is taken in order to remove fluid and air. In the case of complications, acute pancreatitis will last few days.

There are some cases when a person may require nasogastric feeding. In such a case a special liquid given in a long, thin tub. The liquid is inserted through the nose and throat and into the stomach. The whole procedure takes lasts for the period of several weeks. During this time pancreas can heal. Before leaving the hospital, the person is strongly advised to do the following things:

1. not to smoke
2. drink alcoholic beverages
3. eat fatty meals

In some cases, the cause of the pancreatitis can be explained as rather clear. Still, there are cases, when more tests are needed. This is usually happens after the person is discharged and the pancreas is healed.

Bibliography:

Pancreatitis. NIH Publication No. 08–1596. July 2008 http://digestive.niddk.nih.gov/ddiseases/pubs/pancreatitis/

4. Humor in presentations Essay

The significance of humor in general and concrete jokes in particular during presentations.

Essay Questions:

How can humor be the only way to get to the audience? What is the difference between health and unhealthy humor? What jokes are the most appealing for the audience during presentations?

Thesis Statement:

The jokes and humorous stories that are used by the speaker have to relate directly to the topic of his speech, the speaker is not

Humor in presentations Essay

"A little humor goes much farther than you might imagine"
Introduction: Sometimes humor is the only way to deliver a certain point of view to the audience. But one of the main restrictions concerning the usage of humor is its appropriateness. Humor has always to be healthy in the first place. When we talk about presentations it is vital to consider this factor, too. A presentation always means a large number of people and it is very important to point out – different people with different sense of humor. Using humor during presentations can sometimes be a long shot.

The first thing to know is to distinguish healthy and unhealthy humor. Unhealthy humor usually has a victim. If people laugh at this humor it is likely to be a sign of anxiety. It is based on differences. Healthy humor is taken from our ordinary everyday experiences and it is based on the things people have in common, therefore unites them. This factor is of a great importance when dealing with presentations. Another thing is that a good speaker has to "share" humor with the audience and not to "use" it. When "sharing" humor with the audience a speaker has to take in counts what part of the day it is. The "morning" audience can be really tough, because everyone is just getting into the work day and still have a lot of work ahead, "lunch" audience is better, but the best time for "sharing" humor is dinner-time, because people relax after their working-day and are more likely to feel the speaker. A speaker can use short one-liners and simple jokes to waken up the "morning" audience. There certain rules that strongly advised to be followed. The primary rule is not to offend anybody by a joke. For example: a person without a limb may not think a one-armed paper hanger joke is funny. The jokes and humorous stories that are used by the speaker have to relate directly to the topic of his speech, the speaker is not supposed to laugh at his own story or joke, his goal is to make the story or joke clear and to the point. The jokes are not supposed to relate to the audience and the speaker has to speak audibly.

Conclusion: Once a joke is said it may not be repeated once more. So the speaker must not repeat a story or joke that flops and repeat a story or joke that works. The primary topic of the jokes should be the speaker himself. He can kid about his fame, problems, image etc. however, is does not have to belittle himself or sacrifice his reputation for a laugh. When a speaker "shares" through personal stories he will 100% establish rapport with your audience. A speaker has to think over all the particularities of the audience he is appealing to before starting his presentation speech. And he always has to remember tips that always work: personal jokes, one-liners that go well with the speech, statistics presented in a clever way, good choice of vivid words, appropriate body gestures and humor and smiling while "sharing" it.

Bibliography:

1. "Requirements of a Good Toastmaster :The Complete Toastmaster"/ by Herbert V. Prochnow / Stylus Publishing 2003
2. "How To Write and Give A Speech"/ by Joan Detz / Wiley 1988

CHAPTER SIX

EXPOSITORY ESSAYS

What is an expository essay?

An expository essay is an essay which explains something via facts, rather than opinions. So, if you decide to write about the beginning of WWI, you'd simply begin by discussing the tension in Europe, the arms race, the unification of Germany, etc, like a standard essay. But you'd do this without adding your own opinions, just plain information. In other words, an expository essay refers to an essay, which explains or describes a number of things by using facts and not opinions. It has a basic structure just like any other essay and it is does not use first person pronouns.

Expository Essays: Just the Facts

The **expository essay** is an informative piece of writing that presents a balanced analysis of a topic. In an expository essay, the writer explains or defines a topic, using facts, statistics, and examples. Expository writing encompasses a wide range of essay variations, such as the comparison and contrast essay, the cause and effect essay, and the "how to" or process essay. Because expository essays are based on facts and not personal feelings, writers don't reveal their emotions or write in the first person.

An expository essay is meant to describe, explain and inform the reader. The sample expository essay below explains the correlation between the terrorist attacks of 9/11 and gas prices in the USA. While this essay by far exceeds the five paragraph standard, this essay was written to conduct a deep analysis of the situation with gas prices within the USA after the 9/11 attacks. Please note the structure of the essay - despite exceeding the five paragraph format, it still consists of the introduction, body, and conclusion. If you are looking for a top quality, a custom-written expository essay with a proper language and formatting, feel free to visit our order page. Our experienced writers will come up with a tailor-made solution that fully matches your requirements and will help you to master expository writing.

How to write an expository essay?

This type of essay is aimed to explain some subject by presenting a very clear and complete picture of other people's views on this certain situation or event. It may also be in a form of a report. The main idea of any expository essay is to present a certain event or situation in detail to the reader. This essay may also be called a coalition of facts and opinions, which are free from the author's criticism but with a deep analysis of the provided information.

Writing an expository essay outline

In order to create a profession expository essay it is necessary to follow three golden rules:

1. The statements taken from different articles must be clearly stated in the essay and the development of this statement in the essay should not be different from its development in the original article. Therefore no "meaning deformations" will occur, but the main point of the original article will be emphasized.
2. The analyzed event of situation should be review from the position of several sources thus making the expository essay stay focused on the context and very objective.
3. The conclusions in an expository essay should never be a surprise for the reader as they need to be easily traced throughout the essay. The analysis and the conclusions have to be always connected to each other. The reader should never have to guess what the author meant and never have a problem following the essay's reasoning.

Expository essay Structure

A proper structure of an expository essay is a way to make it as effective as possible.

1. A narrow topic is presented
2. A thesis statement must express the main essence of the essay
3. The topic is developed through different opinions
4. The conclusion is made according to the summary of the presented above opinions

Expository essay format

The expository essay format implies some vital specifications:

1. The paragraphs supporting the thesis statement are supposed to have one main topic-line. The rest of the sentences are to be directly related to this topic-line. This makes it easier for the reader to trace the logical movement of the essay.
2. Conclusion is a place of logical end of the essay analysis but not for nay type of new information.
3. The conclusion in an expository essay always restates the thesis sentence and supports the main topic-line of the essay. The ending must be memorable.

What Is the Difference Between Narrative and Expository Essay?

When facing a task of writing a narrative or expository essay, the first thing you should do is understand the difference between these types of papers.

Narrative Essays: Tell a Story

In simple terms, a narrative essay is a story meant to entertain the readers. This writing style is extremely versatile, because it has almost no limitations. Every piece of fiction out there is an example of a narrative essay.

However, this doesn't mean that these stories are purely fictional. If the author tells a story based on personal experience or historical facts, it will still be considered a narrative essay, as long as the work complies with the essential requirements that pertain to this style of writing. They are:

- Switching between points of view of different characters (optional)
- Combination of concrete and abstract language
- No definite chronology of events, flashbacks, etc. (optional)
- Abundance of personal pronouns
- Simple structure common for fiction stories (setting, characters, conflict, plot, resolution)
- When you are writing a narrative essay on some particular subject, the story should be centered on it without deviating to other areas.
- Expository Essays: Inform and Explain

There is no room for fiction and descriptive literary tools in expository essays. These papers are fine examples of informative articles and instructions.

The style of expository essays is concise and simple. All in all, an author should aim to make the essay as clear as possible and edit it in order to remove all information that isn't strictly necessary.

The most common examples of expository essays are:

- Directions, scientific articles and other texts that follow the cause-effect structure.
- Recipes, biographies, history texts that follow some definite chronology.
- Speeches (mostly political) and other types of texts that are based on the pros versus cons structure.
- Some newspaper articles that provide detailed descriptions of events.

- Medical and scientific texts that follow the problem-solution structure.
- Speeches for debates and other events that are based on the position-reason structure.

In general, expository essays can be characterized by lack of descriptive elements and simple structure. They must be based on facts and require extensive research of the subject.

In Conclusion

The core difference between narrative and expository essays is their style. While narrative paper allows the author to be creative and tell a story in a way he or she likes, expository essays follow some strict rules that one must abide. Narrative texts are versatile in structure and style, but they also require some thorough research of the subject.

Examples of Expository Essays

1. Mythology Essay

The word "myth" is closely related to the term "culturology". So, in order to start talking about myths is very important to identify what is culturology. For the majority of the people culturology possesses some degree of uncertainty. Culturology is formed on the bases of the combination of the social and humanitarian knowledge. In other words, culturology is a discipline which tries to understand and explain culture as a phenomenon and trace its development in space and time. Nevertheless, it is impossible to explore culture as a whole entity. It is only possible to study its certain epochs and local manifestations. One of the brightest examples of such manifestations is the myth.

Mythological cognition is different from the scientific knowledge and actually, approaches art in a way that has a figurative character. The primary function of the myth is the satisfaction of the human inquisitiveness by answering the questions "why?", and "where from?". For us the myth which we attribute to the "primitive man" is only a poetic image. We call it a "myth" only in relation to the thoughts of those people who wrote it and of those to whom it was addressed. In the latest poetic products the image is no more but a mean of realization of the value, a mean which breaks into verses. In other words, the integrity collapses each time when it achieves its goal, though its meaning has an allegoric shape.

On the contrary, in a myth, the image and values are various; the allegorical meaning of an image does exist, but is not realized by the subject as the image is entirely transferred to the value. Otherwise: the myth is a verbal expression of such explanation during which the described subjective image gets an objective existence. There are no abstract concepts in a myth. There is nothing in a myth that cannot be presented visually, sensually, plastically.

We use a lot of words that do not carry an image for us: "conscience", "tiredness", "ignorance", "work", "glory" etc. A myth does not life in a word. It is a tale. Any comparison and likening in a myth is stretched really far, inevitably gravitating to a complete identification. The analogy, likening, identification undividedly dominate in a myth. They carry out the same role what in our culture is called the cause –consequence connections. A myth makes a thing axiomatic without demanding the subsequent clearing.

The central characters of any mythology were the Gods. It is a well-known fact, that mythology is definitely polytheistic. The myths aspire not only to sort out but also to form the hierarchy of the gods led by the supreme god. Zeus gets the sky and the superiority over the brothers: the sea one Poseidon and the underground one Hades. Not to mention his children: Apollo, Artemis, Athena, Dionysus etc. Yes, Zeus in the consciousness of the Greeks did win his contenders and was identified with the Supreme deity.

The myth historically was the "filling" of a soul of the "primitive" people and remains the same for modern people due to the fact that it reflects the outlook its "authors". It actually is what we know as theology, philosophy, fiction and science. A man of any primitive society used to mythologize and a modern man creates scientific researches. Therefore our contemporary knowledge is based on the mythological thinking.

Differently, in the beginning it was a question of a myth as of some kind of informative relation, then as of a way of life it presented and eventually of the values which are born by a myth: what is proclaims and what is denies. The myth being a specifically generalized reflection of the reality in the form of sensual representations and the fantastic animated beings, always played a considerable role in religion and religious philosophy.

In the XX century the "political" myth get an extreme value as it leads to the sacralization of the state, of the nation, of the race etc. The brightest example of such myth is the ideology of fascism. This myth managed to contain religious mythology, bourgeois philosophy and demagogically absolutized such real entity as "nation" or "the people".

Some features of mythological thinking can remain in mass consciousness along with elements of philosophical and scientific knowledge resulting in scientific logics. Under some circumstances, the mass consciousness can serve as a base for the distribution of a "social" or "political" myth, but as a whole the mythology as a level of consciousness has historically become outdated.

Various forms of mass consciousness, after a definitive allocation from mythology, still continue to use myth as a "language", expanding and interpreting mythological symbols in a new manner. In particular, the XX century gives demonstrates the turn of the literature to the side of mythology (J. Joyce, T. Mann, Z. Kotto, etc). Reconsideration of various traditional myths takes place along with the creation of new poetic symbols.

It is very hard to underestimate the role of the myth as it teaches people the lessons of life required and used for them in certain situation. It also provides people with a set structure of the cosmic events that are to be accepted. Historically, a whole epoch of the life of humanity, the formation and the blossom of the ancient civilizations was the kingdom of myth created by the imagination of a man. Imagination is a great gift of nature, a priceless quality of people, and their creative energy. It created such masterpieces as the "Iliad", "Ramayana" and the "Aeneis". Through myths people look for the answers to the philosophical questions, they try to unravel the mysteries of the Universe, the man and of the life itself. When the reality does not provide the required answers – the myths comes into play.

A myth is not a fairy-tale. A myth identifies the dream with the reality. The creation of a myth is associated with the absolute knowledge of the "truth" which has to be transferred to other individuals. No one from the contemporaries of Homere could doubt the existence of Zeus because the myth is alive as long as we believe in it!

2. International business and Child Labor

International social responsibility is the approved framework that draws a line between business purposes and moral, ethical and social commitments on a global level. There is a variety of international social responsibility concerns, and child labor is high on the contemporary multinational agenda. For the time being, the number of child laborers exceeds 250 million worldwide. In fact, child labor is defined by the International Labor Organization (2008) as types of work performed by children under 18. For instance, the internationally acclaimed clothing retailers like Nike and Gap conventionally build up their global businesses on contracting factories and suppliers in the developing countries. Therein, local employers apply unethical and illegal practices to the workforce while benefiting the abovementioned global retailers. For a number of times, these organizations were reported as such that are exploiting child labor disregarding set ethical norms and legal regulations. In all cases, the traditional response from the corporate management is limited to the lack of awareness of such unfair instances and injustice applications. This indicates that despite the impacts of pressure groups and advocacy organizations these global brands are unwilling to bear either ethical or legal responsibility for their dishonest employment practices. Fortunately, owing to the enormous efforts of various international pressure groups, the companies like these have recently taken adequate measures to cease unethical applications, particularly those associated with child labor (Gorgemans, n.d).

By placing such enforcements, pressure organizations invaluably contribute to the expansion of civil society based on ethical principles of respect, justice and human right priority. In such a way, various pressure groups, media, and youth rights groups are fighting against dishonest companies and their suppliers to protect children from illegal exploitation. Fact is, it is almost impossible to reveal the truth since suppliers are operating in the areas that are difficult to monitor, which enables the latter to conspire their unethical and illegal practices. Whenever the unethical scandals addressing child labor exploitation are revealed, the corporate managers tend to deny their awareness of such illegal happenings allowed in the contracted factories or suppliers.

Ostensibly, the global problem of child labor is immense and in most instances falls beyond any reasonable ethical or legal control of the responsible authorities. Considering this, it is a common knowledge that legal regulations have always been based on the ethical principles reflecting social morale. Therefore, primarily it is a question of ones ethics and morale to intentionally accept and apply child labor for low pay and in appalling conditions. Nevertheless, in practical terms it seems that many suppliers actually do not mind unethical and illegal exploitation of child labor solely caring about enlarging their profits, expanding consumer markets and winning competitive advantages owing to cheap workforce that consists of ethically and legally unprotected children from Mali, Bangladesh, India, Cambodia, Liberia, Pakistan and many other destinations worldwide. To this end, according to International Labor Organization and the United Nations, the child labor is considered exploitative (UN General Assembly, 1989).

References

Gorgemans, A. n.d., 'Addressing Child Labor: An Industry Approach', [Online] Available at:
http://usinfo.state.gov/journals/ites/0505/ijee/gorgemans.htm
UN General Assembly "Convention on the Rights of the Child", Adopted and opened for signature, ratification and accession by General Assembly resolution 44/25 of 20 November 1989 entry into force 2 September 1990, in accordance with article 49

3. Interracial Dating

Introduction: Two people of different races who originate from the same geographical location can share more than can two people of the same race who originate from different locations. How can that be? When we talk about a personality we can always interpret and even make a prognosis of the values of the person basing on the analysis of the surroundings. No matter what part of a country a person lives in and no matter what nationality he is – he will still be the reflection of the geographical area his lives in and carry the values that are widespread in this area. It is common knowledge that the key factor of the development of personality is socialization and the place of socialization plays a vital part too. Socialization in also very important in interracial dating and of course the geographical location predestines the set of qualities which one will look in a partner along with the stereotypes concerning this or that race.

Geographical location does truly effect how people of different races interact with one another. One of the brightest examples is between the South and the North of the United States of America. A young white woman from the North of the country and a young Afro-American from the South will have a lot of difficulties getting along together, due to the hostility of the South towards white people in general as a race. For instance if two young people come out from the same geographical location which is a multi-cultural area they are less likely to have any kind of problems dating each other. People identify themselves with their environment and two people coming from the same geographical location who are dating each other will have at least the same concept of a relationship, which is set in their area. If an interracial couple has a different geographical location it raises the possibility that each of them lives in a one-race community making it even harder for them to communicate within their communities: they potentially have different interests and feel uneasy coming to visit each other. For example one race community sees a woman as a housekeeper and a mother, while the other views a woman being equal to a man. In one community is normal to greet the neighbors while the other is more isolated. It also creates the difficulty to raise a biracial child in all-white, all-black, all-Asian or all-Hispanic environment. While living in one geographical location makes people closer to each other because their unity is acceptable in the first place as it is a multi-racial community.

Conclusion: A couple from originating from the same geographical location can share much more than the same state codes in their addresses. For instance living in Seattle will not create any difficulties for an interracial couple and Alabama will not greet it, as it demonstrates the "hatred" of the old-south. Basically saying a couple originating from the same geographical location has the same "community anthem": they went to similar school, had the same interests popular in the area, and had the same inter-racial and inter-gender examples. It honestly does make the couple feel more comfortable and gives a lot to share with each other, including the same interracial values.

CHAPTER SEVEN

ARGUMENTATIVE ESSAYS

What is an Argumentative Essay?

An **argumentative essay** is a writing piece meant to persuade someone to think the way you do. Though it's usually organized as an essay, Myrtle's letter to her parents is also a type of argumentative writing. To help Myrtle write her essay, let's take a closer look at the elements and format of an argumentative essay.

In this kind of essay, we not only give information but also present an argument with the PROS (supporting ideas) and CONS (opposing ideas) of an argumentative issue. We should clearly take our stand and write as if we are trying to persuade an opposing audience to adopt new beliefs or behavior. The primary objective is to persuade people to change beliefs that many of them do not want to change. Choosing an argumentative topic is not an easy task. The topic should be such that:

- it should be narrowed down

  ✘ Marijuana should be considered illegal. (Not a good topic because it is too general. In some medical cases, marijuana is prescribed by the doctors and the patients are encouraged to use it in case of suffering from too much pain)

  ✔ Selling and using marijuana in public places should be considered illegal.

- it should contain an argument

  ✘ We should decide whether we want a bicycle or a car. (our stand is not clear: do we support having bicycles or cars?)

  ✔ If we are under the age of 30 and want a healthy life, we should definitely get a bicycle instead of a car.

✘ Are you one of those who thinks cheating is not good for students? (a question cannot be an argument)

✔ Cheating helps students learn.

✘ Considering its geological position, Turkey has an important geopolitical role in the EU. (facts cannot be arguments)

✔ Considering its geopolitical role, we can clearly say that the EU cannot be without Turkey.

- it should be a topic that can be adequately supported (with statistics, outside source citations, etc.)

  ✘ I feel that writing an argumentative essay is definitely a challenging task. (feelings cannot be supported; we cannot persuade other people)

If you believe that you can find enough evidence to support your idea and refute others effectively, you can choose challenging topics as well. You can enjoy writing about such topics:

Cheating is beneficial for students.
Murat 124 is a very good choice for conscientious drivers.
Stress is good for the human body.
Polygamy is quite natural.
For women, there is no need for men.

Organization: All argumentative topics have PROs and CONs. Before starting writing, it is imperative to make a list of these ideas and choose the most suitable ones among them for supporting and refuting.

There are three possible organization patterns:

Pattern 1:

Thesis statement:

PRO idea 1
PRO idea 2

CON(s) + Refutation(s)

Conclusion

Pattern 2:

Thesis statement:

CON(s) + Refutation(s)
PRO idea 1
PRO idea 2

Conclusion

Pattern 3:

Thesis statement:

CON idea 1   ----->   Refutation
CON idea 2   ----->   Refutation
CON idea 3   ----->   Refutation

Conclusion

The sample essay has been written according to the third pattern.

Thesis: Do Reiki instead of taking medicine.

Counter arguments		Refutation
1. People should trust medicine since it is effective and scientifically proven.	----->	Reiki is also scientifically proven and does not have side effects. (refutation method: insufficient claim)
2. Serious illnesses such as HIV/AIDS and cancer cannot be treated without medicine.	----->	Medicine also cannot treat serious illnesses if not diagnosed at an early stage. (refutation method: opponents are partially correct)
3. Reiki, like alternative healing methods, requires a lot of time.	----->	Reiki requires less time if done regularly. (refutation method: opponents are completely wrong)

Supporting our ideas: This is the most important part when persuading others. We are asking some people to change their beliefs or actions. We should be supporting our ideas with such facts, statistics and/or authorities that there should not be room for any doubts. Here are some *faulty* supports we should avoid:

Thesis: Leaving the university and starting to work is good for the adolescent because ...

- Feelings, emotional arguments (... it makes one feel much better.)
- Irrelevant examples (wandering off the topic) (... he would then be able to take his girlfriend to expensive restaurants.)
- Oversimplification (... only then would he understand what it means to be an adult.)
- Hasty generalizations (... it is a widely known fact that all adolescents look forward to earning money.)

- Unreliable, even false outside sources (… according to www. doubtme.com, 80% of working men wish they quit school when they were at university and started working at an earlier age.)

Refuting opposing arguments: Before we start saying that the opponents are wrong, we should *specify* their opposing ideas. Otherwise, it would be like hitting the other person with eyes closed. We should see clearly what we are hitting and be prepared beforehand so that he cannot hit us back. We can do this by knowing what we are refuting.

> e.g. ✘ Some people may say that adolescents should not leave university education; however, they are wrong. (what they say is not wrong. Maybe their supporting idea is wrong /irrelevant /insufficient. We should state their supporting idea specifically to be able to refute it.)

> ✔ Some people may say that adolescents should not leave university education because they are not physically and psychologically mature enough to cope with the problems of the real world. However, they forget one fact: adolescents can vote or start driving at the age of 18 (in some countries even before that age!), which proves that they are considered physically and psychologically mature at that age.

Language: Signposts gain importance in the argumentative essay. They enable the readers to follow our arguments easily.

When pointing out opposing arguments (CONs):
Opponents of this idea claim / maintain that …
Those who disagree / are against these ideas may say / assert that …
Some people may disagree with this idea.

When stating specifically why they think like that:
The put forward this idea because …
They claim that … since …

Reaching the turning point:

However,

but

On the other hand,

When refuting the opposing idea, we may use the following strategies:

- *compromise* but prove that their argument is not powerful enough:
  They have a point in thinking like that.
  To a certain extent they are right.

- completely *disagree*:
  After seeing this evidence, there is no way we can agree with what they say.

- say that their argument is *irrelevant* to the topic:
  What we are discussing here is not what they are trying to prove.
  Their argument is irrelevant.

While some teachers consider persuasive papers and argument papers to be basically the same thing, it's usually safe to assume that an argument paper presents a stronger claim—possibly to a more resistant audience. For example: while a persuasive paper might claim that cities need to adopt recycling programs, an argument paper on the same topic might be addressed to a particular town. The argument paper would go further, suggesting specific ways that a recycling program should be adopted and utilized in that particular area.

To write an argument essay, you'll need to gather evidence and present a well-reasoned argument on a debatable issue.

How can I tell if my topic is debatable? Check your thesis! You cannot argue a statement of fact, you must base your paper on a strong position. Ask yourself...

- How many people could argue against my position? What would they say?
- Can it be addressed with a yes or no? (aim for a topic that requires more info.)
- Can I base my argument on scholarly evidence, or am I relying on religion, cultural standards, or morality? (you MUST be able to do quality research!)
- Have I made my argument specific enough?

Worried about taking a firm stance on an issue?

Though there are plenty of times in your life when it's best to adopt a balanced perspective and try to understand both sides of a debate, this isn't one of them.

You MUST choose one side or the other when you write an argument paper!

Don't be afraid to tell others exactly how you think things should go because that's what we expect from an argument paper. You're in charge now, what do YOU think?

Do...	Don't...
...use passionate language	...use weak qualifiers like "I believe," "I feel," or "I think"—just tell us!
...cite experts who agree with you	...claim to be an expert if you're not one
...provide facts, evidence, and statistics to support your position	...use strictly moral or religious claims as support for your argument
...provide reasons to support your claim	...assume the audience will agree with you about any aspect of your argument
...address the opposing side's argument and refute their claims	...attempt to make others look bad (i.e. Mr. Smith is ignorant—don't listen to him!)

Why do I need to address the opposing side's argument?

There is an old kung-fu saying which states, "The hand that strikes also blocks", meaning that when you argue it is to your advantage to anticipate your opposition and strike down their arguments within the body of your own paper. This sentiment is echoed in the popular saying, "The best defense is a good offense".

By addressing the opposition you achieve the following goals:

- illustrate a well-rounded understanding of the topic
- demonstrate a lack of bias
- enhance the level of trust that the reader has for both you and your opinion
- give yourself the opportunity to refute any arguments the opposition may have
- strengthen your argument by diminishing your opposition's argument

Think about yourself as a child, asking your parents for permission to do something that they would normally say no to. You were far more likely to get them to say yes if you anticipated and addressed all of their concerns before they expressed them. You did not want to belittle those concerns, or make them feel dumb, because this only put them on the defensive, and lead to a conclusion that went against your wishes. The same is true in your writing.

How do I accomplish this?

To address the other side of the argument you plan to make, you'll need to "put yourself in their shoes." In other words, you need to try to understand where they're coming from. If you're having trouble accomplishing this task, try following these steps:

1. Jot down several good reasons why you support that particular side of the argument.

2. Look at the reasons you provided and try to argue with yourself. Ask: Why would someone disagree with each of these points? What would his/her response be? (Sometimes it's helpful to imagine that you're having a verbal argument with someone who disagrees with you.)

3. Think carefully about your audience; try to understand their background, their strongest influences, and the way that their minds work. Ask: What parts of this issue will concern my opposing audience the most?

4. Find the necessary facts, evidence, quotes from experts, etc. to refute the points that your opposition might make.

5. Carefully organize your paper so that it moves smoothly from defending your own points to sections where you argue against the opposition.

A Quick Note before You Begin

Argumentative essays are also commonly known as persuasive essays. However, there are some differences between the two even if they're commonly considered to be the same.

Persuasive essays are short, around five to six paragraphs. They usually focus on your side with occasionally one paragraph devoted to the opposing side. Persuasive essays focus more on the emotions of the reader.

Argumentative essays are usually longer in length, ranging from as little as five paragraphs to as many as necessary. While the focus is mainly on your side, there is also a discussion regarding the opposing side that goes far beyond a single sentence or a paragraph. Argumentative essays focus more on the facts to persuade the reader as opposed to calling to their emotions on a topic or issue.

Before You Write

It's important that you plan your essay out before you write, and that includes several different aspects. You're going to want to pick a topic first, but your topic should be something that has two conflicting points or different conclusions. Only consider topics that interest you – it will make your writing that much easier. Try this list of 100 topics to help you find a topic.

Keep in mind that an argumentative essay is based more on facts as opposed to emotion. When picking a topic you're interested in, be sure to pick one that you can support with evidence and reasoning. Look through the list of topics carefully, and begin making a mental list of the evidence you can use on topics you like.

Once you find an interesting topic, don't just research your side – if you already know it. Do some reading on both sides of the argument, and list the points for both sides. It will come in handy later when you go to write, and this way you'll know that the side you pick is based on the facts instead of just your emotions.

As an example, consider the topic from the above link regarding traditional versus alternative medicine. The AHHA has an excellent page that lists the different points of holistic (alternative) medicine compared to conventional (traditional) medicine. Using a page like this, you can easily find the main points of both sides and consider the side you would take. Afterward, you would do more thorough research on each topic to find evidence to support each point. Write quality paragraphs and essays with this online course.

As You Write

Like all essays, the argumentative essay has three important parts – the introduction, the body, and the conclusion. Each area is described in further detail below. Keep in mind that the length of your essay depends on the assignment given to you. Write better essays with an online class.

- The Introduction

The first paragraph should introduce the topic and give your thesis statement. Your thesis will be the position you're going to be taking on whatever topic you chose. Read this example essay entitled *School Choice: An Unwise Option*, and see if you can find the topic and thesis in the very first paragraph. Your introductory paragraph should be clear and concise just like the example.

• The Body

The next few paragraphs will make up the bulk of your essay. This particular area can include as little as three paragraphs to as many as necessary to complete your assignment requirements. Within the body, you will detail both sides of the argument. Use one paragraph for each point, including the strongest points of the opposing side.

Because the idea of this essay is to argue for your position, be sure to spend more time on your side than on the opposing side. Introduce the opposing side first, and present the strongest points along with any evidence used to support them. Depending on your topic and assignment length, this could take anywhere from one to three paragraphs.

Once you've detailed the opposing side, introduce your position. Again, you should use one paragraph per point, and include all evidence to support your position. You can even include examples of how your evidence refutes the evidence of the opposing side. This particular portion of your essay should be longer than the opposing side.

• The Conclusion

This final paragraph should restate your position. Emphasize that your position is the best by summarizing the main points of your argument. Include the best evidence. Most conclusions are only a paragraph in length as the conclusion is expected to be a summary of the entire essay.

Read this example essay entitled *School Choice: An Educational Fit*, and decide if the conclusion is a good summary for the essay. This is the opposite position from the above example essay.

After You Write

At this point, you may very well be thinking that you're done with your essay, but you're not. The most important part of an argumentative essay is the revision and editing. Without it, your essay could have large holes in the logic, or it could have grammatical issues that make it difficult for your readers to read. Consider a course in proofreading to help you revise and edit your essay.

- Editing and Revising Tools

If you need extra help with editing and revising, there are a couple of free tools available online. Try EditMinion and ProWritingAid to help you. If you're typing up your draft on a computer, most word processors come with some basic built-in editing tools.

- Practice Your Editing and Revising

If you're concerned your skills aren't up to snuff for your own essay, consider editing a couple of example essays first. Read through one of the example essays on this page, and see if you can spot any editing and revising errors. You can also try using the above editing and revising tools to test them out before inputting your own essay.

The Final Check

Before you turn in your assignment, you'll want to look over it one last time. Read through the list below. These are common items that are missed during the first and second reading, and they're usually not caught by editing and revising tools either.

- Emotional Language Should Be Avoided

This is an argumentative essay, not a persuasive essay. You are not attempting to draw people to your side with emotions. The idea behind an argumentative essay is to draw people to your position by detailing the important points of both sides and giving the evidence to support your claim. Let the evidence you provide speak for itself.

- NEVER Make Up Evidence

Your facts should be truthful. If someone were to ever check your evidence, it would only harm your argument if you made something up. Technology makes it easy to find facts on anything, and use that to your advantage when collecting your evidence. Don't make up evidence supporting your side, and don't make up evidence that makes the other side look bad.

- Always Cite Sources

If you're quoting from a book, cite it. Did you paraphrase something from a magazine article? Cite it. Include a reference page or works cited page. Citing your sources will depend on whether you're writing in MLA or APA format. Check with your instructor if you're uncertain which you're writing in.

- Use an Outline for Help

Before you write your essay, you should consider writing an outline. This can include the thesis statement you come up with, a short summary of your topic, and the main points you plan to cover for both the opposing side and the side you support. This outline can be very helpful when it comes to writing your conclusion too.

- Know Your Stuff

Your argument is useless if you don't actually know what you're talking about. Know as much as you can about your side, but know just as much if not more about the opposing side too. This will come in handy if your argument ends up challenged by the instructor or a fellow student.

Structure of the Argumentative Essay Outline

If you distill your argumentative essay outline down to its basics, you'll find that it's made of four main sections:

1. Intro
2. Developing Your Argument
3. Refuting Opponents' Arguments
4. Conclusion

That's not so bad! There's really nothing to be afraid of.

Here's how your argumentative essay outline would look if you turned it into a pretty picture:

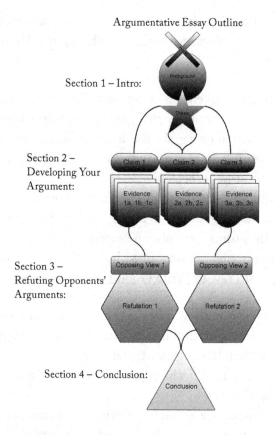

Each of these four sections requires some important elements. Let's break those down now.

Argumentative Essay Outline Section 1: Your Intro

Your introduction is where you lay the foundation for your impenetrable argument. It's made up of a hook, background information, and a thesis statement.

1. Hook. Your first sentence is comprised of a "hook." Don't know what a hook is? A hook is a sentence that grabs your reader's attention just like a good Jackie Chan movie grabs the attention of a martial arts fan.

Let's say I'm writing an argumentative essay about why American people should start eating insects.

My hook could be, "For those interested in improving their diets and the environment, say 'goodbye' to eating chicken, fish, and beef and 'hello' to eating silk worms, crickets, and caterpillars."

If you're having trouble coming up with a good hook, I recommend reading my blog post <u>How to Write Good Hook Sentences</u>.

2. Background information. The next part of your intro is dedicated to offering some detailed background information on your topic.

Try answering the following questions:

What is the issue at hand? Who cares? Where is this issue prevalent? Why is it important?

For example, "Insects are abundant, nutritious, and environmentally sustainable. Currently, people in the United States shun the idea of eating insects as part of their diets, favoring instead less nutritious and environmentally destructive food options, such as beef and pork. The UN recently issued a statement calling for more world citizens to embrace the many benefits of eating insects."

3. Thesis. Your thesis typically makes up the last sentence of your intro paragraph. This is where you clearly state your position on the topic and give a reason for your stance.

For example, "A diet of insects can help fix problems related to starvation, obesity, and climate change, and therefore, United States citizens should learn to rely on a variety of insects over chicken, beef, and fish as their main source of protein and nutrition."

Notice the word "should" in my thesis statement? Using this word makes it clear I'm taking a stance on the argument.

You'll also notice that my thesis statement sets up the three claims I'm going to expand on later: a diet of insects can help fix problems related to starvation, obesity, and climate change.

Here are even more example argumentative thesis statements.

Let's talk about adding those claims to our argumentative essay outline now.

Argumentative Essay Outline Section 2: Developing Your Argument

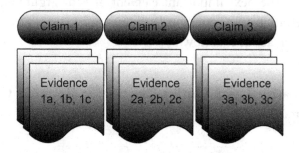

Now that you have filled in the general points of your topic and outlined your stance in the introduction, it's time to develop your argument.

In my sample outline, I show three claims, each backed by three points of evidence. Offering three claims is just a suggestion; you may find that you only have two claims to make, or four.

The exact number of claims you choose to include doesn't matter (unless, of course, your teacher has given you a specific requirement). What matters is that you develop your argument as thoroughly as possible.

1. What is a claim? A claim is a statement you make to support your argument.

For example, "Bugs are highly nutritious and eating them can fix the problem of hunger and malnutrition in the United States."

Great! So I've made my claim. But who's going to believe me? This is where evidence comes into play.

2. What is evidence? For each claim you make, you need to provide supporting evidence. Evidence is factual information from reliable sources.

It is not personal knowledge or anecdotal.

For example, "Researchers at the Food and Agricultural Organization of the United States state that 'Termites are rich in protein, fatty acids, and other micronutrients. Fried or dried termites contain 32–38 percent proteins.'"

My outline shows three pieces of evidence to support each claim, but you may find that each claim doesn't necessarily have three pieces of evidence to back it. Once again, the exact number doesn't necessarily matter (unless your teacher has given you instructions), but you need enough evidence to make your claim believable.

Once you have gathered your evidence to support your claims, it's time to add the next important element of your argumentative essay outline: refuting your opponents' arguments.

Let's talk about that now.

Argumentative Essay Outline Section 3: Refuting Opponents' Arguments

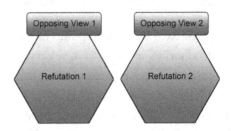

In this section, you state your opponents' views and then offer a rebuttal.

For example, "Opponents of insect eating from the Beef Council of America say that it is too difficult and time consuming to catch crickets, so it is not easy to gather enough food for a meal, whereas a cow is large and contains a lot of meat for many meals."

Oh diss! We know the Beef Council just wants us to keep eating McD's hamburgers and skip the cricket soup. (By the way—I just made that up. The Beef Council did not say that. In your essay, make sure to use *real* facts.)

Now it's time to set the opponents straight with a refutation that is full of hard evidence and that will bring them to their knees.

For example, "According to researchers Cerritos and Cano-Santana, the best time to harvest crickets is to catch them in the hour just before sunrise when they are least active. What's more, it is easy to develop the infrastructure to farm crickets in a way that is more sustainable than cattle farming."

Booyah! The Beef Council has been served (crickets).

Once you have refuted your opponents' viewpoints, it's time to sail to the finish line with your conclusion.

Argumentative Essay Outline Section 4: Conclusion

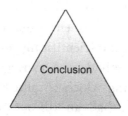

In your conclusion, you are going to accomplish two important tasks.

1. Restate the importance of your issue. Similar to what you did in your introduction, you want to restate why this topic is critical.

For example, "Simply by incorporating insects into their diets, U.S. citizens can improve the sustainability and nutrition of the American diet."

2. Paint a picture of the world if your argument is (or is not) implemented. In the final part of your conclusion, make your audience think about the ramifications of your argument. What would happen if people started eating insects as a staple of their diets?

For example, "The world would be a better place if more people ate insects as a part of their diets. Fewer people would go hungry, more people would get the vitamins, minerals, and micronutrients they need to live healthy lifestyles, and our planet would be relieved of the burden of an unsustainable food system.

Closing with a clear picture of the world as you would like it to be can leave your reader convinced that your argument is valid.

Examples of an Argumentative Essays

1. Health and Healing at Your Fingertips

Throw out the bottles and boxes of drugs in your house. A new theory suggests that medicine could be bad for your health, which should at least come as good news to people who cannot afford to buy expensive medicine. However, it is a blow to the medicine industry, and an even bigger blow to our confidence in the progress of science. This new theory argues that healing is at our fingertips: we can be healthy by doing Reiki on a regular basis.

Supporters of medical treatment argue that medicine should be trusted since it is effective and scientifically proven. They say that there is no need for spiritual methods such as Reiki, Yoga, Tai Chi. These waste our time, something which is quite precious in our material world. There is medicine that can kill our pain, x-rays that show us our fractured bones or MRI that scans our brain for tumors. We must admit that these methods are very effective in the examples that they provide. However, there are some "every day complaints" such as back pains, headaches, insomnia, which are treated currently with medicine. When you have a headache, you take an Aspirin, or Vermidon, when you cannot sleep, you take Xanax without thinking of the side effects of these. When you use these pills for a long period, you become addicted to them; you cannot sleep without them. We pay huge amounts of money and become addicted instead of getting better. How about a safer and more economical way of healing? When doing Reiki to yourself, you do not need anything except your energy so it is very economical. As for its history, it was discovered in Japan in the early 1900s and its popularity has spread particularly throughout America and Western Europe. In quantum physics, energy is recognized as the fundamental substance of which the universe is composed. Reiki depends on the energy within our bodies. It is a simple and effective way of restoring the energy flow. There are no side effects and it is scientifically explained.

Opponents of alternative healing methods also claim that serious illnesses such as HIV/AIDS and cancer cannot be treated without drugs. They think so because these patients spend the rest of their lives in the hospital taking medicine. How can Reiki make these people healthy again? It is very unfortunate that these patients have to live in the hospital losing their hair because of chemotherapy, losing weight because of the side effects of the medicine they take. Actually, it is common knowledge that except for when the cancer is diagnosed at an early stage, drugs also cannot treat AIDS or cancer. Most of the medicine these patients use are to ease their pain and their sufferings because of the medical treatment they undergo. Instead of drugs which are expensive and have many side effects, you can use your energy to overcome the hardships of life, find an emotional balance, leave the stress of everyday life and let go of the everyday worries. Most of the chronic conditions such as eczema or migraine are known to have causes such as poor diet and stress. Deep-rooted anger or other strong emotions can contribute to viral infections as well. Since balancing our emotions and controlling our thoughts are very important for our well-being, we should definitely start learning Reiki and avoid illnesses before it is too late.

Some people may still maintain that in our material world, everything depends on time. It is even "lacking time" that causes much of the stress that leads to the illnesses we mentioned. How would it be possible to find time to do Reiki to ourselves and the people around us when we cannot even find time to go to the theater? This is one good thing about Reiki; it does not require more than 15 minutes of our time. There is no need for changing clothes or special equipment. It is a wonderfully simple healing art, an effective method of relaxation and stress-relief. Most important of all, it is less time consuming than medicine if we think of all the time we spend taking medicine for some complaints and taking some more for the side effects as well.

Having said these, resistance to Reiki would be quite illogical. Reiki is natural and drug-free. What is more, it is easy to learn by anyone, regardless of age and experience. It can be used anywhere, anytime. It also enhances physical, mental, emotional and spiritual well-being and the benefits last a lifetime. It is definitely high time to get away from the drug boxes we store in our drug cabinet!

2. Child Obesity Essay: I see fat kids

The main causes of obesity are: the decreased level of nutrients intake, and sedentary lifestyle. In spite of all available information about nutrition in schools, hospitals, Internet, it is apparent that overeating is a problem. For example, the intake of fast food meals tripled between 1977 and 1995, and calorie level magnified four times during the same period. Nevertheless, it is insufficient explanation of phenomenal rise in the obesity levels in the well-developed countries. Overall, obesity is a significant health and social problem, which has reached pandemic levels. In accordance with numerous reports, energy intakes from food in England have decreased over the last 30 years, while the prevalence of obesity has tripled over 20 years, and continue to increase at an alarming rate.

Optimal nutrition therefore is deemed an important issue on the healthy food agenda and therefore nutrition security systems are applied to lower the levels of energy deficiency. As well as this, proper systems increase dietary intake (Tenth Five Year Plan, 2002-07). A well-balanced diet therefore provides energy and nourishment necessary to lead normal life, and therefore to keep fit. Hence, it is important to provide our body with all the necessary resources and fuels to stay in good health (Lysol, 2006). An unhealthy diet and physical inactivity, on the other hand, increase our chances of getting heart disease, cancer, stroke, type 2 diabetes, high blood pressure, breathing problems, arthritis, gallbladder disease, and osteoarthritis (HHS, 2007). Hence, it is possible to support human immune system to prevent various types of disease and illness by eating the right foods. Eating variety of fruits and vegetables given by nature will strength the body, and allow healing the diseases. Proper nutrition will be much more successful in defending body. This connection between nutrition and Immune System is the key to health. Nowadays, foods are full of chemicals and pesticides, as a consequence, plant food now have nutrition losses (Bio Net, 2007). Taking the aforementioned into account it is apparent that in order to receive optimal health, humans require a various, well-balanced diet that includes a complex mixture of both macronutrients and micronutrients.

Understanding sufficient nutrition as a component of nutrient metabolism helps us to control and maintain proper health condition. For instance, eating a good breakfast sets the tone for the rest of the day. Nonetheless, many people tend to miss breakfasts to lose their weight. Furthermore, people who eat breakfast maintain a healthy weight. A great number of scientists proved that children who eat breakfast produce better results at school, while adults feel and work better too. Ideally, a healthy breakfast should include some protein and some fiber. As was mentioned above, protein is a component of low fat meats, eggs, beans, and soy. Grains, vegetables and fruits consist of fiber. A perfect example of healthy breakfast is often limited to boiled egg, orange, or low fat milk. As is known, protein and fibre satisfy hunger (Jegtvig, 2007).

Right nutrition helps us to achieve health and reduce risk of diseases, for instance, heart disease, stroke, cancer, diabetes and osteoporosis. Additionally, nutritional therapy may also be included to the treatment of Parkinson's disease. Several studies proved that the importance of nutrition regulate humans health. Consequently, it is significant to understand the importance of nutrition in order to be healthy from day-to day. Nowadays, people are making changes in their lifestyle and include proper nutrition. Hence, understanding sufficient nutrition as a component of nutrient metabolism helps us to control and maintain proper health condition (Jegtvig, 2007).

Functional foods mainly consist of vitamins and minerals normally consumed by humans. Overall, these additives are approved and recommended by most governments, and are well-known to everyone (Food Additives and Ingredients, 2007). To this end, Vitamins are components of organic origin present in food and necessary to our body. The most widely known vitamins are: A, B1, B2, and B3 (niacin), B5, B6, B7, B9, B12, C (ascorbic acid), D, E, and K. The B and C vitamins are soluble in water, while A, D, E, and K vitamins are fat-soluble, and accumulated in the body fat. In turn, minerals are important to our life because they are the main building blocks that create muscles, tissue, and bones. Additionally, they are significant components of many important life systems, in particular, hormones, oxygen transport, and enzyme systems. At that, there are two types of minerals: the main (macro) minerals and the trace minerals. A body in considerable amounts requires Main minerals. Particularly, main minerals include sodium, potassium, sulphur etc, required to build muscles, blood, nerve cells, teeth and bones. The main minerals and trace minerals are required in small amounts due to the fact that they are very significant to our body. These important minerals participate in the majority of chemical reactions run in a body. Additionally, they are important to produce hormones.

Teenagers need special nutrients in order to support growth. This period brings dynamic increase in height as well as hormonal changes. Especially significant is iron. Requirement for calcium growth while skeletal mass increases. Calcium is significant for young adults. Teenager's caloric needs vary depending on their growth rate and activity level. Males generally have higher energy requirements than females due to their larger proportion of lean body mass to adipose tissue (Kid Source, 2007).

Alternatively, performing physical exercise is an effective approach to self-care maintenance along with mental and spiritual practices. Overall, life satisfaction depends on physical state and this study suggests that quality of life and life satisfaction depend on self care and sound motivation. Self-care is achieved by maintaining physical, mental and spiritual harmony. However, a combination of both internal and external motivators is needed to make person work on his/her self-improvement. To this end, the contribution of social work practice has served as valuable external factor that put client in a certain format of performing definite physical activities.

Consequently, a well-balanced diet provides energy and nourishment necessary to lead normal life, and therefore to keep fit. Hence, it is important to provide our body with all the necessary resources and fuels to stay in good health (Lysol, 2006). Conversely, an unhealthy diet and physical inactivity increase our chances of getting heart disease, cancer, stroke, type 2 diabetes, high blood pressure, breathing problems, arthritis, gallbladder disease, and osteoarthritis (HHS, 2007).

Works Cited

HHS. 2006, 'Obesity and Weight Loss', [Online]: Available at: http://www.4women.gov/faq/weightloss.htm

Jegtvig, S. 2007, 'Are Genetically Engineered Foods Healthy?' [Online]: Available at: http://nutrition.about.com/od/askyournutritionist/f/gmo_foods.htm

Kid Source. 2007, 'Nutrients Needs' [Online]: Available at: http://www.kidsource.com/kidsource/content3/ific/ific.teen. trends.html

Lysol, 2007, 'Health Eating', [Online]: Available at: http://www. lysol.com/topic_eating.shtml

TENTH FIVE YEAR PLAN 2002-07 FOOD AND NUTRITION SECURITY, [Online]: Available at: http:// planningcommission.nic.in/plans/planrel/fiveyr/10th/volume2/ v2_ch3_3.pdf

3. The Negative Effects of Television Essay

Essay Questions:

Is TV by itself a straight danger for the viewer?

Why do contemporary parents use the TV as a babysitter?

What are the most terrible possible consequences of exposure to television?

Thesis Statement:

The television negative effect facts that are well known to every single parent, but are ignored by them in order to put the responsibility for bringing up kids and showing them examples through interaction on the shoulders of somebody else.

"…Like the sorcerer of old the television set casts its magic spell, freezing speech and action, turning the living into silent statues so long as the enchantment lasts…"

Urie Brofenbrenner

Introduction: Television has become a "member" of almost every single family on our planet. And not just an ordinary member, but a very important one, because the time spent next to it exceeds the amount of time spent together with any other family member. You do not have to apply any efforts to talk or listen to complaints while "communicating" with it. You do not have to play with your little son after a hard working day. You are SO tired! Can anybody respect that? You can simply turn the TV on and everything is done: kids are quiet, your wife is not complaining and you feel absolutely happy. It is so simple that it has become an integral part of the culture of every family. It is the only time, when a person can forget about all the family troubles and the failures of the day. The sofa opposite the TV set has become the place of "reconciliation and spiritual unity" of the family. And instead of playing together and having emotional talks people prefer to watch an episode from a thriller. It is senseless to deny the all-embracing negative effect the existence of television has brought to our lives. But to make our point of view ultimately convincing we will introduce to your attention certain facts that people do not want to accept and often try to justify. The base of the tomorrow's society – are children today. And on the way they develop depends how are world is going to look like tomorrow. The television negative effect facts that are well known to every single parent, but are ignored by them in order to put the responsibility for bringing up kids and showing them examples through interaction on the shoulders of somebody else.

Contemporary parents work a lot, but when they come back home they are not eager to spend time with their child, the consequences of this fact are the following: kids are given to themselves and watch everything they want or TV plays a role of a babysitter. Therefore children learn moral principles from the television, where by the age of 16 they observe 100,000 violent acts and 33,000 murders. The models of life interactions given in the television are very exaggerated and garbled. Children learn that they can gain what they want through being stronger and subordinating other people that they can become popular through killing and that even if you are a "good" guy killing is o.k. Statistics have proved that the growth of time spent next to the TV-set scales up the development of aggression. Many years before the examples of imitation for children were their own parents; now these examples come from hit-thrillers and violent films where the personages imitated are cruel, impartial and often purely negative personages. Nowadays, resulting this phenomenon, children instead of playing leap-and–frog on the open air pretend to be "terminators" and run around "killing" each other. The fact of child's identification with a "negative" destructive image has a vital impact on the development of his or her personality. Violence becomes an ordinary way of interaction, alongside with anger. Early exposure to sexual scenes may lead to early sexual contacts, with destroy the healthy development of a child. Young people are pressured by such an amount of sexual scenes and these scenes normalize casual sexual encounters. They do not to evaluate what they see – they take it as the reality. All the listed above may cause a trauma to a young consciousness and in combination with the violence may produce an unbalanced and unhealthy conduct. We do not have to go far away for examples when kids get guns and go to their schools shooting their teachers and schoolmates. This becomes a call to get somebody's attention on them, the result of the TV violence and examples influences that overfills their minds. Television has also a great influence on the self-image of people watching it. We see perfectly shaped bodies hundred of times per day. All the men shown on the TV screen have big muscles and are handsome, and all the women shown are very skinny and their faces and bodies look like a complete perfection. This has caused numerous eating disorders, especially in the teenage group. Such things as bulimia, anorexia and self-mutilation became a well-spread phenomenon.

A person, especially a child that spends a lot of time next to the TV-set has a very high probability of damaging the eye mechanics and the ability to focus and pay attention. Another negative influence that is connected with the sight is the spoiling of the hearing due to the shortage of auditory stimulation. Even if the programs watched are not violent, if they are watched per hours may have a deep impact on the personality, causing psychological and physiological problems. All the hidden effects in the films and commercials subconsciously depress children and grown-ups. Another reaction of a child to the TV violence besides his aggression is fair. A child, or a person may become so much scared of what they had observed in the television that it might cause their depression and emotional misbalance. Television prevents children from doing their homework and adults from completing their work, influencing in a very bad manner the school grades and work productivity. It lowers the overage level of physical fitness of a person, breaking the coordination. Children being attached to the TV-set loose the possibility to learn the world through real nature, games, sports, etc. They do not feel the world with all its colors and peculiarities. They do not read, and get acquainted with the unforgettable characters of Robinson Crusoe or Tom Sawyer. They do not learn the messages that a book carries inside. Due to that the personality of a person loses a very important piece and may not by called complete.

Conclusion: Television has converted or lives into a nightmare. A nightmare where children kill not only on the TV screen and adults lose their will sitting next to the TV-set eating "junk food". A nightmare where the time spent by a family next to the TV-set watching a soup-opera is considered to be "family time". It is a nightmare where violent television performs the role the parents. What else can be said to show that television destroys the healthy development of a child's personality. All the negative effects listed above concern grown-ups as well, but through the special sensitivity of children towards the influences we wanted to show to the full the destructive power of television. It has turned our lives into an addiction that suppresses the beauty of our real life by the violent substitution. And can without any doubts be called one of the worst inventions of modern times.

Bibliography:

1. "Stop teaching our kids to kill: a call to action against TV, movie and video game violence" by Dave Grossman & Gloria Degaetano /Crown/ 1999.
2. "The other parent: the inside story of the media's effect on our children" by James Steyer /Atria/ 2003.

4. Marriage and Happiness Essay: Everyday happiness is sharing commitments

Have you ever wondered where love disappears after marriage? And why it does? What happens to it after two loving hearts united themselves in the bonds of matrimony? Probably, many different specialists - psychologists, sociologists, medical doctors, public servants, teachers and others will give you different answers. It may happen that all those answers will be correct. Let us consider several causes of such "light-minded" and stubborn behavior of love - it does not want to be stored on the dusty shelves or dark corners of a family unit. Crucial challenges and changes in the modern society have affected the reasons for marriages and the challenges families face in the course of the past few decades - they have modified the traditional view on family and married life and are even threatening the existence of the institute of formal marriage thus generating special needs for strengthening the family.

Reasons for creating a family can strongly influence its well-being, unity and moral atmosphere. For example, marriage for getting independence from parents may result in loosening bonds, since after a short period of time the couple realizes that, firstly, real independence was not gained (and possibly is very unreal at all) and, secondly, the reason for such marriage was only temporary and not powerful enough to keep two different people together.

Likewise, marriage for financial reasons can turn out to be a disaster since money and riches are disappearing even sooner than love. Moreover, day-to-day survival of a couple shows that family cannot be considered as an enterprise or a successful financial investment. It simply does not work that way and does not obey the same laws as business. In addition, financial inequality of spouses in the beginning may lead to deep misunderstandings and disrespect. Instead, more and more people will find the solution of their financial problems and satisfaction of their material aspirations outside of marriage much more successfully.

Marriage because of love is one of the most widely spread reasons for creating a family. A man and a woman feel deep attraction to each other and want to get together for good. However, sometimes they do not realize that those emotions of infatuation and sexual desires are just a very strong prelude of a deeper feeling that can be born later and only in marriage. So they are expecting that those nice moments of mutual intimacy and adoration will follow them automatically through cruel routine and turmoil of housekeeping, financial problems, illnesses, family relationship, child-bearing, etc. When they do not recognize their beloved ones who turned into grungy husbands and grumpy wives they say that love has disappeared and their marriage was a big mistake. As a result many people will look for love outside of marriage, which is a threatening factor by itself.

Overall, only optimum combination of factors analyzed could guarantee the happiness in family life. For traditional family faced numerous changes over the recent decades, modern family does not follow purely conventional attitudes any longer. Neither does financial success guarantee internal closeness of two people united by family bonds. Therefore, love and mutual respect should be rationally combined with daily commitments

CHAPTER EIGHT

PERSUASIVE ESSAYS

What is a persuasive essay?

A persuasive essay, also known as an argumentative essay, argues the writer's position on a controversial topic with an intention to persuade the reader to agree with the writer's stance. The main point of a persuasive essay, is to convince the reader to think the same way you do. Remember that it is not an informative essay, and try not to include conversational tone. Your thesis and supporting statements should be strongly written. In a persuasive essay, never use "I" statements, such as "I believe, or I think." because it makes your opinion sound more one-sided and weak. State your opinions as if they were facts, even if they are just your own opinions.

Persuasive essays include an introductory paragraph that establishes the writer's purpose and position, body paragraphs that provide supporting arguments for the overall argument and a conclusion that summarizes the main points to leave a lasting, persuasive impression. A *persuasive essay* is an essay used to convince a reader about a particular idea or focus, usually one that you believe in. Your persuasive essay could be based on anything about which you have an opinion. Whether you're arguing against junk food at school or petitioning for a raise from your boss, the persuasive essay is a skill that everyone should know.

What is a call to action in persuasive writing? When writing a persuasive essay, the key to persuading the reader involves making the position clear from the start. The introduction should include background information to establish the problem or controversy and a thesis statement that shows the writer's stance on the issue. Many times, the thesis is solution-seeking, which prompts the reader to consider taking action. The body paragraphs provide supporting arguments to support the writer's position. For example, a persuasive essay on eliminating the death penalty may offer supporting ideas about detail the cost, ethical ramifications and potential errors associated with employing the death penalty. The body of the essay should also recognize the opposing views to establish the writer's ability to look at the issue objectively. However, a rebuttal statement or paragraph should refute the opposing views. Finally, the persuasive essay should end with a summary of the main arguments and reiterate the persuasive thesis statement.

Tips on Writing a Persuasive Essay

Writing a persuasive essay is like being a lawyer arguing a case before a jury. The writer takes a stand on an issue—either "for" or "against"—and builds the strongest possible argument to win over the reader.

In a persuasive essay, it's the writer's job to convince the reader to accept a particular point of view or take a specific action. Persuasive essays require good research, awareness of the reader's biases, and a solid understanding of both sides of the issue. A good persuasive essay demonstrates not only why the writer's opinion is correct, but also why the opposing view is incorrect.

Persuasive writing is a fixture of modern life—found in advertising, newspaper editorials, blogs, and political speeches. Often persuasive writing assignments and test prompts concern contemporary issues, for example: "The school board is debating on whether or not to ban cell phone use in school. Write an essay convincing the board to adopt your position." As shown in this persuasive writing prompt, the main purpose is not to inform, but to "persuade" or "convince" an audience (the school board) to think or act a certain way.

How to Write a Persuasive Essay

Students all over the world are required to write argumentative academic papers for high school and college classes. Unfortunately, a majority of these students have not mastered proper literary structure. Without a clear organizational plan, one's ideas are not worth much. However, before we get to the abstract, let's talk about the fundamentals. So, what is a persuasive essay?

Taking a look at the **definition**, the term itself means to influence and convince. Logically, this is a type of literary writing in which the writer uses their personal opinions to attempt and adjust the reader's point of view about the topic. The persuader will use certain rhetoric to try and grow their appeal on the audience. Whether you're arguing about global warming or sending a petition to a president for same-sex marriage, the persuasive essay is an important skill that everyone should know. Right now we are going to help you to find a way out.

Although all types of writing have a specific set of rules, norms, and conventions, the style is commonly used within the 5 paragraph format. The main purpose of this type of assignment is to give an argumentative analysis on a particular topic. It is used as a tool for high school and college students to develop their critical thinking skills and train them to explain their analysis in a structured format.

How to Choose a Topic

Choosing a good essay topic is crucially important. That's why if you are not aware of the thing that you are talking about you will just kill your time, and get not as good mark as you want to. Try to choose your topic wisely and if necessary do some research about your particular theme. Most academic essay topics usually ask you to pick a side in an argument or to defend a particular side against criticism. These are some common samples of questions you might receive as assignments:

- Should marijuana be legal for medicinal purposes?
- Should people who download music and movies illegally be punished?
- Should abortions be legal?
- Should the death penalty be used to punish violent criminals?
- Should tobacco manufacturers be allowed to advertise on television?

- Should state colleges be free to attend?
- Should students have to wear uniforms?
- Should teens be allowed to buy violent video games?

Though these are just some general knowledge questions, they are effective in training the student towards writing effective persuasive essays. Most of the time, students will write about topics specific to their course or subject, but regardless the format stays the same for all essays.

Winning Topics for College

Unlike topics for middle school or high school, good college topics are more challenging to find. While one's primary school education may test their ability to put together a well-structured piece of writing, college tends to be a little more demanding. As most students can follow simple guidelines, an emphasis is placed on creating unique content rather than paraphrased ideas. This is why persuasive essays on topics such as abortions, gun control and cyber bullying will never earn recognition higher than a decent grade. When choosing an argument for your essay, aim for something out of the ordinary with untapped possibilities. In other words, if your college professor were to raise their eyebrows after glancing on your front page, then that is an excellent sign!

- "Is government surveillance of personal information via Google warranted?"
- "Should illegal immigrants with clean criminal records and work experience avoid deportation?"
- "Does social media improve one's people skills and overall socialization level?"
- "Is the movie rating system rigged and or judged on incomplete criteria?"
- "Have technological advancements decreased the value of individual skill?"
- "Is there a correlation between cell-phone and lowered concentration?"

- "Should college network have filters to prevent access to inappropriate materials?"
- "Should chronic mental patients be housed in "halfway houses" in the community, rather than suffer further in mental hospitals?"

These are some of the best topics that make for a great debate. Not only are they original, but a lot of informational variety can be used to make one's argument stronger. So, for university students looking to craft great arguments in their writing, follow these models for guaranteed success!

Developing a title

Creating a title is one of the hardest things that student might deal with. That's why we have created a tutorial to provide you with some of the best the best information on the internet. Let's start with the determination of purpose. So, the main purpose of a title is to: Predict content, catch the reader's attention, identify the tone of your piece of writing.

- **Read your assignment instructions carefully.** Were there any specific requirements related to the essay title? If yes, just follow them. Does the essay assignment ask any questions? Asking a question in a title is a good way to arouse the curiosity of readers.
- **Write an essay first, title last.** If you need to create a title by yourself, the first thing you need to do is to write an essay, and just then develop a title. If you write a title first, your essay will have to be based on your title, but it should be vice versa.
- **Consider your audience.** Keep your target audience in mind before and while writing an essay. Spend some time thinking about who will be reading your essay when choosing a title.
- **Use a quote or main idea of your essay as a title.** Read through the quotes used in your work for ones that seem exceptionally strong or powerful. Find some quotes or phrases that sum up

your essay as a whole or highlight a central theme or idea in your essay.

- **Search for the title in the introduction or body.** Your introduction should include your thesis and the general ideas of your essay. Your conclusion should also restate your thesis and sum up your analysis. Both sections may be good places to find keywords that could lead to a strong title for your essay.
- **Sum up your essay.** Sum up your essay in few words; try to put commas between them and if after this everything sounds good, it might become your title.

Understanding the Format

As mentioned before, the persuasive structure is in the classic 5 paragraph style. Many high school students are trained to write their paper in the five paragraph format to follow national standards, especially in the USA. However, several topics simply cannot be analyzed and explained in a mere five 5 paragraphs, which is why the persuasive essay has flexibility in this scenario. In most high school settings, you will be tested on your ability to write one of these assignments in the classroom, and this assessment will take 30 minutes to an hour. However, in several college courses, this standard style is rarely ever used, and the type of content you must research and analyze becomes much longer and way more in depth. To put it in simpler terms, the outline is very much dependent on the topic and the sort of question you are asked to respond about.

Persuasion techniques

- As was mentioned in the beginning, the term "persuasive essay" means to influence and convince. It supposed to be hard to persuade someone in something without any knowledge. That is why we have gathered some techniques which you can use in your writing.

- **Focus on your best audience.** Don't try to persuade everyone, it is simply impossible. Focus on the audience which is more likely to benefit from your content and write for them; that will bring you more results.
- **Use the right tone of voice.** Of course, it is important what you say, but how do you say it is vital as well. Tone determines how audience understands the message, so pick yours and use it consistently.
- **Put yourself in reader's shoes.** Decide what would grab your attention if you were the reader. When you are writing this type of essay, you have to become the reader to understand what allures them.
- **YES, YES, YES.** Concentrate and create a situation in which the reader will not be able to answer anything except yes. At first sight it seems to be hard, but actually, it is not. All you need to do is make general statements or ask questions that are difficult to challenge:
  - o Do you want to be healthy?
  - o Do you want to study better?
  - o Do you want to earn good money?
- **Touch the emotions.** Arouse emotions in the reader. Everybody knows that emotions stand behind making a purchase or making a deal. Remember that emotions arouse desire.

How to Outline Your Essay

The structure looks like some variation of this:

- **Introduction**
  - o Emphasis on a strong introduction;
  - o Brief presentation of both parts;
  - o Present your side of the argument;
  - o Thesis statement expressing the validity of your whole argument.
- **Body**
  - o **Paragraph 1:**

- An informative topic sentence that gets to the point (stating 1st reason);
- Provide evidence that is logical and applicable;
- Connection of evidence with explanation;
- Closing statement about the overall paragraph.
    o **Paragraph 2:**
    - An informative topic sentence that gets to the 2nd point (stating 2nd reason);
    - Provide evidence that is logical and applicable;
    - Connection of evidence with explanation;
    - Closing statement about the overall paragraph.
    o **Paragraph 3:**
    - An informative topic sentence that gets to the point (stating 3rd reason);
    - Provide evidence that is logical and applicable;
    - Connection of evidence with explanation;
    - Closing statement about the overall paragraph.
- **Conclusion**
    o Restatement of thesis;
    o Summed up explanation of each argument;
    o Give the text an overall conclusion that calls to action.

Introduction

- **Hook Statement**: Need some help starting your <u>argumentative essay</u>? Well, there is no better way than with the trusty hook statement: a sentence that excites the reader about your essay, and must in some way relate to your topic of persuasion.
- **Brief Intro/Background**: The length of this varies based on how much content and analysis you will provide. Each subject of analysis should have about one sentence of the introduction.
- **Thesis Statement**: The core argument/point of persuasion that the entire essay is based around. It is recommended to write your body paragraphs first, and then create your thesis after seeing what your content is truly about.

Learn how to write a killing <u>THESIS</u>

It's much easier to create a thesis at the end, rather than align your statements towards your thesis because most of the time this harms the quality of your analysis and the strength of your sentences.

Read more about how to write a great <u>INTRODUCTION</u>

Body Paragraphs

- **Topic Sentence**: Sentence that introduces your argument; needs to include words of emphasis. These are strong and supportive words that defend your statement.
- **Argument**: This is the meat of your paper, the statements that really serve the purpose of audience persuasion.
- **Explanation/Evidence**: These statements are either facts or data analysis and serve to defend your main argument and prove its authenticity.
- **Concluding Sentence**: After fully explaining your defending argument, the concluding sentence is used to sum up your point with the most effective words possible. Think of it as a short but efficient summary! Depending on the subject of analysis, thesis, or the requirements such as word length or page length, the number of body paragraphs in your persuasive essay will vary! However, this is the general structure of the paper.

Conclusion

- **Restatement of Thesis**: After proving your thesis throughout the essay, it's important to make it known in the conclusion. Rephrase it and start making conclusion points.
- **Summarize Key Points**: Briefly explain how your main arguments defended your thesis statement and show that these explanations are reasonable and logical.
- **Overall Concluding Statement**: Make sure the reader understands the value and importance of your essay and the argument that you portrayed throughout the paper. If the reader has taken your persuasive argument into serious consideration,

that's when you know that you have written an awesome piece of work.

General Tips

- **MLA and Chicago style formats** are usually used for persuasive and argumentative writings. They provided the physical alignments, margins, titles and other similar aspects of the essay.
- **Avoid overusing vocabulary:** try to provide some variety but don't go overboard either. If you are trying to become the young Shakespeare, do it cleverly.
- **Use different persuasion techniques.** You can surf the web and find a couple of techniques which suit your style.
- **Show why your point of view is more credible than the opposing.** It's good to defend your side, it's even better if you can counterattack afterward.
- **Double-check to make sure that your essay has proved the thesis.** If the paper has proved something slightly different, then edit the thesis accordingly.
- **Use clear and directed sentences to start each paragraph.** Make the beginning of each paragraph as a mini-thesis statement.
- **Get a second pair of eyes:** have a friend read it from a fresh perspective to make sure it makes sense to others.

Persuasive Essay Rubric

When being graded on the quality of work presented, the instructors will usually base the final grade around certain criterion. Although each piece of criteria follows its own instructions, the combination of them being accurately fulfilled is what really makes for a high ranking paper!

- **Focus:** Does the thesis statement state a concrete point of view instead of being neutral? Is the writing on-track and continuously defending the thesis statement?
- **Positional Support:** How well is the thesis statement defended? Is there a minimum of 3 supporting points presented? Does the arguments idea decisively confirm the validity of the thesis?
- **Organization:** How smoothly does the writer transition from one idea to the next? Do transitional sentences really fill the gap between ideas? Were the arguments presented in the most suitable order?
- **Conclusion:** After reading the essay, does the reader feel that they have fully understood the writer's point of view? Is it stated well enough to make the reader possibly sway their opinion towards the writer's?
- **Conventions:** Are there little to no grammatical errors? Is there a good mix of short and long sentences? Is punctuation appropriately placed?

The Five-Step Writing Process for Persuasive Essays

At Time4Writing, we believe the five-step writing process is the best approach to learning how to write a persuasive essay. Here are persuasive essay tips for each phase of the writing process.

1. Prewriting for the Persuasive Essay

The prewriting phase of writing a persuasive essay is extremely important. During this phase, students should plan every aspect of the essay:

- **Choose a position.** Students should think about the issue and pick the side they wish to advocate.
- **Understand the audience.** In order to write an effective persuasive essay, the writer must understand the reader's perspective. Is the reader undecided or inclined to favor one side or the other?

Persuasive Essay Outline

Introductory Paragraph

- Grab the reader's attention by using a "hook."
- Give an overview of the argument.
- Close with a thesis statement that reveals the position to be argued.

Body Paragraphs

- Each body paragraph should focus on one piece of evidence.
- Within each paragraph, provide sufficient supporting detail.

Opposing View Paragraph

- Describe and then refute the key points of the opposing view.

Concluding Paragraph

- Restate and reinforce the thesis and supporting evidence.

2. Drafting the Persuasive Essay

When writing the initial draft of a persuasive essay, consider the following suggestions:

The introductory paragraph should have a strong "hook" that grabs the reader's attention. Open with an unusual fact or statistic, a question or quotation, or an emphatic statement. For example: "Driving while talking on a cell phone, even hands-free, is the equivalent of driving drunk."

The thesis statement should leave no doubts about the writer's position.

Each body paragraph should cover a separate point, and the sentences of each paragraph should offer strong evidence in the form of facts, statistics, and quotes from experts, and real-life examples.

Consider various ways to make the argument, including using

an analogy, drawing comparisons, or illustrating with hypothetical situation (e.g., what if, suppose that...).

Don't assume the audience has in-depth knowledge of the issue. Define terms and give background information.

The concluding paragraph should summarize the most important evidence and encourage the reader to adopt the position or take action. The closing sentence can be a dramatic plea, a prediction that implies urgent action is needed, a question that provokes readers to think seriously about the issue, or a recommendation that gives readers specific ideas on what they can do.

3. Revising the Persuasive Essay

In the revision phase, students review, modify, and reorganize their work with the goal of making it the best it can be. Keep these considerations in mind:

- Does the essay present a firm position on the issue, supported by relevant facts, statistics, quotes, and examples?
- Does the essay open with an effective "hook" that intrigues readers and keeps them reading?
- Does each paragraph offer compelling evidence focused on a single supporting point?
- Is the opposing point of view presented and convincingly refuted?
- Is the sentence structure varied? Is the word choice precise? Do the transitions between sentences and paragraphs help the reader's understanding?
- Does the concluding paragraph convey the value of the writer's position and urge the reader to think and act?

If the essay is still missing the mark, take another look the thesis. Does it present the strongest argument? Test it by writing a thesis statement for the opposing viewpoint. In comparison, does the original thesis need strengthening? Once the thesis presents a well-built argument with a clear adversarial viewpoint, the rest of the essay should fall into place more easily.

4. Editing the Persuasive Essay

Next, proofread and correct errors in grammar and mechanics, and edit to improve style and clarity. Having a friend read the essay helps writers edit with a fresh perspective.

5. Publishing the Persuasive Essay

Sharing a persuasive essay with the rest of the class can be both exciting and intimidating. Learn from the experience and use the feedback to make the next essay even better.

- **Do the research.** A persuasive essay depends upon solid, convincing evidence. Don't rely on a single source. Go to the library and enlist the help of the librarian. Speak with community experts and teachers. Read and take notes. There is no substitute for knowledge of both sides of the issue.
- **Identify the most convincing evidence,** as well as the key points for the opposing view.

Organizing the Persuasive Essay: Outline and Structure

Next, create an outline. Organize the evidence to build the strongest possible argument. If the teacher has specified an essay structure, incorporate it into the outline. Typically, the persuasive essay comprises five or six paragraphs:

What is a tentative thesis?

A tentative thesis, or working thesis, is the writer's overall promise to the reader regarding what the essay will deliver. For example, when writing an argumentative essay, the tentative thesis should detail the writer's primary argument or position. A tentative thesis in an analysis paper details the topic the writer will be investigating, evaluating and analyzing.

The working thesis should strive to tell the reader something new and innovative and reach for unique theories versus common ideas. For example, if a writer chooses to write a persuasive essay about the death penalty, the working thesis should detail if the writer is for or against the death penalty and show with details and facts why the position is justifiable, logical and ethical. Regardless of the type of essay a writer is composing, the tentative thesis should serve as the guiding idea or primary angle of the topic to clarify the contents of the paper for the reader.

Examples of Persuasive Essays

1. Effects of alcohol on the human body Essay

Essay Topic:

The impact and the dramatic effects of alcohol on the human body. Essay Questions:
Why is alcohol considered to be a destructive substance?
How does social drinking influence the alcohol habits of the society?
What are the side effects of the alcohol abuse side effects?
What major physical changes occur in the human body of an alcoholic?

Thesis Statement:

The contemporary medical world is very much concerned with the female alcohol abuse phenomenon and the appearance of a group of inclinations that both female and male abusers experience.
Effects of alcohol on the human body
Table of contents:
1. Introduction
2. Alcohol abuse and possible outcomes

3. Changes in the human organism
   a. Physical change
   b. Mental changes
4. Conclusion

Introduction: Humanity has always yielded to the pressure of different chemical substances that eventually caused it irreparable damage. Finding the "cure" from the damage obtained was the next step. And it seems that only now, when the number of the diseases caused by different substances has reached its peak, people have finally understood that the best "cure" is the prevention of any forms of substance abuse. Alcohol is not the last one in the list of these destructive substances. It is the "companion" of any significant event occurring in the life of modern people or even an everyday way to relax and get away from all the difficulties. People relax and forget that they are supposed to think not only about their health but also about the health of the people around them. This especially concerns women, as they are the ones to deliver the next generation into the world. A woman's organism is a lot more influenced by any external chemical influences and alcohol becoming woman's frequent "companion" becomes a real threat for the health of the nation. The contemporary medical world is very much concerned with the female alcohol abuse phenomenon and the appearance of a group of inclinations that both female and male abusers experience. Alcohol abuse is the giant problem, which needs to be fixed desperately. It is very important to understand its nature and the possible effects that it can make to the human body.

2. Alcohol abuse and possible outcomes

The "disabilities" caused by alcohol last a lifetime and therefore completely change the life of any person and those people who will take care of him. Some people start being exposed to alcohol during their fetal development and therefore suffer throughout their whole lives sometimes not even having a small hope to find their places in the world and not being even "comparatively" independent. They cannot concentrate, talk too much and are not capable of making proper decisions. Such people are completely helpless and unprotected. The outcomes of alcohol abuse for the body are severe. Alcohol or sometimes called ethanol is a volatile liquid can easily burn oxidizes and is composed of oxygen, hydrogen and carbon, having the formula of C2H5OH. Alcohol influenced the whole human body, even including the central nervous system and the brain of a man. After the process of drinking alcohol people start feeling pleasure and more open to the outer world. Nevertheless, even though the person feels comfortable and more self-confident the most dangerous thing is often forgotten – alcohol's side effects. If a person drinks large amounts of alcohol in a very small period of time it may result in the person's brain being suppressed by the chemicals and lead to a fatality. If the amount of alcohol in a human body is exceeding a person can die in his sleep, because the body will not have enough resources to cope with the suppression. It is also extremely dangerous to combine alcohol with other chemical substances.

3. Changes in the human organism

The changes that occur in the human organism for the reason of alcohol abuse are terrible. The whole body is damaged and the person stops being able to either move and think properly. The effect of alcohol throughout the period of human's life is immense and even the lesser amount of alcohol may cause some changes. These destructive processes, which occur inside the organism, cause irreparable damage that it made on the genetic level. Even "social drinking" causes changes in intellectual and behavior activity of children [2]. Heavy abuse, causing disorders has nowadays become unbelievably widespread. All this changes throughout the period the development of the alcohol dependency cause mental disabilities and severe changes in the human body.

3. a. Physical changes

Very often it is said that alcohol heavy drinkers look the same. This happens because in the first place all of them experience problems with their skin. As the vessels of the skin widen, the blood flow to the person's face become more intensive. This is the reason people who drink alcohol have a flushed skin color and constantly feel that they are hot. Alcohol also often causes serious weight problem. As a fact, alcohol prevents people from consuming healthy food on a regular basis and it direct influences the heart of a drinker. This is one of the primary reasons why people who prefer to drink alcohol can experience a heart failure. Another part of the body that is directly damaged by alcohol is the liver. This is primarily due to the fact that it is liver that works the most to "clean" the organism from the chemicals in alcohol. When alcohol get to the blood of a person rather often, the blood in its turn damages the process of functioning of the liver cells and some of them start dying. The majority of people do not keep in mind the fact that even a one-time alcohol abuse makes the liver cells die, but it is the body of the person, who is not an alcohol heavy drinker, still has time to recuperate from the damage. In case the person drinks alcohol on a regular base the liver becomes weaker and weaker from day to day.

One other important physical sphere that is seriously damaged is the reproductive system of a human body. The reason of this type of dysfunction is that alcohol deprives the impulses that the nerves pass, and especially those that cause ability to erect, as for men. Women alcohol abuse it on of the first to be prevented as the fetus changes negatively and a lot of disabled children are born into to the world. Females metabolize alcohol very quickly and this is the primary cause of their necessity to abstain from alcohol. The fetus is already in high danger of obtaining FAS if the pregnant female consumes around 3 ounces of pure alcohol per day1[1]. Alcohol does not need to make much efforts to cross the placenta and therefore to enter the fetus's organism. Alcohol may cause spasm of placenta vessels and the umbilical cord. This leads to the oxygen "starvation" of the fetus. As the amount of zinc in the cells is rapidly reduced their growth and development is damaged. Through these effects alcohol causes changes called "mutations" in the DNA of the fetus cells. In its turn, the mutation of DNA in the fetus cells leads to pathologies of the development of different organs and tissues [6]. Alcohol also influences the person's ability to perceive sounds and the direction they are coming out from. The taste and smell are lost and the speech becomes unclear. As alcohol constantly burns the throat of the drinker in may result in severe pain, vomiting and even cancer. The body itself starts being very weak, the muscles suffer from atrophy, pain and spasms.

3. b. Mental changes

If a person constantly abuses alcohol it will eventually lead to a set of permanent transformations in the brain morphology. One of the most significant transformations concerns the reduction of the total amount of brain tissue and the growing size of the ventricles. The basic reason the body stops being able to produce brain tissue to cope with the chemical is because it lacks natural vitamins that a healthy body produces. Another reason because the body is deprived of vitamins is that alcohol abusers often experience a problem of systematic eating and do not consume food at the required time, making the body weak and unable to resist the alcohol effects. As the brain of a person under alcohol dependency does not have enough vitamins it turns out to be the first step to the beginning of mental retardation. What happens to a person is that he completely losses the ability to control his behavior, his judgments become illogical and his ability to concentrate decreases tremendously. It is common fact that alcohol very often is a "companion" of crimes for the listed reason, as the inability to control the behavior results in extreme mood swings and emotional outbursts. Alcohol does not let the brain properly control the manifestations of the body, as the central nervous system becomes damaged through the depression of the nerve cells in the brain. The cells cannot respond to the impulses and a group of body function failures appear: anesthesia, respiratory failure, coma and death. As alcohol destroys the central nervous system the drinker experiences impaired visual abilities, loss of pain perception, slow reactions, impaired motor skills, altered perception of time and space and many others.

Conclusion: The consumption of alcohol beverages has strongly entered the tradition of celebration any significant events in the life of people. Anybody can hardly imagine celebrating Christmas or a birthday without a gulp of champagne. Seemingly, there is nothing bad in that and nothing bad can happen after a gulp of champagne or a gulp during a routine "social drinking". But the reality is cruel... Therefore even small doses of alcohol can do harm to the human body. Most people do not understand the consequences alcohol abuse can have of their health nevertheless the abuse occurs primarily because people do not know the destructive power of alcohol. The consequences of the alcohol abuse do not decrease with time, though specific manifestations change when doses of drinking become smaller. These factors prevent people from proper social adaptation and therefore make their life incomplete. Social impracticability of people suffering from the alcohol abuse is one of major problems of the contemporary medical society. And the only way to solve this problem is to prevent people from drinking alcohol in any amounts. There is no cure better than alcohol abstention!

Note

1. Women have lesser enzyme that known as alcohol dehydrogenate and that is the reason about 30% more alcohol is absorbed into their bloodstream than in men.
2. **Parental Rights Essay**
   Father Parental Rights

Introduction

We are used to the situation when the rights of children and parents in families are clearly defined. We promote widely accepted beliefs, that parents are responsible for their children, and are obliged to take care of children, providing them with home, food, clothes, and various social opportunities. Traditional family will imply the existence of a happy married couple with at least two children, who possess sufficient freedom and are provided with everything they need daily. However, what happens when fathers leave? Are fathers responsible for taking care of their children after the law separates them? How do father parental rights and obligations impact the quality of the child's social development? All these questions lack clear answers, but one thing is evident: fathers invariably impact the child's worldviews and attitudes toward social environment. The role, which fathers play in their children's lives help children develop specific socialization patterns, which they later use in their own families.

Socialization is important for successful social and psychological development of a child. Recent researches suggest that children usually go through the three different socialization stages: first, children are impacted by socialization patterns which their parents use early in life; second, children are impacted by socialization patterns which they learn when their parents separate; third, children tend to develop new types of socialization approaches when they create their own family unions (Archard 49). Thus, fathers should participate in the children's development, to guarantee that children are prepared to the difficulties that await him (her) ahead. Unfortunately, fathers are not always able (willing) to fulfill their parental obligations. Daughters who are separated from their fathers find themselves in a virtually incomplete social environment, due to the fact that mothers are not always able to address the issues they face in their daily interactions with others.

Officially, "the natural father has no custodial right of the child once the parental rights are given up. Also, after relinquishing the parental rights the father has no legal rights and privileges on his child" (Montaque 14). Thus, the father who does not live with his daughter and has relinquished his parental rights is not obliged to provide his daughter with spiritual and moral support. While daughters are particularly vulnerable to external threats and may need their father's support, fathers may appear unprepared to supporting their children through difficult times. Unfortunately, laws do not provide us with reliable instruments that would grant us with fathers' loyalty and devotion; furthermore, laws seem to separate us with our fathers when they realize their inability to support us. For example, "the court allows voluntary giving up of parental rights for other than adoption cases if it is convinced that a good and sound reason exists for this and it serves the best interest of the child" (Archard 53); but how does the court know what is the best for me? Can the court realize the importance of my being with father? These legal issues will hardly be resolved in the nearest future. Evidently, fathers who do not live with their daughters break the eternal structure of legal and social relationships between parents and children, making their daughters unprepared to adult life.

Fathers invariably impact the quality of family relations between their daughters, mothers, and themselves. From my personal experience, fathers tend to display more tender attitudes towards their daughters than mothers do. This paradox may be the result of fathers being more realistic about their daughters' weaknesses and vulnerabilities. Fathers tend to view themselves as their daughters' safeguards; that is why providing fathers with clearer parental roles is essential for the successful social development of future generations.

Every day and every hour we face serious misbalances and inconsistencies in the current system of family law. These legal inconsistencies lead to unequal distribution of parental responsibilities between mothers and fathers. Fathers who do not support any relations with their daughters have the right and are not restricted from neglecting their daughters' spiritual needs. While mothers are fighting to provide their daughters with continuous material and moral support, fathers may not display any willingness to develop closer ties with them. The law cannot make fathers maintain close relationships with their children; nor can the law push fathers to realizing the importance of participation in their daughters' lives. "Disciplining the child, choosing and providing for the child's education, being responsible for the child's property, and allowing confidential information about the child to be disclosed" (Archard 30) – all these responsibilities are laid on mothers, when fathers leave. The father's absence and his unwillingness to maintain close relationships with his daughter will negatively impact the girl's moral status. From the legal viewpoint, separation and divorce will officially deprive a young girl of a chance to have father; as a result, she will appear completely unprotected in the face of the most serious life issues.

The fact that parents are not legally responsible for their separated daughters generates a set of legal, ethical, and moral concerns. On the one hand, the law voluntarily deprives a young girl of her natural right to be loved by her father. By signing off their parental rights, parents do not think of the consequences of their legal actions and the impact, which separation will produce on their daughters' lives. On the other hand, family law and legal obligations will never grant us with our father's love, and if our fathers are not able to fulfill their natural obligations, they should be better relieved of this "fatherhood" burden (Archard 80). The state should develop and implement a set of clear criteria for determining whether the parent is really unprepared or physically unable to support his daughter. The father unwilling to reside with his daughter may have numerous reasons for such unethical conduct: he might be involved into a new type of relationship that may prevent him from seeing his child; he may be physically or mentally unable to fulfill his parental obligations; or he may be simply unwilling to recognize the fact of being father. Regardless the particular situation, daughters will need to adapt to the situation where they have no one to rely on, except for their mothers and themselves. The law does not work to support daughters in their striving to restore close family relationships with their fathers.

Objectively, mothers are able to fulfill the majority of obligations and responsibilities parents have toward the child. Mothers are able to work, earn, support their children and promote their interests further in life. Laws do not consider fathers to be directly responsible for their daughters' wellbeing; rather, their parental responsibilities are limited to a set of biological functions (or better, gender and sexual reflexes) that result in the emergence of a new life, and end as soon as the child is born (Montaque 16). By giving fathers unlimited freedom and the chance to voluntarily distance themselves from their natural parental obligations, the law shrinks the notion of father to a small biological concept, where fathers are used to maintain the continuous human evolution but are not responsible for what happens to children as they grow up. I think that this problem extends far beyond traditional legal domains; and it should be re-evaluated through the whole complex of motivational issues, which may change fathers' attitudes towards their daughters. Termination of father rights is a painful experience, and fathers should realize the importance of being with their daughters, when they enter the most responsible and the most difficult phases in their lives.

Fathers who have voluntarily terminated their relationships with their daughters are legally obliged to support their children materially; however, the law does not require that fathers love them. Material issues can be resolved, but they cannot improve the quality of relationships between fathers and their daughters. Those living separately may view material support as an effective substitute for parental love, but they may be deeply wrong in the way their life priorities are evaluated. Under the current law, community and future generations may face the need for shifting the emphases from legal to moral and spiritual aspects of father-daughter relationships, but the time will pass before fathers realize the wide scope of their responsibilities toward their daughters. The law may become the foundation for reconsidering father attitudes towards daughters. The law may become the source of reliable and unbiased knowledge about the roles fathers play in their daughters' lives – roles that go far beyond primitive biological reactions. Fathers should be provided with a complex vision of their obligations, as well as the opportunities they have to make their daughters' dreams real. Material support required by law is not the ultimate source of moral and spiritual satisfaction for daughters. Law is a reliable basis for developing innovative approaches to parental roles in families, and while fathers do not display any willingness to change their attitudes toward their daughters, the law may help them adopt new approaches and philosophies in their closer relationships with children.

Conclusion

Fathers have the right to voluntarily relinquish themselves from their natural parental responsibilities. The problem is in that daughters cannot rely on law when seeking fathers' support. The law shrinks the role of father to a biological subject, but laws can also become the starting point for changing father attitudes towards their daughters. Even when fathers and daughters live separately, the law may provide the basis for restoring their relationships. Currently, fathers and daughters who live separately do not have any legal stimuli for maintaining high quality of their relationships; that is why a clear set of criteria should be developed to determine whether fathers are able to fulfill their parental obligations, and whether daughters deserve to grow and mature in the balanced social environment.

Works Cited

Archard, D. *Children: Rights and Childhood*. Routledge, 2004.

Montaque, P. "The Myth of Parental Rights." *Social Theory and Practice*, vol. 26 (2000): pp. 12-18.

3. Essay on obesity: healthy Food vs fast food essay

Malnourishment in the United States

Malnourishment in the United States is caused mainly by the consumption of unhealthy, cheap foods that are low in nutrition and staffed with calories and fat. This eventually leads to obesity. As surprising as it may seem, one of the factors affecting obesity is poverty. As a matter of fact, there can be no doubts that poverty and obesity are interconnected. Provided more attention is focused on this link, the health of the Americans can be improved.

According to the statistics, about two-thirds of all American adults and more than one-tenth of American children are either overweight or obese. One-tenth of families suffer from food insecurity such as obesity and hunger, which take place when access to nutritionally satisfactory and safe foods is either restricted or unstable. At first glance it seems illogical as scarcity of food should result in underweight people. Nevertheless, children from families with low income are about 2.6 times as likely as children from rich families to get obese. It means that poor citizens are in some kind of unfavorable conditions when it comes to obesity.

The reality is that not all American households have the financial capabilities to provide satisfactory housing, transportation, commodities, medical assistance, education, food, and clothing that all families need. Many families often have to buy less healthy but cheaper foods instead of healthy but more expensive foods. Unfortunately, usually the most inexpensive option available to these people are foods with low nutritional value as to calorie content. That is why lower income families are at the highest disadvantage of malnutrition.

It has been revealed by a recent study that such health problems linked to obesity, like hypertension and diabetes, are more widespread among people with low income. Each year about $70 billion is spent on health-care due to obesity. Obesity, the condition of an abnormal accumulation of body fat, has a negative effect on different body systems (psychological, pulmonary, gastrointestinal, renal, musculoskeletal, neurological, cardiovascular, and endocrine). Solving the obesity problem can save health care money which could be used for improvement of the living conditions of low income citizens by paying for housing or college education, for instance.

One of the factors that help bring about obesity in poor families is fast food restaurant chains. They don't make it a secret in their advertising campaigns that their target customers are lower-class neighborhoods and families. Families that live in the poorest parts of cities and towns are much more exposed to fast food than people living in the richest places. Consequently, families with low income have more chances to buy fast food, although it is much less nutritious than other foods that can be bought for the same price. Despite their cheap price, these foods contain enormous amounts of calories and fat. Typically, calories in junk food come from sugar and fat, but not from whole-grain carbohydrates and fiber that satisfy hunger cravings and provide you with energy.

As a consequence, one will be hungry soon after eating fast food because the body was not satisfied with the lack of nutrition during the last meal. After that, if food is available, more food is ususaly consumed, which helps the progress of obesity.

The consumption of more organic foods can combat obesity and malnourishment. Unlike fast food, organic foods are not toxic and have more useful nutrients. However, their price is usually high, and families with low income cannot afford them.

Organic food is expensive due to a number of different factors. Today only one-tenth of American citizens buy organic foods on a regular basis. If the demand for organics grows, ultimately, the price should go down.

To stop the trend of increasing obesity among the families with low income, the first thing to be done is helping the poor abandon poverty. The government should provide money for college education to poor students, so that they could get the opportunity to receive a costly education that would give them higher-income jobs and reduce the current poverty level. In addition, it would be great if more affordable housing could be built for destitute families to have a safe place to live. After these reforms are made, the poverty level should be reduced and the current problem with obesity will improve.

Moreover, other measures must be taken. It is possible to improve opportunities for exercise and physical education. Currently, physical education courses in poor school areas are usually the first courses to be cut because of insufficient funding. Only upper-class students have access to high-tech gyms and workout facilities to help with weight management and fitness, whereas the lower-class students cannot afford to subscribe to these facilities.

In many poor urban areas there is no space for recreation which is safe for children. The only form of recreation or exercise for the majority of children is physical education. Typically, physical education is offered only once or twice a week, which is insufficient. The governments should do something to re-evaluate its standards for physical education. School is a place where children should be educated about healthy lifestyles. Consequently, physical education should be a part of this educational tool and should be provided most days of the week in public schools.

Improvements can be made to cut the prices of organic food so that people with different incomes can afford buying healthy foods. If organic foods get more popular, their prices will be much lower. Additionally, grocery stores should be stocked with locally grown food but not with food imported across the country or world because the shipping affects the product's price. Farmers would be able to economize on shipping fees; the environment wouldn't be so polluted because less gas has to be consumed to ship the products; finally, people would be able to purchase healthy foods at less expensive prices.

Farmers markets and local vendors are a nice alternative to grocery stores and a great way to buy foods. Not having to pay stores to sell their products, farmers get the entire price of the product, so they can reduce the selling price. State governments should cooperate with farmers and small businesses so that these markets could stay afloat. Not only do farmers markets offer healthy food at low prices, but also they nurture positive relationships between farmers and community members.

References

Ebbeling, Cara B., Ludwig, David S., and Pawlak, Dorota B. "Childhood Obesity: Public Health Crisis, Common Sense Cure."

"Obesity and Hunger in the United States." May 2003. Bread for the World Institute. Online. 5 Sept. 2005.

Overweight and Obesity: Obesity Trend. (2006). Retrieved from http://www.cdc.gov/nccdphp/dnpa/obesity/trend/maps/index.htm.

CHAPTER NINE

COMPARING AND CONTRASTING

What is a Compare and Contrast Essay?

An informative **essay** in which you talk about **what is** similar **and** different between two things. Compare and contrast essays are the bringing together two or more subjects, such as people, business or even events and shows their similarities and differences. This type of essay is used in business, as well as in college. There are two ways to write this type of essay. You can either compare or contrast the topics throughout the entire essay or you can talk on one topic and then talk on the other topic and so on. This is a personal preference, as well as a formatting preference. However, some topics work better one way or the other when reading them. To determine which way to write the essay, a Venn diagram can be completed to break the topics up and look at how they may read on paper. Remember, a Venn diagram shows circles that overlap each other and the similarities are placed in the overlapping section of the circles and the differences are put in the non-overlapping section of the circles. When writing a compare and contrast essay keep in mind to stay focused on the topics you are covering. You may not want to cover all similarities and differences between the chosen topics. Depending on how many similar and contrasting points there are, you may want to choose to narrow down the most poignant pieces of information to show a stark comparison as well as a sharp contrast between the topics.

This lesson will help you first to determine whether a particular assignment is asking for comparison/contrast and then to generate a list of similarities and differences, decide which similarities and differences to focus on, and organize your essay so that it will be clear and effective. It will also explain how you can (and why you should) develop a thesis that goes beyond how "Thing A and Thing B are similar in many ways but different in others."

The purpose of a compare and contrast essay is to analyze the differences and/or the similarities of two distinct subjects. A good compare/contrast essay doesn't only point out how the subjects are similar or different (or even both!). It uses those points to make a meaningful argument about the subjects. While it can be a little intimidating to approach this type of essay at first, with a little work and practice, you can write a great compare-and-contrast essay!

A compare and contrast essay therefore examines two or more topics (objects, people, or ideas, for example), comparing their similarities and contrasting their differences. You may choose to focus exclusively on comparing, exclusively on contrasting, or on both-or your instructor may direct you to do one or both. First, pick useable subjects and list their characteristics. In fact, their individual characteristics determine whether the subjects *are* useable. After that, choose a parallel pattern of organization and effective transitions to set your paper above the merely average.

1. Picking a subject

Focus on things that can obviously be compared or contrasted. For instance, if you are examining an idea (political or philosophical) examine the opposite of that idea. Or, if you are examining a person, like a president, pick another president for comparison or contrast. Don't try to compare a president and a cab driver, or existentialism and a legislative bill on car tax refunds.

2. Listing characteristics

Divide a piece of paper into two sides. One side is for the first subject, the other for the second subject. Then, begin to list the similarities and differences that immediately come to mind. Concentrate on characteristics that either are shared or are opposing between the two subjects. Alternately, you may construct a Venn diagram of intersecting circles, listing the subjects' differences to either side or their similarities where the circles intersect. Keep in mind that for a balanced paper, you want to make point-by-point, parallel comparisons (or contrasts).

Similarities between my math and English instructor:
Both are welcoming and available to students.
Both are organized and keep a neat office.
Both are knowledgeable and professional.
Differences between my math and English instructors
Math teacher listens to classic rock. English teacher listens to jazz.
Math teacher drinks Earl Grey tea. English teacher drinks strong black coffee.
Math teacher likes to chat about movies. English teacher sticks to business.

As you create your list, is it clear why you are comparing and contrasting these two subjects? Do you have a preference for one or the other? If so, make sure you are evaluating each side fairly. A point-by-point list helps you maintain balance.

Once you have a list, decide whether there are more similarities or differences between the topics. If there are more similarities, concentrate your paper on comparing. If there are more differences (or if, as in the example above, the differences are simply more interesting), concentrate on contrasting. If there is a balance of similarities and differences, you might concentrate on discussing this balance.

3. Organizing

There are at least two ways to organize a compare/contrast essay. Imagine you are examining Robert E. Lee and Ulysses S. Grant, both Civil War generals. In your list you have uncovered important points of dissimilarity between them. Those points are their background, personalities, and underlying aspirations. (Call these three points A, B, and C.) You have decided to contrast the two subjects.

Here is one way to organize the body of this paper, addressing points A, B, and C for each subject. This paper will follow parallel order–A, B, and then C–for each subject:

A. Lee's background

    B. Lee's personality
    C. Lee's underlying aspirations
    D. Grant's background
    E. Grant's personality
    F. Grant's underlying aspirations

However, here is another way to organize the same paper:

    A. Lee's background
    A. Grant's background
    B. Lee's personality
    B. Grant's personality
    C. Lee's underlying aspiration
    C. Grant's underlying aspiration

For a shorter paper, the above might represent three paragraphs; if you are writing a long paper and have a great deal of information, you may choose to write about each point, A, B, and C, in separate paragraphs for a total of six. However you decide to organize, make sure it is clear *why* you are examining this subject. You might be able to compare apples and oranges, for example, but why would you? Include any insights or opinions you have gathered. And yes, in general, three is the magic number. While there is no hard-and-fast rule that precludes creating a paper based on two points, or four, or five, a three-point discussion is manageable, especially for complex or abstract subjects. At the same time, a three-point structure helps you avoid oversimplifying, especially when addressing controversial topics in which discussions tend to become polarized–right or wrong, black or white, for or against. Three-point treatments encourage discussion of the middle ground.

4. Signaling transitions

Learn to use expressions that precisely convey contrast or comparison. These expressions, or transitions, signal contrast:

- *on the contrary*
- *on the other hand*

- *however*
- *otherwise*
- *whereas*
- *still*
- *yet*

These expressions signal comparison:

- *as well as*
- *both*
- *like*
- *in common with*
- *likewise*
- *also*

Signal words such as these help the reader understand the relationships between your sentences, paragraphs, and ideas. In particular, if you are both comparing and contrasting, signal words help sort out what's what. Second only to effective organization, effective use of these expressions will go a long way toward helping produce a good compare/contrast paper.

How to Write a Comparative Analysis

Throughout your academic career, you'll be asked to write papers in which you compare and contrast two things: two texts, two theories, two historical figures, two scientific processes, and so on. "Classic" compare-and-contrast papers, in which you weight A and B equally, may be about two similar things that have crucial differences (two pesticides with different effects on the environment) or two similar things that have crucial differences, yet turn out to have surprising commonalities (two politicians with vastly different world views who voice unexpectedly similar perspectives on sexual harassment).

In the "lens" (or "keyhole") comparison, in which you weight A less heavily than B, you use A as a lens through which to view B. Just as looking through a pair of glasses changes the way you see an object, using A as a framework for understanding B changes the way you see B. Lens comparisons are useful for illuminating, critiquing, or challenging the stability of a thing that, before the analysis, seemed perfectly understood. Often, lens comparisons take time into account: earlier texts, events, or historical figures may illuminate later ones, and vice versa.

Faced with a daunting list of seemingly unrelated similarities and differences, you may feel confused about how to construct a paper that isn't just a mechanical exercise in which you first state all the features that A and B have in common, and then state all the ways in which A and B are different. Predictably, the thesis of such a paper is usually an assertion that A and B are very similar yet not so similar after all. To write a good compare-and-contrast paper, you must take your raw data—the similarities and differences you've observed—and make them cohere into a meaningful argument. Here are the five elements required.

Frame of Reference. This is the context within which you place the two things you plan to compare and contrast; it is the umbrella under which you have grouped them. The frame of reference may consist of an idea, theme, question, problem, or theory; a group of similar things from which you extract two for special attention; biographical or historical information. The best frames of reference are constructed from specific sources rather than your own thoughts or observations. Thus, in a paper comparing how two writers redefine social norms of masculinity, you would be better off quoting a sociologist on the topic of masculinity than spinning out potentially banal-sounding theories of your own. Most assignments tell you exactly what the frame of reference should be, and most courses supply sources for constructing it. *If you encounter an assignment that fails to provide a frame of reference, you must come up with one on your own.* A paper without such a context would have no angle on the material, no focus or frame for the writer to propose a meaningful argument.

Grounds for Comparison. Let's say you're writing a paper on global food distribution, and you've chosen to compare apples and oranges. Why these particular fruits? Why not pears and bananas? The rationale behind your choice, the grounds for comparison, lets your reader know why your choice is deliberate and meaningful, not random. For instance, in a paper asking how the "discourse of domesticity" has been used in the abortion debate, the grounds for comparison are obvious; the issue has two conflicting sides, pro-choice and pro-life. In a paper comparing the effects of acid rain on two forest sites, your choice of sites is less obvious. A paper focusing on similarly aged forest stands in Maine and the Catskills will be set up differently from one comparing a new forest stand in the White Mountains with an old forest in the same region. You need to indicate the reasoning behind your choice.

Thesis. The grounds for comparison anticipates the comparative nature of your thesis. As in any argumentative paper, your thesis statement will convey the gist of your argument, which necessarily follows from your frame of reference. But in a compare-and-contrast, the thesis depends on how the two things you've chosen to compare actually relate to one another. Do they extend, corroborate, complicate, contradict, correct, or debate one another? In the most common compare-and-contrast paper—one focusing on differences—you can indicate the precise relationship between A and B by using the word "whereas" in your thesis:

Whereas Camus perceives ideology as secondary to the need to address a specific historical moment of colonialism, Fanon perceives a revolutionary ideology as the impetus to reshape Algeria's history in a direction toward independence.

Whether your paper focuses primarily on difference or similarity, you need to make the relationship between A and B clear in your thesis. This relationship is at the heart of any compare-and-contrast paper.

Organizational Scheme. Your introduction will include your frame of reference, grounds for comparison, and thesis. There are two basic ways to organize the body of your paper.

- In *text-by-text*, you discuss all of A, then all of B.
- In *point-by-point*, you alternate points about A with comparable points about B.

If you think that B extends A, you'll probably use a text-by-text scheme; if you see A and B engaged in debate, a point-by-point scheme will draw attention to the conflict. Be aware, however, that the point-by- point scheme can come off as a ping-pong game. You can avoid this effect by grouping more than one point together, thereby cutting down on the number of times you alternate from A to B. But no matter which organizational scheme you choose, you need not give equal time to similarities and differences. In fact, your paper will be more interesting if you get to the heart of your argument as quickly as possible. Thus, a paper on two evolutionary theorists' different interpretations of specific archaeological findings might have as few as two or three sentences in the introduction on similarities and at most a paragraph or two to set up the contrast between the theorists' positions. The rest of the paper, whether organized text- by-text or point-by-point, will treat the two theorists' differences.

You can organize a classic compare-and-contrast paper either text-by-text or point-by-point. But in a "lens" comparison, in which you spend significantly less time on A (the lens) than on B (the focal text), you almost always organize text-by-text. That's because A and B are not strictly comparable: A is merely a tool for helping you discover whether or not B's nature is actually what expectations have led you to believe it is.

Linking of A and B. All argumentative papers require you to link each point in the argument back to the thesis. Without such links, your reader will be unable to see how new sections logically and systematically advance your argument. In a compare-and contrast, you also need to make links between A and B in the body of your essay if you want your paper to hold together. To make these links, use transitional expressions of comparison and contrast (*similarly, moreover, likewise, on the contrary, conversely, on the other hand*) and contrastive vocabulary (in the example below, *Southerner/Northerner*).

As a girl raised in the faded glory of the Old South, amid mystical tales of magnolias and moonlight, the mother remains part of a dying generation. Surrounded by hard times, racial conflict, and limited opportunities, Julian, *on the other hand*, feels repelled by the provincial nature of home, and represents a new Southerner, one who sees his native land through a condescending Northerner's eyes.

Creation or Evolution?

After Sir Charles Darwin introduced his original theory about the origins of species and evolution, humanity's faith in God, which remained undisputed for hundreds of years, had reeled. The former unity fractured into evolutionists, who believed life as we see it today developed from smaller and more primitive organisms, and creationists, who kept believing life in all its diversity was created by a higher entity. Each side introduced substantial arguments to support their claims, but at the same time, the counter-arguments of each opponent were also credible. Therefore, the debates between the evolutionists and the creationists seem to be far from ending. And though their arguments are completely opposite, they can coexist and even complement each other.

Evolutionists often come with the argument about fossil findings serving as a proof of the evolutionary process; bones of such creatures as dinosaurs, or the remains of even more ancient beings found by archaeologists are much older than the age of our world according to the Bible. Therefore, claim the evolutionists, creationists are wrong. Creationists, however, came up with a strong counter argument. They say all fossil findings are already fully formed, and appear to have not changed much over time; in other words, they remained in a stasis condition (Geological Society of America). This means there are no intermediate links between simpler and more complex life forms, which witnesses in favor of the claim of each species having been created.

Evolutionists—as well as atheists—state, despite the enormous scientific and technological progress, despite ultra-sensitive observation systems, such as orbital telescopes, there are still no factual evidence of God's existence. At the same time, creationists appeal to the fact that though God has not yet been heard or seen, a multitude of indirect evidence exists of its existence. For example, creationists name an incredible complexity both of living organisms, and the ecosystems they inhabit. The compound eyes of night creatures are extremely difficult to develop, especially on their own. Ecosystems function in such a way that the absence, even of several smallest components, causes the ruin of the environment. It is difficult to believe such complexity and diversity appeared and established balance on its own, whereas evolutionists suggest the idea of random development through survival of the fittest.

Evolutionists believe over time, the matter that formed our universe shaped out into stars, planets, chemicals, and finally, living organisms. According to evolutionists, before the Big Bang, there existed nothing (or at least what could be observed with our laws of physics), but after it, the matter self-organized in ordered structures, which become even more structured and organized as time flowed on. Surprisingly, creationists refer to science to oppose this thesis. They say that, according to the second law of thermodynamics, everything, be it living creatures, chemicals, or substances, tend to blend and mix with their environment over time, finally reaching the steady-state, which does not happen in nature (BestBibleScience.com).

At the same time, both sides seem to forget one point of view that does not necessarily contradict another one. It is possible God could have planned everything, prepared certain elements for the universe's development, and then just pressed a metaphysical "Start" button, letting its ideas self-embody, watching the results. Or, God could have created the possibility of life, but after this, it could leave this life to find its own ways. Besides these, many other compromise variants can be suggested; anyways, it is ridiculous in the debate about the most complex and incomprehensible subject in the world if only two points of view exist.

The clash between evolutionists and creationists seems to be far from its finale. Both sides come up with potent arguments in favor of their positions. Evolutionists stress the absence of factual evidence in favor of God's existence, point to fossils as a proof of the evolutionary process, and name the Big Bang as the reason of the universe's appearance and further development. Creationists, in their turn, stress there are no intermediate links between species in found fossils, consider complexity and diversity of nature to be an indirect evidence of God's existence, and refer to the second law of thermodynamics to argue against the Big Bang theory. However, none of these sides seem to see how both points of view can not only coexist, but be successfully combined. Such a combination could explain everything at once.

Outline your essay. Outlining your essay will help you work out the main organizational structure and will give you a template to follow as you develop your ideas. No matter how you decided to organize your essay, you will still need to have the following types of paragraphs:

- o *Introduction.* This paragraph comes first and presents the basic information about the subjects to be compared and contrasted. It should present your thesis and the direction of your essay (i.e., what you will discuss and why your readers should care).
- o *Body Paragraphs.* These are the meat of your essay, where you provide the details and evidence that support your claims. Each different section or body paragraph should tackle a different division of proof. It should provide and analyze evidence in order to connect those proofs to your thesis and support your thesis. Many middle-school and high-school essays may only require three body paragraphs, but use as many as is necessary to fully convey your argument.
- o *Acknowledgement of Competitive Arguments/Concession.* This paragraph acknowledges that other counter-arguments exist, but discusses how those arguments are flawed or do not apply.
- o *Conclusion.* This paragraph summarizes the evidence presented. It will restate the thesis, but usually in a way that offers more information or sophistication than the introduction could. Remember: your audience now has all the information you gave them about why your argument is solid. They don't need you to just reword your original thesis. Take it to the next level!

Introduction

In your career as a student, you'll encounter many different kinds of writing assignments, each with its own requirements. One of the most common is the comparison/contrast essay, in which you focus on the ways in which certain things or ideas—usually two of them—are similar to (this is the comparison) and/or different from (this is the contrast) one another. By assigning such essays, your instructors are encouraging you to make connections between texts or ideas, engage in critical thinking, and go beyond mere description or summary to generate interesting analysis: when you reflect on similarities and differences, you gain a deeper understanding of the items you are comparing, their relationship to each other, and what is most important about them.

- o Body Paragraph 1: Discuss first difference between woods and beaches: climate/weather.
    - Woods
    - Beach
- o Body Paragraph 2: Discuss second difference between woods and beaches: types of activities.
    - Woods
    - Beach
- o Body Paragraph 3: Discuss third difference between woods and beaches: available facilities.
    - Woods
    - Beach
- o Conclusion

Outline your body paragraphs based on compare then contrast. This type of organization works best for when you want to emphasize the contrasts between your subjects. First, you discuss how your subjects are similar. Then, you end with how they're different (and, usually, how one is superior). Here's how your essay could look with this organization:

- o Introduction
- o Body Paragraph 1: Similarity between woods and beaches (both are places with a wide variety of things to do)
- o Body Paragraph 2: First difference between woods and beaches (they have different climates)
- o Body Paragraph 3: Second difference between woods and beaches (there are more easily accessible woods than beaches in most parts of the country)
- o Body Paragraph 4: Emphasis on the superiority of the woods to the beach
- o Conclusion

Organize your individual body paragraphs. Once you've chosen an organizational method for your body paragraphs, you'll need to have an internal organization for the body paragraphs themselves. Each of your body paragraphs will need to have the three following elements:

o Topic sentence: This sentence introduces the main idea and subject of the paragraph. It can also provide a transition from the ideas in the previous paragraph.
o Body: These sentences provide concrete evidence that support the topic sentence and main idea.
o Conclusion: this sentence wraps up the ideas in the paragraph. It may also provide a link to the next paragraph's ideas.

Use your brainstorming ideas to fill in your outline. Once you've outlined your essay, it should be fairly simple to find evidence for your arguments. Look at the lists and diagrams you generated to help you find the evidence for your comparisons and contrasts.

o If you are having trouble finding evidence to support your argument, go back to your original texts and try the brainstorming process again. It could be that your argument is evolving past where it started, which is good! You just need to go back and look for further evidence.

Remember to explain the "why." A common error many writers make is to let the comparisons and contrasts "speak for themselves," rather than explaining why it's helpful or important to put them together. Don't just provide a list of "ways Topic A and Topic B are similar and different." In your body paragraphs as well as your conclusion, remind your readers of the significance of your evidence and argument.

o For example, in a body paragraph about the quality of ingredients in frozen vs. homemade pizza, you could close with an assertion like this: "Because you actively control the quality of the ingredients in pizza you make at home, it can be healthier for you than frozen pizza. It can also let you express your imagination. Pineapple and peanut butter pizza? Go for it! Pickles and parmesan? Do it! Using your own ingredients lets you have fun with your food." This type of comment helps your reader understand *why* the ability to choose your own ingredients makes homemade pizza better.

Recognizing comparison/contrast in assignments

Some assignments use words—like compare, contrast, similarities, and differences—that make it easy for you to see that they are asking you to compare and/or contrast. Here are a few hypothetical examples:

- Compare and contrast Frye's and Bartky's accounts of oppression.
- Compare WWI to WWII, identifying similarities in the causes, development, and outcomes of the wars.
- Contrast Wordsworth and Coleridge; what are the major differences in their poetry?

Notice that some topics ask only for comparison, others only for contrast, and others for both.

But it's not always so easy to tell whether an assignment is asking you to include comparison/contrast. And in some cases, comparison/contrast is only part of the essay—you begin by comparing and/or contrasting two or more things and then use what you've learned to construct an argument or evaluation. Consider these examples, noticing the language that is used to ask for the comparison/contrast and whether the comparison/contrast is only one part of a larger assignment:

- Choose a particular idea or theme, such as romantic love, death, or nature, and consider how it is treated in two Romantic poems.
- How do the different authors we have studied so far define and describe oppression?
- Compare Frye's and Bartky's accounts of oppression. What does each imply about women's collusion in their own oppression? Which is more accurate?

- In the texts we've studied, soldiers who served in different wars offer differing accounts of their experiences and feelings both during and after the fighting. What commonalities are there in these accounts? What factors do you think are responsible for their differences?

You may want to check out our handout on Understanding Assignments for additional tips.

Using comparison/contrast for all kinds of writing projects

Sometimes you may want to use comparison/contrast techniques in your own pre-writing work to get ideas that you can later use for an argument, even if comparison/contrast isn't an official requirement for the paper you're writing. For example, if you wanted to argue that Frye's account of oppression is better than both de Beauvoir's and Bartky's, comparing and contrasting the main arguments of those three authors might help you construct your evaluation—even though the topic may not have asked for comparison/contrast and the lists of similarities and differences you generate may not appear anywhere in the final draft of your paper.

Discovering similarities and differences

Making a Venn diagram or a chart can help you quickly and efficiently compare and contrast two or more things or ideas. To make a Venn diagram, simply draw some overlapping circles, one circle for each item you're considering. In the central area where they overlap, list the traits the two items have in common. Assign each one of the areas that doesn't overlap; in those areas, you can list the traits that make the things different.

To make a chart, figure out what criteria you want to focus on in comparing the items. Along the left side of the page, list each of the criteria. Across the top, list the names of the items. You should then have a box per item for each criterion; you can fill the boxes in and then survey what you've discovered.

As you generate points of comparison, consider the purpose and content of the assignment and the focus of the class. What do you think the professor wants you to learn by doing this comparison/contrast? How does it fit with what you have been studying so far and with the other assignments in the course? Are there any clues about what to focus on in the assignment itself?

Here are some general questions about different types of things you might have to compare. These are by no means complete or definitive lists; they're just here to give you some ideas—you can generate your own questions for these and other types of comparison. You may want to begin by using the questions reporters traditionally ask: Who? What? Where? When? Why? How? If you're talking about objects, you might also consider general properties like size, shape, color, sound, weight, taste, texture, smell, number, duration, and location.

Two historical periods or events

- When did they occur—do you know the date(s) and duration? What happened or changed during each? Why are they significant? What kinds of work did people do? What kinds of relationships did they have? What did they value? What kinds of governments were there? Who were important people involved? What caused events in these periods, and what consequences did they have later on?

Two ideas or theories

- What are they about? Did they originate at some particular time? Who created them? Who uses or defends them? What is the central focus, claim, or goal of each? What conclusions do they offer? How are they applied to situations/people/things/ etc.? Which seems more plausible to you, and why? How broad is their scope? What kind of evidence is usually offered for them?

Two pieces of writing or art

- What are their titles? What do they describe or depict? What is their tone or mood? What is their form? Who created them? When were they created? Why do you think they were created as they were? What themes do they address? Do you think one is of higher quality or greater merit than the other(s)—and if so, why? For writing: what plot, characterization, setting, theme, tone, and type of narration are used?

Two people

- Where are they from? How old are they? What is the gender, race, class, etc. of each? What, if anything, are they known for? Do they have any relationship to each other? What are they like? What did/do they do? What do they believe? Why are they interesting? What stands out most about each of them?

Deciding what to focus on

By now you have probably generated a huge list of similarities and differences—congratulations! Next you must decide which of them are interesting, important, and relevant enough to be included in your paper. Ask yourself these questions:

- What's relevant to the assignment?
- What's relevant to the course?
- What's interesting and informative?
- What matters to the argument you are going to make?
- What's basic or central (and needs to be mentioned even if obvious)?
- Overall, what's more important—the similarities or the differences?

Suppose that you are writing a paper comparing two novels. For most literature classes, the fact that they both use Calson type (a kind of typeface, like the fonts you may use in your writing) is not going to be relevant, nor is the fact that one of them has a few illustrations and the other has none; literature classes are more likely to focus on subjects like characterization, plot, setting, the writer's style and intentions, language, central themes, and so forth. However, if you were writing a paper for a class on typesetting or on how illustrations are used to enhance novels, the typeface and presence or absence of illustrations might be absolutely critical to include in your final paper.

Sometimes a particular point of comparison or contrast might be relevant but not terribly revealing or interesting. For example, if you are writing a paper about Wordsworth's "Tintern Abbey" and Coleridge's "Frost at Midnight," pointing out that they both have nature as a central theme is relevant (comparisons of poetry often talk about themes) but not terribly interesting; your class has probably already had many discussions about the Romantic poets' fondness for nature. Talking about the different ways nature is depicted or the different aspects of nature that are emphasized might be more interesting and show a more sophisticated understanding of the poems.

Your thesis

The thesis of your comparison/contrast paper is very important: it can help you create a focused argument and give your reader a road map so she/he doesn't get lost in the sea of points you are about to make. As in any paper, you will want to replace vague reports of your general topic (for example, "This paper will compare and contrast two pizza places," or "Pepper's and Amante are similar in some ways and different in others," or "Pepper's and Amante are similar in many ways, but they have one major difference") with something more detailed and specific. For example, you might say, "Pepper's and Amante have similar prices and ingredients, but their atmospheres and willingness to deliver set them apart."

Be careful, though—although this thesis is fairly specific and does propose a simple argument (that atmosphere and delivery make the two pizza places different), your instructor will often be looking for a bit more analysis. In this case, the obvious question is "So what? Why should anyone care that Pepper's and Amante are different in this way?" One might also wonder why the writer chose those two particular pizza places to compare—why not Papa John's, Dominos, or Pizza Hut? Again, thinking about the context the class provides may help you answer such questions and make a stronger argument. Here's a revision of the thesis mentioned earlier:

- Pepper's and Amante both offer a greater variety of ingredients than other Chapel Hill/Carrboro pizza places (and then any of the national chains), but the funky, lively atmosphere at Pepper's makes it a better place to give visiting friends and family a taste of local culture.

You may find our handout Constructing Thesis Statements useful at this stage.

Organizing your paper

There are many different ways to organize a comparison/contrast essay. Here are two:

Subject-by-subject:

Begin by saying everything you have to say about the first subject you are discussing, then move on and make all the points you want to make about the second subject (and after that, the third, and so on, if you're comparing/contrasting more than two things). If the paper is short, you might be able to fit all of your points about each item into a single paragraph, but it's more likely that you'd have several paragraphs per item. Using our pizza place comparison/contrast as an example, after the introduction, you might have a paragraph about the ingredients available at Pepper's, a paragraph about its location, and a paragraph about its ambience. Then you'd have three similar paragraphs about Amante, followed by your conclusion.

The danger of this subject-by-subject organization is that your paper will simply be a list of points: a certain number of points (in my example, three) about one subject, then a certain number of points about another. This is usually not what college instructors are looking for in a paper—generally they want you to compare or contrast two or more things very directly, rather than just listing the traits the things have and leaving it up to the reader to reflect on how those traits are similar or different and why those similarities or differences matter. Thus, if you use the subject-by-subject form, you will probably want to have a very strong, analytical thesis and at least one body paragraph that ties all of your different points together.

A subject-by-subject structure can be a logical choice if you are writing what is sometimes called a "lens" comparison, in which you use one subject or item (which isn't really your main topic) to better understand another item (which is). For example, you might be asked to compare a poem you've already covered thoroughly in class with one you are reading on your own. It might make sense to give a brief summary of your main ideas about the first poem (this would be your first subject, the "lens"), and then spend most of your paper discussing how those points are similar to or different from your ideas about the second.

Point-by-point:

> Rather than addressing things one subject at a time, you may wish to talk about one point of comparison at a time. There are two main ways this might play out, depending on how much you have to say about each of the things you are comparing. If you have just a little, you might, in a single paragraph, discuss how a certain point of comparison/contrast relates to all the items you are discussing. For example, I might describe, in one paragraph, what the prices are like at both Pepper's and Amante; in the next paragraph, I might compare the ingredients available; in a third, I might contrast the atmospheres of the two restaurants.

If I had a bit more to say about the items I was comparing/contrasting, I might devote a whole paragraph to how each point relates to each item. For example, I might have a whole paragraph about the clientele at Pepper's, followed by a whole paragraph about the clientele at Amante; then I would move on and do two more paragraphs discussing my next point of comparison/contrast—like the ingredients available at each restaurant.

There are no hard and fast rules about organizing a comparison/ contrast paper, of course. Just be sure that your reader can easily tell what's going on! Be aware, too, of the placement of your different points. If you are writing a comparison/contrast in service of an argument, keep in mind that the last point you make is the one you are leaving your reader with. For example, if I am trying to argue that Amante is better than Pepper's, I should end with a contrast that leaves Amante sounding good, rather than with a point of comparison that I have to admit makes Pepper's look better. If you've decided that the differences between the items you're comparing/contrasting are most important, you'll want to end with the differences—and vice versa, if the similarities seem most important to you.

Cue words and other tips

To help your reader keep track of where you are in the comparison/ contrast, you'll want to be sure that your transitions and topic sentences are especially strong. Your thesis should already have given the reader an idea of the points you'll be making and the organization you'll be using, but you can help her/him out with some extra cues. The following words may be helpful to you in signaling your intentions:

- like, similar to, also, unlike, similarly, in the same way, likewise, again, compared to, in contrast, in like manner, contrasted with, on the contrary, however, although, yet, even though, still, but, nevertheless, conversely, at the same time, regardless, despite, while, on the one hand … on the other hand.

For example, you might have a topic sentence like one of these:

- Compared to Pepper's, Amante is quiet.
- Like Amante, Pepper's offers fresh garlic as a topping.

- Despite their different locations (downtown Chapel Hill and downtown Carrboro), Pepper's and Amante are both fairly easy to get to.

Examples of Compare and Contrast Essays

1. Differences between Good and Bad Bosses

Everyone knows how important it is to have favorable conditions at the workplace. Starting from trivial things such as air conditioners or coolers with fresh water, and ending up with flexible schedules and good relationships with colleagues—all this, as well as many other factors, impact employees' productivity and quality of work. In this regard, one of the most important factors is the manager, or the boss, who directs the working process. It is not a secret that bosses are often a category of people difficult to deal with: many of them are unfairly demanding, tyrannic, and prone to shifting their responsibilities to other workers, and so on. At the same time, there are many bosses who not only manage to maintain their staff's productivity at high levels, but also treat them nicely, fairly, with understanding, and are pleasant to work with. Let us try to figure out the differences between good and bad managers, or bosses.

There are numerous cases when a boss sees his or her staff as personal attendants. The scales of this attitude can vary: some bosses may from time to time ask an employee to bring them a cup of coffee—this is tolerable, and in many cases this can be evaluated as a friendly favor a coworker would do for another coworker without feeling inferior or exploited. However, there are managers whose personal demands go far beyond friendly requests. Highly qualified workers sometimes have to face humiliating demands; for example, Jennifer (the name is changed)—a finance executive in a big company—had to dress up like a Japanese woman, because her boss demanded her to do so. Or, another victim of unfair chief-subordinate relationships, Marisa, had to stay in the office late after work, because her boss required her to (attention!) trim his ear hair (Everwise).

A "good" boss would obviously not treat his or her subordinates like this. Respecting their feelings, dignity, and personal space, such a boss would not demand colleagues to do personal favors, making use of a higher position in a company's hierarchy. As it has been mentioned before, asking for a cup of coffee or some other small favor can be tolerable if it does not harm a worker's productivity and/or somehow infringes upon their dignity. Such favors are often made by subordinate employees for each other, and probably cannot be evaluated as exploitation. Things like those described in the previous paragraph, however, go far beyond a friendly attitude, and feel more like exploitation.

There are bosses who are typical "emotional vampires." These people are extremely difficult to work with, and even though they may possess traits necessary for performing their duties excellently, their subordinates usually suffer severe stress because of their bosses' psychological peculiarities. According to the clinical psychologist Albert Bernstein, vampires fall under four categories: anti-socials, who pursue excitement in all of its forms; obsessive-compulsives, who meticulously seek for the slightest flaws in their subordinates' work and micromanage everything; histrionics, who need other people's attention, and narcissists, who believe they are the most spectacular, valuable, and professional employees in the company (Everwise). Each of these types can be emotionally dangerous for employees. For example, anti-social bosses may provoke conflicts within the office environment, and then enjoy the emotional dramas following up; narcissists will criticize everything and everyone, never satisfied with the work their subordinates do, but never "stooping low enough" to organize it in such a way that benefits everyone; obsessive-compulsive bosses can drive employees crazy with trying to handle and regulate every little detail of the working process—implementing rules for ridiculous things like how sharp should pencils be, or what angle monitors should be. It does not mean that emotional vampires do it on purpose: rather often, such traits are subconscious behavioral patterns, but this still does not make employees' lives easier.

A "good boss," on the contrary, does not try to regulate everything, or put himself or herself on a pedestal. Such a person is supportive, knows the weak and the strong professional traits of each of his or her subordinates, listens to what staff has to say (and not just listens, but cares about implementing good ideas), encourages personnel, and cares not just about the work done but also about the team in general and about each of the team's members. "Bad" bosses may be highly competent in the latest theories regarding their field of work, but it is the skill to manage personnel, to inspire rather than to enforce, which makes yet another difference between the good and the bad boss (Developing People). And even though it is important for a manager to care about the tasks his or her team must accomplish, a good manager will always consider the capabilities and skills of his or her team, instead of blatantly demanding results without regarding how people in the team feel.

All this does not mean that a good boss is one who is nice and tender to his or her subordinates, and a bad boss is one who demands too much, though. In fact, a "good" boss can possess all the traits of a "bad" one: he or she can criticize, yell, or force people to do a lot of work within a short period of time, for example. However, it is the sense of limits that makes the difference. Robert Sutton, a professor of management at Stanford University, says that: "The best bosses have that ability to sort of turn up the volume, to be pushy, to get in people's faces when they need it, maybe to give them some negative feedback, and to back off when it's the right time to do that as well. We want people leading us who are confident, who are competent, who act like they're in charge, who make firm decisions, but we don't want to work for arrogant, pigheaded bastards who can't take input. And so what you end up with is sort of this challenge—what great bosses do is find a way to walk the line between these two things" (Business Insider). In other words, many of the "nasty" things "bad" bosses do can be done by "good" bosses as well, but a "good" boss uses such tactics only when it is necessary and knows when to stop being pushy—unlike "bad" bosses, who know no other manner of management.

The relationships between bosses and their employees greatly affect the productivity and the quality of work within any company—this is why it is important that these relationships are, if not friendly, then at least constructive and respectful. Unfortunately, not all managers know how to treat their personnel well. There are traits that indicate a bad boss with almost 100% accuracy: such bosses often treat their subordinates as personal attendants, are demanding, pushy, and offensive for no real reason, or may let their negative traits of character loose, turning the life of regular employees into psychological hell (as in the case of emotional vampires). On the contrary, good bosses treat their subordinates with respect, consider their emotions and professional capabilities, care about teamwork, try to inspire employees instead of forcing them to do something, and even when they need to be pushy and harsh, such bosses always know when to stop.

Works Cited

Giang, Vivian. "This is the Difference Between a Good and Bad Boss." Business Insider. Business Insider, 02 Jan. 2014. Web. 16 June 2017.

"The Difference Between Good and Great Managers." Everwise. N.p., 13 June 2016. Web. 16 June 2017.

"Good Manager vs. Bad Manager—What is the Difference?" Developing People. N.p., 01 Jan. 1970. Web. 16 June 2017.

Shermer, Michael. "25 Creationists' Arguments & 25 Evolutionists' Answers." Geological Society of America. N.p., n.d. Web. 06 Aug. 2013.

"Top Evidences for Creation." BestBibleScience.org. N.p., n.d. Web. 06 Aug. 2013.

1. Nature and Nurture, Then and Now

By Timandra Harkness

'Oklahoma, 1973', begins the documentary account of an experiment to teach a baby chimpanzee human language and thus, in the words of one of the researchers, 'test the nature versus nurture hypothesis'. And through today's eyes, the eyes of film-maker James Marsh (of Man on Wire fame), much of that experiment seems bizarre if not downright wrong. Nim's first surrogate mother, Stephanie Lafarge, takes the baby chimp into her home like another baby, changing its nappies, dressing it and even breastfeeding the animal for several months.

The film is a mixture of interviews, archive footage. and

reconstruction, and the testimony of the humans involved is, of course, far more revealing about them than about Nim. Both Stephanie and her daughter recall how Nim quickly learned to manipulate the dynamics of the family, playing off the jealousy of Stephanie's poet husband (who was not consulted before the baby ape moved in) and defying the authority of the project's supervisor, professor Herb Terrace, when he visited.

But while chimps are social animals with a strong sense of power relationships, it is also clear that Stephanie was playing games of her own. The ostensible purpose of the project was to teach Nim sign language, but at one point, she says 'words became the enemy' in her relationship with writer husband and linguistic psychologist (and ex-lover) Herb. And when Herb removes the chimp, and puts Nim in the care of attractive 18-year-old student Laura-Ann Pettito, the human dynamics continue to overshadow the scientific study of an ape learning sign language.

Yet the excitement of the researchers is clear. If they can teach a chimpanzee to communicate, they can find out how it 'thinks'. They are well aware of how radical an idea this is, a potential breaking down of the barrier between humans and animals. It is an ideal that sits well in their hippy era and milieu. Unfortunately for them, a chimpanzee is not a child. From the start, Nim uses violence to assert himself in social interactions, and as he grows stronger physically, this makes the 'chimp as child' conceit harder and harder to sustain. The researchers suffer bites that sever arteries and tendons, and one has her face torn open. Nim uses the sign for 'sorry' after these attacks, but they continue. Eventually, Herb decides to return Nim to the research facility where he was born.

Marsh's interviews reveal just how emotionally involved the humans became with Nim, but the story itself is told as a biography of the chimp. So, it is impossible to avoid seeing how the contradictions of the human attitudes to the ape—treating it like a baby and then like the dangerous animal it is—added to Nim's distress. One minute he is a spoilt pet with the run of a country house, the next he is in a cage with other chimpanzees, a social group he has never learned to live in. So, while we are invited to empathize with the humans, still crying all these years later as they recall leaving Nim in his cage, it also implicitly criticizes them for having taught him to live around humans and then thrown him back in with the other experimental subjects. And yet, the film humanizes Nim in our eyes too, so when he is sold on to a medical research establishment, we identify not with the human scientists but with the apes.

If this 1970s experiment reveals that era's confusion about where apes end and humans begin, the film says much about today's ambivalent attitudes too. So, it is worth comparing it to Francois Truffaut's L'Enfant Sauvage, a 1970 feature film based closely on Dr Jean Itard's account of his own experiment 170 years earlier. In 1798, a boy is found in the woods, apparently without language and completely unsocialised. Dr Itard reads about the boy and brings him to Paris to be the subject of his own experiment in nature and nurture, to see whether a child of around 11 can be transformed by education from a near-animal into a civilized man.

At first, there are many parallels in the behavior of the boy, whom the doctor names 'Victor', and that of Nim. Both show instinctive fear and resistance, bite their captors, and have to be restrained with a rope from running away. Both learn table manners and to ask for food and drink. Both—in strikingly parallel scenes—love to be wheeled around at high speed, Nim in a child's pushchair and Victor in a wheelbarrow. But there are vital differences in the two experiments. Dr Itard wants to teach Victor language not to see the world through the eyes of a boy who survived in the forest for 10 years, but to equip him to communicate with the wider world and—crucially—to be able to ask for things which are not in front of his eyes. He is thrilled by Victor's spontaneous tool making, when the boy fashions a chalk-holder, but even more thrilled when he shows that Victor has developed a sense of justice and thus become 'a moral being'.

This investigation into human nature happened in revolutionary France—supported by a grant—and aspired to prove that the most savage human being had the potential to be civilized—that human potential outstrips what initial circumstances endow on us, and that we are all capable of learning not only the superficial trappings of human society but to be free, moral agents. Through the prism of 1970, the

1798 experiment looks cruel at times, but though Dr Itard treats Victor harshly, he sees the fellow human in him. The educator's struggle to turn a wild child into a full member of human society, and the implicit faith that we are all capable, given the right conditions, of thus flourishing, is an echo of Enlightenment optimism in 20th century France.

By contrast, the Project Nim experiment saw the capacity for language as not uniquely human. It was based on the idea that nurture alone is responsible for making us human—that even an ape can have essentially human characteristics if it is reared with humans. Though the film, with 21st century eyes, is critical of confusing chimpanzee nature with human nature because of its adverse effects on Nim's happiness, it does not entirely reject the basis of the failed experiment. As well as criticizing human willingness to treat animals as experimental subjects, Project Nim draws implicit parallels between Nim's behavior and that of the humans studying him. It takes care not to elevate Nim to human status, but it does, at times, reduce the humans to primate social groups, with dominant males and nurturing females. Nim may be ruled by the desire for instant gratification, but so are the researchers, is the implication.

Both films tell us something about human nature, but they tell us more about how our view of that nature, and that potential, has changed since 1798 and since 1970. And not for the better.

Source:

Written under a Creative Commons License, with edits: https://creativecommons.org/licenses/by/1.0/

3. Comparing and Contrasting London and Washington, DC

By Scott McLean in *Writing for Success*

Both Washington, DC, and London are capital cities of English-speaking countries, and yet they offer vastly different experiences to their residents and visitors. Comparing and contrasting the two cities based on their history, their culture, and their residents show how different and similar the two are.

Both cities are rich in world and national history, though they developed on very different time lines. London, for example, has a history that dates back over two thousand years. It was part of the Roman Empire and known by the similar name, Londinium. It was not only one of the northernmost points of the Roman Empire but also the epicenter of the British Empire where it held significant global influence from the early sixteenth century on through the early twentieth century. Washington, DC, on the other hand, has only formally existed since the late eighteenth century. Though Native Americans inhabited the land several thousand years earlier, and settlers inhabited the land as early as the sixteenth century, the city did not become the capital of the United States until the 1790s. From that point onward to today, however, Washington, DC, has increasingly maintained significant global influence. Even though both cities have different histories, they have both held, and continue to hold, significant social influence in the economic and cultural global spheres.

Both Washington, DC, and London offer a wide array of museums that harbor many of the world's most prized treasures. While Washington, DC, has the National Gallery of Art and several other Smithsonian galleries, London's art scene and galleries have a definite edge in this category. From the Tate Modern to the British National Gallery, London's art ranks among the world's best. This difference and advantage has much to do with London and Britain's historical depth compared to that of the United States. London has a much richer past than Washington, DC, and consequently has a lot more material to pull from when arranging its collections. Both cities have thriving theater districts, but again, London wins this comparison, too, both in quantity and quality of theater choices. With regard to other cultural places like restaurants, pubs, and bars, both cities are very comparable. Both have a wide selection of expensive, elegant restaurants as well as a similar amount of global and national chains. While London may be better known for its pubs and taste in beer, DC offers a different bar-going experience. With clubs and pubs that tend to stay open later than their British counterparts, the DC night life tend to be less reserved overall.

Both cities also share and differ in cultural diversity and cost of living. Both cities share a very expensive cost of living—both in terms of housing and shopping. A downtown one-bedroom apartment in DC can easily cost $1,800 per month, and a similar "flat" in London may double that amount. These high costs create socioeconomic disparity among the residents. Although both cities' residents are predominantly wealthy, both have a significantly large population of poor and homeless. Perhaps the most significant difference between the resident demographics is the racial makeup. Washington, DC, is a "minority majority" city, which means the majority of its citizens are races other than white. In 2009, according to the US Census, 55 percent of DC residents were classified as "Black or African American" and 35 percent of its residents were classified as "white." London, by contrast, has very few minorities—in 2006, 70 percent of its population was "white," while only 10 percent was "black." The racial demographic differences between the cities is drastic.

Even though Washington, DC, and London are major capital cities of English-speaking countries in the Western world, they have many differences along with their similarities. They have vastly different histories, art cultures, and racial demographics, but they remain similar in their cost of living and socioeconomic disparity.

In sum, a comparison and contrast essay is one of the most common assignments in high schools and universities. In this type of essay students have to compare two (in some essays several) things, problems, events or ideas and evaluate their resemblances and differences. This type of essay advances and develops your critical thinking as well as your argumentation and understanding of importance of the events and things that you compare.

Examples of the headings in compare/contrast assignments are:

- Compare and contrast the weather conditions for cotton-growing areas of Lagos and Zaria.
- Compare the approach to the Soviet Union of F. D. Roosevelt and H. Truman. What are the similarities differences of their policy?
- Compare and contrast the movies "God Farther" and "Once upon a time in America."

- Sometimes, you may be asked to compare, sometimes you can be requested to contrast, and on several occasions both actions mentioned should be performed.
- Yet, at the same time comparison/contrast can be a part of an essay as well. In this case, you compare and contrast some events or things in order to develop an argument later.

Here are the examples of several topics, where compare/contrast parts should be included.

- Hatred and love, how these topics are treated in Hamlet?
- How two main historians we have studied define the term "d`etente"?
- Compare the programs to reduce the level of pollution in New York and Los Angeles. Which one is more effective?
- Comparison/contrast techniques.

Some students use comparison/contrast techniques in their essays, in order to develop argument in later stages of their essay writing assignments. For example if you assert that the approach to the USSR was more effective during Truman's presidency than during Roosevelt's presidency, then the comparison/contrasting technique will help you to develop your contention.

Comparison/contracting techniques.

One of the most effective ways of comparison/contracting techniques is the drawing of Venn diagram. Drawing this diagram allows you to compare and contrast two or even several things/events. To design a Venn diagram, draw several overlapping circles, each should represent some event or idea that you research. In the space of overlapping, write down the similarities, which two objects have. In the space that does not overlap, list the features that make things/events different.

In order to draw a chart you should understand the features of the things to be compared.

The left side is assigned to one criterion. The names of the items are listed across the top. Each box right now corresponds to one criteria.

Write down existing facts in the boxes that help you understand what features you have discovered.

Once all major points of comparison/ contrast have been listed, one should concentrate on the main aim of the comparison/contrast assignment. On this stage of the writing process you should have a clear idea of the purpose of this essay.

Try to answer the following questions: Why was this type of essay assigned to you? Does this type of assignment have any similarities with the ones you have completed before? What should be emphasized in this type of essay?

The following is a list of some questions on several topics that might be helpful in designing of your comparison/contrast essay. Certainly, you should use them as the guide, only. Try to formulate your own questions and arguments after you have studied the listed questions.

First ask several typical questions, such as: Who? How? Where? What? Why? If you research some objects you might try to concentrate on its physical features, like size, weight and height.

If you are assigned to compare two historical events, one should ask the following questions: When did it happen? Who was involved in it? Why did it happen? How did it influence further events? **Why is this event important?**

If you are assigned to compare two ideas/theories. you can pose the following questions to help you get on the right track.

What are these ideas? Who comes up with them? Why are they defended? How have they influenced people? How are they used? Which one is more credible?

After you have completed your list of differences and similarities, you should evaluate which of them are more interesting and important for your essay. In order to facilitate this process, you should ask these questions:

What differences and similarities are relevant to my assignment?

In your opinion, which similarities or differences are more important?

If you are assigned to compare and contrast two novels, you should cautiously evaluate the importance of different facts and features. Some physical features of the characters would be of less importance for this type of assignment; emphasize on psychological differences and similarities of the characters, the differences of the plots and attempts of the writer to research and investigate some problems or events.

In some essays it is pivotal to stress particular points of comparison. If you are assigned to compare the novels of Charles Dickens and Wilkie Collins for example, you should not emphasize that both of these authors are classical English writers. This fact is common knowledge and it is well-known to your tutor, essay writers and students. Talking about different analysis approaches to human minds would better show your understanding of the novels.

Thesis.

Thesis is one of the most important parts of your comparison/contrast essay. It is the central feature of your essay, the guide of your writing process. Unlike thesis in other types of essays, thesis of compare/contrast essay should be specific and backed up with highly argumentative analysis. The most common question that should be asked in the designing of this type of the thesis is "why?". You should show the importance of things and events that you compare.

The plan of your essay.

As we have mentioned earlier, the contrast/compare essay is a specific type of essay. That is why composing this type of an essay might differ from other ones. The following are several methods of organizing and designing this type of essay.

Item by item.

First, list all information on the first subject of comparison. Then you should go further, and list all points of another subject of comparison. Then you should do the same with the third subject (and so forth, depending on the number of subjects of comparison).

Certainly, if your paper is not long, one paragraph might comprise several items; however it is better to devote one paragraph to one item of comparison. The danger of such comparison is that your paper might be transformed into a simple list of points of comparison. Do not succumb to this mistake. Remember, your tutor would like you to compare and contrast these subjects, and not only provide the list of differences and similarities. In other words analytical work is expected from you. In order to complete this type of essay one should develop and design analytical thesis and paragraph (one or several of them, depending on the topic of your essay) that can combine your several points together.

This item-to-item comparison is frequently used when you design so called "lens" comparison. In this assignment you are asked to use one thing for better understanding of another. In this case you should describe in a nutshell the main points on the first thing and then move on discussing how the points mentioned are similar/different to another thing.

Point-by-Point.

This method is used to compare each point of the objects, rather than describe one thing at a time. For example, if you are assigned to compare two sport venues, your first paragraph might comprise the comparison of their locations. Your second one can be devoted to the description of the designs of the venues. In the third paragraph you may describe sport events that these venues host.

There is no universal rule in designing of compare/contrast essay. Certainly, it should have logical, comprehensive and consistent structure. Remember that the last point is of particular importance, because your reader will judge your essay by it. If, for example, you attempted to prove that the stadium "Universal" is much better than the stadium "Albano" you should wind up by stressing the fact that stadium "Universal" is better, rather than leaving reader with the statement that "Albano" might look better as well. If you think that differences rather than similarities are more important for your essay, you should end up with stressing differences, and vice versa.

CHAPTER TEN

REFLECTIVE ESSAYS

What Is a Reflective Essay?

A reflective essay is one in which you *reflect* on your personality, places you've been, people you've met, or experiences that have influenced you. This type of essay lets you tell the reader who you are and what/who has made you that way. Unlike most other types of essays you may have written, reflective essays typically don't deal with researching facts and figures. They are much more personal in nature and can be more fluid in structure and style. It can be tempting to just jump right into writing, but hold on! A good reflective essay can be a *great* reflective essay with the proper planning. In a reflective essay, the writer captures an image of his own mind.

Writing a reflective essay is like taking a "selfie" photo in words or holding a mirror to your psyche and memorializing the details of the image. In a reflective essay, you examine your own mind and articulate the process. Reflective essays focus on a specific experience, whether taking a course or going through a major crisis, and explain to the reader what its effects and ramifications are and how you have been affected or changed.

Benefits of Reflective Essay Writing

When you write things down, creating a visual image, you enhance your brain's ability to remember what you have written as opposed to merely thinking a thought or saying it aloud. Therefore, reflecting on learning solidifies the intellectual benefit gained, both in remembering the material that was taught and by analyzing the experience and cognitive processes involved. Writing down your reflections and having them at hand to rewrite can also generate fresh insight.

Uses of Reflective Essays

A teacher may assign a reflective essay to analyze how much material his students have absorbed, how well they have integrated it and what parts of his instructional strategy were most beneficial or flawed. A reflective essay provides a deeper, more detailed picture of the learner's experience than short-answer or multiple-choice testing possibly can. This type of essay is a part of most applications for admission to private school, college or graduate school, because it gives admissions officials a more complete picture of the individual they're considering. Reflective essays are also used in disciplinary contexts, where a misbehaving child or an individual convicted of offenses such as drunken driving or shoplifting may be asked to participate in an educational program and sum up the ways in which the program has (or has not) changed her.

Structure of a Reflective Essay

A reflective essay typically offers the writer considerably more flexibility than a research paper or critical essay, but the basic structure is the same. In your introduction, explain to the reader the purpose of the essay and who you were when the experience began; in terms of the essay topic, for example, you might characterize yourself as overly shy, lacking an understanding of theoretical physics or blind to the feelings of others. State whether you feel the course or experience has effectively changed you or not. In the body of your essay, identify specific parts of the experience and their specific impact on you. In your conclusion, briefly revisit who you were before and summarize the ways in which you have or have not changed. You may include ways in which your new understanding will affect your future behavior.

Reflective Essay Tips

Although reflective writing is more casual than other types of academic writing and does not usually require extensive research and citations, it will be held to the same standards as any other type of writing in terms of punctuation, grammar, clarity and logic. Don't get sloppy. Take the time to reflect in depth on your metacognitive processes -- not just the facts you have learned, but the way in which your mind analyzed and organized these facts. After you've written a first draft, reread it with an eye to uncovering deeper layers of insight and previously unseen connections. And be honest. Insincerity is often easy to spot and makes the entire exercise pointless

So you may be asking yourself what a reflective essay is exactly. You've written many other types of essays for many different classes, so how is this any different? First things first... a reflective essay is one in which you *reflect* on your personality, places you've been, people you've met, or experiences that have influenced you. This type of essay lets you tell the reader who you are and what/who has made you that way.

Unlike most other types of essays you may have written, reflective essays typically don't deal with researching facts and figures. They are much more personal in nature and can be more fluid in structure and style. It can be tempting to just jump right into writing, but hold on! A good reflective essay can be a *great* reflective essay with the proper planning.

Types of Reflective Essays

Teachers often assign these sorts of essays to get students to think about what they are learning and to delve deeper into an experience. Here are some examples of class assignments:

- **Literature:** This type of essay asks you to summarize and then respond to a piece of literature in order to understand it better and relate it to your own life and experiences.
- **Professional:** Teachers, doctors, and social workers often use this type of writing in their training in order to analyze their

own behavior in response to other people so that they can understand more clearly how to better do their jobs.

- **Educational:** Sometimes instructors will ask students to respond to a lecture or other school assignment so that they can show what they understand. Writing about what you are learning can also help you share and interact with other students as well as the instructor.

- **Personal Growth:** This kind of writing can help you learn how to understand and analyze their own life experiences. It can also help you grow emotionally as you learn to understand yourself better.

How to Write a REFLECTIVE Essay

Look into a mirror. The first thing you probably see is yourself looking back at you. Keep looking though and you'll also see what's behind you. Writing a reflective essay is similar to looking into a mirror except that instead of seeing objects reflected in the room behind you, you "see" reflections of a past experience.

Reflective essays are usually written at the completion of a milestone. For instance, a scientist may write a reflective essay at the completion of an experiment or a student may be asked to write a reflective essay at the end of a course of study or the completion of an individual or class project.

An essay on "My Summer Vacation" could be a reflective essay. However, a reflective essay is not to be confused with an informative essay. While an informative essay relates facts like where you went, what you did, and how much things cost, a reflective essay is an evaluation. It's a record of your feelings and findings from the beginning of your experience until the end. In addition to concluding with a summary of your subject, the conclusion to a reflective essay usually also includes what you learned from the experience.

The essay format of introduction, body, and conclusion is at its strongest when used to write a reflective essay. Begin writing your essay by describing your subject, your feelings and/or expectations at the beginning of the project and by partly disclosing or hinting at your conclusion.

> Ex: "I didn't want to go to South Dakota last summer, but by the end of our summer vacation I learned that the Black Hills are really more green than black and the Badlands really aren't so bad at all."

Your essay body would go on to describe your Black Hills vacation, examining not just the points of interest but also why you found them interesting. This particular essay might conclude with the trip's highlights and the reasons you came away feeling that, "the Badlands really aren't so bad at all."

In most reflective essays, as well as describing what went right, you'll also want to describe what went wrong or what could be improved and how. For instance, in the example you might describe attractions you didn't visit that you would like to see and/or side trips that disappointed you and why. Alternatively, you might describe things you packed that you didn't need and things you didn't pack that you wished you had brought with you.

The most important factor to remember in writing a reflective essay is that your opinions and conclusions should directly relate to the experiences you examine in the essay body.

Reflective essays are about you, so you go home and take a good long look in the mirror. Before you start writing about what you see on the surface, keep in mind that a reflective essay involves more than just a cursory glance. It requires taking a deeper look at yourself, stepping *through the looking glass*, so to speak, to discover and show important parts of yourself to your readers.

Using a Reflective Essay Outline to Organize Your Thoughts

The goal of any essay is to write clearly and concisely about whatever topic you choose or are assigned. Unfortunately, with reflective essays, some people tend to get a little disorganized and start sounding like the Walrus, talking about anything and everything in no particular order.

Don't be like the Walrus!

Using a reflective essay outline can help your writing in a few ways

- **An outline can help lay out exactly what details you want to use before you start writing.** This is tremendously helpful because you won't end up on your last paragraph and suddenly realize that you forgot to include a crucial element or two.
- **An outline gives you a clear roadmap instead of curvy paths and dead ends.** You don't have to wonder what's supposed to come next because it'll all be in the outline. In other words, you won't have to spend time "in Wonderland."
- Because you can look at your reflective essay outline and follow it as you're writing, **ultimately you'll** save some time in your writing. Second-guessing what comes next, in what order the supporting details should go, or going back for big revisions because you forgot something important are all wastes of time.

Are you convinced yet that creating a reflective essay outline is the best option?

Good! Now let's get to actually making that outline!

Stuck on Your Essay?

Check out thousands of example essays.

How to Craft a Good Reflective Essay Outline

Because the subject of reflective essays is different from that of, say, an argumentative essay, the structure and organization can also be quite different. However, some rules still apply. To start organizing, your reflective essay outline should include sections for the introduction, body and conclusion.

For the purposes of giving examples, let's say Alice just got back from her adventures in Wonderland and is working on a reflective essay outline to tell about her experience there.

Introduction

As with any essay, your reflective essay should begin with an introduction. The parts of your introduction to include in your outline are:

- **The <u>hook</u>:** you want to grab your reader's attention from the very start. If you're telling about an experience, give a quick preview of the most exciting part of that story.
- **The thesis statement:** In a reflective essay, the thesis statement will usually include a brief statement of what your essay is about as well as how the specific person, place, or experience has influenced you. You will expand on this later, so don't give away *too* much in the beginning.

Alice's introduction might go something like this:

I don't know how I had gotten myself into such a mess, but I found myself running down a seemingly endless path with the Red Queen's entire court shouting, "Off with her head!" I had long yearned for adventure and excitement, but my time in Wonderland made me realize that adventure comes with some serious risks.

Body

The next part of your outline is perhaps the most important. Without your reflective essay outline, the body can get muddled and confusing. I can't tell you *exactly* how to organize the body of your essay because every essay is going to be different. However, I do have a couple of tips.

- If you are writing about an experience or an event, **use a chronology that makes sense**. It doesn't have to be completely linear, but if you jump around in the timeline too much, it can confuse both you and the reader. Laying out the important parts in the outline will help you figure out in what order to put everything.

- No matter what you're writing your reflective essay about–an experience, person or place–you should **include the impact it has made and what, if anything, you learned**. This should be at least as long of a section as the description of the event, person or place. It's what shows off who you are and it's what the reader will be most interested in.

The body paragraphs of Alice's reflective outline may look something like this:

1. Following the white rabbit down the rabbit hole
   1. Description of what happened
   2. Learning to look before I leap
2. Meeting the Caterpillar
   1. Description of what happened
   2. I learned how to control my size
   3. I started to realize just how strange the people were in Wonderland
3. Mad Tea Party
   1. Description of what happened
   2. Although a lot of fun, the tea party was very stressful
   3. The people I met were progressively crazier
4. Croquet with the Red Queen
   1. Description of what happened
   2. It's very hard to play croquet when the other person is cheating and threatening to behead you
   3. It was at this point when I realized that Wonderland had no rules, and that a world without rules is insane

As you can see, Alice's timeline includes different events within the entire experience and with a moment of reflection on each. The final lesson learned is the epiphany–the aha! moment.

Your outline does not have to look just like this. It could be a summary of the entire experience, followed by what you learned from it. Like I said, every essay is different.

The conclusion of your reflective essay should be the finishing touch that brings the whole piece of writing together nicely. Include a brief summary of your main points (as stated in the body paragraphs), as well as the overall takeaway from your reflection.

For example, Alice's conclusion would be similar to this:

The White Rabbit, Caterpillar, Mad Hatter, and the Red Queen are certainly faces that I'll never forget. They each contributed to the sheer madness of Wonderland. But those people—that madness—made me thankful for the peace and security of my own home and family and its rules.

Step-By-Step Instructions

Step One: Choose a Topic Idea

If you haven't been assigned a topic, look at my table below for an idea, or follow the link to the right about 100 Reflection Topic Ideas.

Example: I'm visiting my mom who lives near the beach that I went to a lot growing up, so I'm going to write about that.

Step Two: Study your Subject

Depending on your topic, you may need to close your eyes and remember, read, watch, listen or imagine. Spend a few minutes vividly thinking or experiencing your subject.

Example: I went to walk along the beach today and just enjoyed the sand, water, and wind. I thought about many other beach walks I've taken and filled my mind with memories of other beach trips.

Step Three: Brainstorm

Write down everything you can think of about your subject. You want to describe this subject as vividly as you can, so think about smells, tastes, noises, and tastes along with what you see. Try to write down vivid adjectives which describe these sensory experiences. Look at the "Sense Describing Words" chart for help. You can write this in sentences or just phrases. Just get as much down as you can. Later you will turn this into a paragraph.

Example: I see the roll of the waves coming in a roar up to the shore. The waves beat over and over on the beach. Each wave is the same and yet every wave is unique. I saw the sun covered by a cloud which reflected the light so that rays spread out in all directions. The salt smell of the spray felt fresh and clean. The cool foam of the edge of the wave covered my feet as they sank down in the sand. I walked along swinging my sandals in one hand. I took pictures of the sand, the gulls, the waves, then embarrassed, I took a selfie of myself against the ocean waves.

Step Four: Pick Reflection Questions

Look at my list of "Reflection Questions" below and pick at least 3 you want to answer.

Example: I pick the questions: What did I notice? What does this event mean to me? How did this place shape my life?

Questions for Reflection

1. What did I notice?
2. How did I feel about this?
3. Why did it make me feel this way?
4. How was my experience of this unique to me? How did others who were there experience it differently? Why?
5. How has this changed me?
6. What might I have done differently?
7. What is the meaning of this event in my life?
8. How is this similar to something else that I've experienced?
9. How can I use this to help someone else?

10. How does this event relate to the rest of my life?

11. How is this typical in my life?

12. Was this a good or a bad thing for me?

13. How did this experience foretell things that would happen later?

14. Was my experience the same as someone else's or different?

15. What skills did I learn?

16. How can I apply what I learned to my life?

17. How can I apply this experience to my studies?

18. How can this help me in my career?

19. What about this experience challenged me socially?

20. In what way did this expand my understanding of my own culture? or a different culture?

21. How was this emotionally important? or emotionally difficult?

22. How did this experience relate to my understanding of theology, God or religion?

23. What questions did this experience make me have?

24. How has this changed the way I think?

25. How has this made me realize someone else was right?

26. How was this unexpected? Or how did this fulfill my expectations?

27. Would I want to repeat this experience?

28. Would this experience be the same if I did it again?

29. How did this affect me and why?

30. Why did I have the reaction I did to this?

Step Five: Answer Questions

Read your question and then answer it. This doesn't have to be in a formal essay form or perfect sentences. You just want to get as many ideas down as possible.

Example:

1. What did I notice? *I heard the call of the seagulls and the sound of families calling to one another. Couples walked hand in hand. Parents played in the sand with their children. I saw the holes in the sand where I knew sand crabs were scrambling to hide. I noticed the cool wind on my face and the homes right up against the sand.*

2. ***What does this event mean to me?*** *Often, when I visit my mother, I never actually make it to the beach, even though it is just a few miles away from her house. I'm usually too busy helping her or spending time with relatives. This trip, however, a friend of mine named Rhonda, who is also a caregiver to her mother, told me to go to visit the beach for her. As a native Texan, Rhonda has only gotten to visit the beaches in California a few times. So today, I went to the beach for Rhonda. I smelled the beach air and walked along all by myself and took an hour to not think about responsibilities to others. Then I wrote "For Rhonda" in the sand and took a picture of it.*

3. ***How did the beach shape my life?*** *I've gone to the beach ever since I was a little girl and have many family memories of walking along the beach with my father looking for shells. When I went through the struggles of growing up, I remember feeling soothed by the waves. They always seemed to keep on going. That reminded me to not give up. To know that there is always something to look forward to ahead. To remember that laughter and tears are both a part of everyone's life. To me, the waves reminded me to have faith in a God who is in control of everything and has a bigger purpose for me than I can imagine.*

Step Six: Decide Main Meaning

Only one thing is left and you will be ready to write your essay. You need to decide what is the most important thing that you learned from this experience, or what is the memory you will carry with you. That "most important thing" will be the thesis of your paper.

Example: What I learned from this trip to the beach is that I need to remember that in the midst of being a caregiver to my mother, my husband, my five kids, my students and my friends, that I also need to care for myself and create a space for myself where I can rest and renew.

How to Organize

Take your notes and use those to write your final draft. Here are some tips:

Introduction: Either start with a vivid description of the place, your experience, or a summary of what you are reflecting about. End with your thesis idea. Sometimes you may want to put a question first and then the answer

Example Thesis: Why was I feeling so peaceful while walking down this beach? I realized it was because the beach had always been a place of rest to me.

Body: Each of the questions you've answered can be a paragraph in the body of your essay. Take your notes and expand them. Add more details and examples from your experience and your life story.

Conclusion: Explain and expand on your thesis idea. Tell how this experience taught you something new or how it helped you to understand something. Another way to conclude is to suggest where you might like to go from this point in thinking about your thesis idea.

Example Conclusion: I sent my photo of "For Rhonda" to my friend along with a text letting her know how much I appreciate her help in letting me know that we can always find places to relax and renew in the midst of our busy lives. Now, I want to find a way to help Rhonda have a day off of her own, and I'm hoping someday we can take a trip to the beach together.

Reflective Essay Question

What experience is most meaningful for you?

- Going to the beach, mountain, or other place in nature.
- Spending time talking with a friend.
- Finishing a task.
- Having someone notice something you've done.

Professional Uses

Reflection essays are not just a school exercise. Thinking about a real experience and drawing conclusions from help you learn. Here is how professionals use these sorts of essays:

- **Medical Students** write about patients they see. They can use this essay type to carefully describe the patient and the thoughts they have as they determine the correct treatment. They can reflect on how well they interacted with the patient and draw conclusions on what worked and what didn't so that they can better interact with patients.

- **Doctors** can use reflective essays to better fine-tune their ability to provide effective health care in a caring manner that makes patients not only believe them but also follow their advice. They can reflect on how well their body language, words, and tone of voice convinced the patient to make good lifestyle choices or helped a patient deal with difficult medical information.

- **Nurses and medical assistants** write about their care of patients. By thinking back on different cases and their own responses to patient requests, nurses can better understand how they can help patients deal with pain, stress, and illness. This sort of writing can also help nurses deal with the stress of the emotions they must handle from both doctors and patients, and help them understand their role in helping both.

- **Teachers** benefit from writing about experiences in teaching and doing case studies of difficult students. By reviewing their emotions about their teaching and examining patterns in what worked or did not work, teachers can better plan their lessons and solve problems with student learning and behavior.

- **Social Workers** can use this kind of paper to help them analyze the environment and problems of their clients. They can also encourage their clients to write out their experiences in order to help them see the causes and effects of their behavior and circumstances, as well as to see ways they can change.

- **Business People** use this type of written assignment to analyze the interactions in a business setting and to help them to envision how they can better present their service or product to customers.

EXAMPLES

Why Travelling is the Best Way to Change Your Life

How many times, when finding yourself in a difficult situation, you heard something like, "You just need to go somewhere, change your environment, and meet new people?" Based on my experience, I know such advice can be annoying: going through hard times, you rather expect help, compassion, or at least something more practical, rather than, "You know, you should travel." However, the surprising truth is that this is probably one of the most useful and practical pieces of advice you can get.

Of course, you cannot abandon everything and set off to go on a world trip. All of us have duties, responsibilities, debts, connections, and these kinds of ties are probably the most effective means to bind you to one place. However, the advice to travel does not necessarily imply something like departing to Nepal, living among monks, meditating, and living on alms for years—or whatever else people usually imagine when thinking about travelling. In fact, small but regular journeys are available almost to everyone, and the positive effects they can have on your mental condition and your ability to cope with difficulties are as significant as if you undertook a long "spiritual" journey.

A huge part of our daily problems remains in the context in which these problems appeared, and thus you think about them regularly. When you are stressed, your thoughts obviously cannot be positive and optimistic. So, whether you want it or not, you will view your life situation from a rather pessimistic perspective, assuming the worst case scenarios, and so on. However, when you board a plane, fly over seas (or at least head to the neighboring state where you have never been before), you almost immediately start to feel your problems fade. "Out of sight, out of mind," as the saying goes, and pulling yourself out of the environment where everything reminds you of your misfortunes can curative. Of course, I am not saying the easiest way to feel better is to escape from problems; I rather mean that taking a break, allowing yourself to breathe in some fresh air can give you a new perspective, or at least distract your mind from ruminating on the same situation over and over again. Having a good rest is a necessary condition of any recovery, and your mind definitely needs rest from time to time.

Speaking of new perspectives, when travelling, you will inevitably meet a lot of new people. Some of them will become friends of yours, some will remain strangers. Regardless of whether you prefer hotels or hostels, hitchhiking or airplanes, tropical resorts or ancient European towns, you will be always surrounded by people. **A good idea would be to make some acquaintances and communicate.** For a rather long time, psychologists have known that perhaps the most honest and sincere communication often occurs between strangers; this is called "the companion effect." Use it to your advantage. Whether you need advice, condolence, or a person who would quietly listen to you as you share your hardships, there is no better opportunity to get all this then while travelling. Besides, at some point, you might discover that people you meet had gone through the same or similar difficulties; you will be surprised that you and your problems are not unique, that people all over the world suffer from the same things, have the same feelings, and behave in similar ways. This can be a powerful source of psychological support; knowing you are not the only person in the world going "through all this," you might find yourself a bit invigorated, a bit more brave to power through your life situation.

Besides, when travelling, you learn to live in the moment. "Enjoy your life, live in the moment!" is the phrase usually associated with doing all kinds of reckless things, and is often used by hysterically-optimistic "positive-thinking" people around their 30s. However, living in the moment might imply something more than swimming with sharks naked, sniffing cocaine, or jumping from skyscrapers with a pilot chute. **You might feel the moment as you watch the sun rise over the canals of Venice; you might feel it when contemplating the grandeur of the Great Canyon;** you might live in the moment when you find yourself playing football with teenagers in Malawi. Every new experience, every impression you have is a gateway to the present moment—and this moment can be what you need to recover from a long period of stress and loss.

When travelling, you will have to learn to improvise and adapt to new situations on the go. Sometimes you arrive at a hotel you booked two weeks ago only to find out your room was given to someone else and there are no free hotels in the town left; sometimes you might have valuable belongings stolen or lost; or you might find yourself in a situation when the whole plan of your trip does not work, because you did not know what challenges you would face in a new country. When you are at home, where everything is so familiar and safe, you do not have the chance to improvise; you drift with the flow hoping it brings you to where you need. Any journey, however, is a fresh set of situations, circumstances, coincidences, all of which intertwine in the most peculiar combinations, so you cannot apply your previous life experiences to them; therefore, you need to adapt. You need to seek new decisions, sources of help, you learn to solve your problems, and solve them on your own—in a new country, you cannot afford sitting and whining about how unfair life is. You need to solve your problems: find food, shelter, transport, or whatever else you encounter on your trip. And these skills—improvisation and adaptation—are probably the most valuable ones in terms of problem-solving.

Travelling is not a panacea. It will not eradicate your pain if you have lost someone dear, or go through a divorce, or go bankrupt. It will not magically dissolve your problems: when you come back home, they will still be there. Travelling will do nothing about the unfair/complicated/rough world you live in. But it will do something to you. It will teach you that you are not alone: that millions of people around the world rejoice and suffer in the same ways you do; that they face the same problems as you do; that they fight and overcome obstacles in the same ways you do. Along with some psychological support and comfort you might get from this knowledge, you will learn to enjoy the simple beauty of moments: seeing or experiencing something for the first time will draw your mind away from mentally chewing on the same, old topics, and push your consciousness into the stillness of perceiving novelty. You will become more flexible and adaptive, because you will have no other choice: being a traveler will quickly teach you to improvise. All this, as well as other effects travelling will have on you, will help you recover from your mental wounds, get rid of the excessive stress, and give you the skills (and energy!) to deal with your hardships as you return home. In my book, this is totally worth the time and effort.

Examples of a Reflective Essays

1. My Dream Career and How I Realized It

Prompt: Write an essay on the dreams you had for further education when you were in secondary school. In your essay, include three challenges you faced in keeping those dreams alive as well as three ways you worked towards realizing those dreams.

In high school, I was not interested in much else besides writing. Other subjects seemed dry, just about memorization. In writing, I could express myself and be creative. It had an openness to it that other subjects did not have, at least in my perspective at the time.

Around 16 years old, I began to write poetry on a regular basis and eventually incorporated stories into my repertoire. From that time forward, I knew I wanted to study writing and literature in college. There was no doubt that I wanted to be a writer—every other subject was boring to me.

I saw many pathways for my career after college: being a journalist, being a book editor, being a novelist, being a writing teacher, being a teacher of English, and so on. But there were several obstacles that were in my way in having a future writing career.

My mother was against me becoming a writer, as my father was a writer, and they had a troubled marriage, resulting in divorce. My father would go on long writing trips, leaving us at home. Also, my mother attributed my father's in-and-out depression to writing. There are many negative stereotypes about writers, and unfortunately, my father had lived out some of them.

Though my mother allowed me to go to college eventually for writing, she was in constant disagreement with my choice. In addition, my step father, who I was living with at the time, continually stated that my chosen profession would not make any money and that I should be more practical.

Besides parental disagreement, I had the pressure from American society's ideal of being a man and how writing poetry was not a manly activity. Throughout my secondary school, there was a pressure to do something else besides poetry, as I was called a "girly guy," "gay" or "fruity" by my classmates, friends, and even my parents. In American society, especially with teenagers, males are not supposed to show their emotions and be open in their expression. I believe I had a lack of friends due to my interest in being a writer, and from the act of writing itself, which is often done in solitude.

And that brings me to my next struggle. Throughout my college years, I had bouts of depression due to being away from friends and being closer to books than people for at least two years: my junior and senior year of my bachelor's degree. Being mostly alone, occupied by my writing projects, the ups and downs of depression my father had was seemingly inherited by me.

Once out of college, obstacles did not stop giving me trouble. Finding a job was not easy, especially in the financial crisis of 2008. I took low-paying jobs as a tutor and freelance writer for a few years before I could get stable office jobs. I had to live with many people in one house to pay the rent and paid for food communally. But after I got an internship and later was offered to be hired as a staff writer at a scientific report writing company, I finally became a professional writer. I was no longer working as a part-time tutor or freelance writer, but was offered my own desk, computer, and stack of research to pore through.

After receiving this position, I did not look back. I became a book editor, book marketer, and now a content coordinator for websites. How did I achieve a full-fledged career as a writer and editor?

From the time I was about 24 years old and onward, I wrote every single day. I did not let myself go to sleep without writing a poem, a story, a part of a novel, or ideas for future writing projects. This consistency in practice aided me in improving my writing skills continually.

I also kept in touch with mentors on a regular basis. I communicated, and still communicate, with my poetry mentor often. Having a master of writing look over your work and supply feedback is crucial for making progress in one's writing skills.

From college and after, I have made many writing friends. I keep in contact with these writing friends on a daily basis through emails, online forums, and in-person meetings. Getting constructive criticism almost daily has given me the perspective I need to edit and revise my work to have it ready for publication in journals, books, and other publications.

Being a writer is definitely hard work, but I believe that if one loves writing enough, one can make a career as a writer. Through the obstacles of parental disagreements, standards of American society, depression from solitude, and working at low-paying jobs hardly enough for living, the love of writing has carried me.

2. What Life Means to Me

This an essay written by Jack London in 1905, with some minor changes.

I was born in the working-class. Early I discovered enthusiasm, ambition, and ideals; and to satisfy these became the problem of my child-life. My environment was crude and rough and raw. I had no outlook, but an up look rather. My place in society was at the bottom. Her life offered nothing but sordidness and wretchedness, both of the flesh and the spirit; for here flesh and spirit were alike starved and tormented.

Above me towered the colossal edifice of society, and to my mind the only way out was up. Into this edifice I early resolved to climb. Up above, men wore black clothes and boiled shirts, and women dressed in beautiful gowns. Also, there were good things to eat, and there was plenty to eat. This much for the flesh. Then there were the things of the spirit. Up above me, I knew, were unselfishnesses of the spirit, clean and noble thinking, and keen intellectual living. I knew all this because I read "Seaside Library" novels, in which, with the exception of the villains and adventuresses, all men and women thought beautiful thoughts, spoke a beautiful tongue, and performed glorious deeds. In short, as I accepted the rising of the sun, I accepted that up above me was all that was fine and noble and gracious, all that gave decency and dignity to life, all that made life worth living and that remunerated one for his travail and misery.

But it is not particularly easy for one to climb up out of the working-class — especially if he is handicapped by the possession of ideals and illusions. I lived on a ranch in California, and I was hard put to find the ladder whereby to climb. I early inquired the rate of interest on invested money, and worried my child's brain into an understanding of the virtues and excellences of that remarkable invention of man, compound interest. Further, I ascertained the current rates of wages for workers of all ages, and the cost of living. From all this data I concluded that if I began immediately and worked and saved until I was fifty years of age, I could then stop working and enter into participation in a fair portion of the delights and goodness that would then be open to me higher up in society. Of course, I resolutely determined not to marry, while I quite forgot to consider at all that great rock of disaster in the working-class world — sickness.

But the life that was in me demanded more than a meager existence of scraping and scrimping. Also, at ten years of age, I became a newsboy on the streets of a city, and found myself with a changed up look. All about me were still the same sordidness and wretchedness, and up above me was still the same paradise waiting to be gained; but the ladder whereby to climb was a different one. It was now the ladder of business. Why save my earnings and invest in government bonds, when, by buying two newspapers for five cents, with a turn of the wrist I could sell them for ten cents and double my capital? The business ladder was the ladder for me, and I had a vision of myself becoming a bald headed and successful merchant prince.

Alas for visions! When I was sixteen I had already earned the title of "prince." But this title was given me by a gang of cut-throats and thieves, by whom I was called "The Prince of the Oyster Pirates." And at that time I had climbed the first rung of the business ladder. I was a capitalist. I owned a boat and a complete oyster-pirating outfit. I had begun to exploit my fellow-creatures. I had a crew of one man. As captain and owner I took two-thirds of the spoils, and gave the crew one-third, though the crew worked just as hard as I did and risked just as much his life and liberty.

This one rung was the height I climbed up the business ladder. One night I went on a raid among the Chinese fishermen. Ropes and nets were worth dollars and cents. It was robbery, I grant, but it was precisely the spirit of capitalism. The capitalist takes away the possessions of his fellow-creatures by means of a rebate, or of a betrayal of trust, or by the purchase of senators and supreme-court judges. I was merely crude. That was the only difference. I used a gun.

But my crew that night was one of those inefficient against whom the capitalist is wont to fulminate, because, forsooth, such inefficient increase expenses and reduce dividends. My crew did both. What of his carelessness he set fire to the big mainsail and totally destroyed it. There were not any dividends that night, and the Chinese fishermen were richer by the nets and ropes we did not get. I was bankrupt, unable just then to pay sixty-five dollars for a new mainsail. I left my boat at anchor and went off on a bay-pirate boat on a raid up the Sacramento River. While away on this trip, another gang of bay pirates raided my boat. They stole everything, even the anchors; and later on, when I recovered the drifting hulk, I sold it for twenty dollars. I had slipped back the one rung I had climbed, and never again did I attempt the business ladder.

From then on I was mercilessly exploited by other capitalists. I had the muscle, and they made money out of it while I made but a very indifferent living out of it. I was a sailor before the mast, a longshoreman, a roustabout; I worked in canneries, and factories, and laundries; I mowed lawns, and cleaned carpets, and washed windows. And I never got the full product of my toil. I looked at the daughter of the cannery owner, in her carriage, and knew that it was my muscle, in part, that helped drag along that carriage on its rubber tires. I looked at the son of the factory owner, going to college, and knew that it was my muscle that helped, in part, to pay for the wine and good fellowship he enjoyed.

But I did not resent this. It was all in the game. They were the strong. Very well, I was strong. I would carve my way to a place among them and make money out of the muscles of other men. I was not afraid of work. I loved hard-work. I would pitch in and work harder than ever and eventually become a pillar of society.

And just then, as luck would have it, I found an employer that was of the same mind. I was willing to work, and he was more than willing that I should work. I thought I was learning a trade. In reality, I had displaced two men. I thought he was making an electrician out of me; as a matter of fact, he was making fifty dollars per month out of me. The two men I had displaced had received forty dollars each per month; I was doing the work of both for thirty dollars per month.

This employer worked me nearly to death. A man may love oysters, but too many oysters will disincline him toward that particular diet. And so with me. Too much work sickened me. I did not wish ever to see work again. I fled from work. I became a tramp, begging my way from door to door, wandering over the United States and sweating bloody sweats in slums and prisons.

I had been born in the working-class, and I was now, at the age of eighteen, beneath the point at which I had started. I was down in the cellar of society, down in the subterranean depths of misery about which it is neither nice nor proper to speak. I was in the pit, the abyss, the human cesspool, the shambles and the charnel-house of our civilization. This is the part of the edifice of society that society chooses to ignore. Lack of space compels me here to ignore it, and I shall say only that the things I there saw gave me a terrible scare.

I was scared into thinking. I saw the naked simplicities of the complicated civilization in which I lived. Life was a matter of food and shelter. In order to get food and shelter men sold things. The merchant soled shoes, the politician sold his manhood, and the representative of the people, with exceptions, of course, sold his trust; while nearly all sold their honor. Women, too, whether on the street or in the holy bond of wedlock, were prone to sell their flesh. All things were commodities, all people bought and sold. The one commodity that labor had to sell was muscle. The honor of labor had no price in the market-place. Labor had muscle, and muscle alone, to sell.

But there was a difference, a vital difference. Shoes and trust and honor had a way of renewing themselves. They were imperishable stocks. Muscle, on the other hand, did not renew. As the shoe merchant soled shoes, he continued to replenish his stock. But there was no way of replenishing the laborer's stock of muscle. The more he sold of his muscle, the less of it remained to him. It was his one commodity, and each day his stock of it diminished. In the end, if he did not die before, he sold out and put up his shutters. He was a muscle bankrupt, and nothing remained to him but to go down into the cellar of society and perish miserably.

I learned, further, that brain was likewise a commodity. It, too, was different from muscle. A brain seller was only at his prime when he was fifty or sixty years old, and his wares were fetching higher prices than ever. But a laborer was worked out or broken down at forty-five or fifty. I had been in the cellar of society, and I did not like the place as a habitation. The pipes and drains were unsanitary, and the air was bad to breathe. If I could not live on the parlor floor of society, I could, at any rate, have a try at the attic. It was true, the diet there was slim, but the air at least was pure. So I resolved to sell no more muscle, and to become a vender of brains.

Then began a frantic pursuit of knowledge. I returned to California and opened the books. While thus equipping, myself to become a brain merchant, it was inevitable that I should delve into sociology. There I found, in a certain class of books, scientifically formulated, the simple sociological concepts I had already worked out for myself. Other and greater minds, before I was born, had worked out all that I had thought and a vast deal more. I discovered that I was a socialist.

The socialists were revolutionists, inasmuch as they struggled to overthrow the society of the present, and out of the material to build the society of the future. I, too, was a socialist and a revolutionist. I joined the groups of working-class and intellectual revolutionists, and for the first time came into intellectual living. Here I found keen-flashing intellects and brilliant wits; for here I met strong and alert-brained, withal horny-handed, members of the working-class; unfrocked preachers too wide in their Christianity for any congregation of Mammon-worshipers; professors broken on the wheel of university subservience to the ruling class and flung out because they were quick with knowledge which they strove to apply to the affairs of mankind.

Here I found, also, warm faith in the human, glowing idealism, the sweetness of unselfishness, renunciation, and martyrdom — all the splendid, stinging things of the spirit. Her life was clean, noble, and alive. Her life rehabilitated itself, became wonderful and glorious; and I was glad to be alive. I was in touch with great souls who exalted flesh and spirit over dollars and cents, and to whom the thin wail of the starved slum child meant more than all the pomp and circumstance of commercial expansion and World Empire. All about me were nobleness of purpose and heroism of effort, and my days and nights were sunshine and star shine, all fire and dew, with before my eyes, ever burning and blazing, the Holy Grail, Christ's own Grail, the warm human, long-suffering and maltreated, but to be rescued and saved at the last.

And I, poor foolish I, deemed all this to be a mere foretaste of the delights of living I should find higher above me in society. I had lost many illusions since the day I read "Seaside Library" novels on the California ranch. I was destined to lose many of the illusions I still retained.

As a brain merchant I was a success. Society opened its portals to me. I entered right in on the parlor floor, and my disillusionment proceeded rapidly. I sat down to dinner with the masters of society, and with the wives and daughters of the masters of society. The women were gowned beautifully, I admit; but to my naive surprise I discovered that they were of the same clay as all the rest of the women I had known down below in the cellar. "The colonel's lady and Judy O'Grady were sisters under their skins" — and gowns.

It was not this, however, so much as their materialism that shocked me. It is true, these beautifully gowned, beautiful women prattled sweet little ideals and dear little moralities; but in spite of their prattle the dominant key of the life they lived was materialistic. And they were so sentimentally selfish! They assisted in all kinds of sweet little charities, and informed one of the fact, while all the time the food they ate and the beautiful clothes they wore were bought out of dividends stained with the blood of child labor, and sweated labor, and of prostitution itself. When I mentioned such facts, expecting in my innocence that these sisters of Judy O'Grady would at once strip off their blood-dyed silks and jewels, they became excited and angry, and read me preachment about the lack of thrift, the drink, and the innate depravity that caused all the misery in society's cellar. When I mentioned that I could not quite see that it was the lack of thrift, the intemperance, and the depravity of a half-starved child of six that made it work twelve hours every night in a Southern cotton mill, these sisters of Judy O'Grady attacked my private life and called me an "agitator" — as though that, forsooth, settled the argument.

Nor did I fare better with the masters themselves. I had expected to find men who were clean, noble, and alive, whose ideals were clean, noble, and alive. I went about among the men who sat in the high places — the preachers, the politicians, the business men, the professors, and the editors. I ate meat with them, drank wine with them, automobiled with them, and studied them. It is true, I found many that were clean and noble; but with rare exceptions, they were not alive. I do verily believe I could count the exceptions on the fingers of my two hands. Where they were not alive with rottenness, quick with unclean life, they were merely the unburied dead — clean and. noble, like well-preserved mummies, but not alive. In this connection I may especially mention the professors I met, the men who live up to that decadent university ideal, "the passionless pursuit of passionless intelligence."

I met men who invoked the name of the Prince of Peace in their diatribes against war, and who put rifles in the hands of Pinkertons with which to shoot down strikers in their own factories. I met men incoherent with indignation at the brutality of prize-fighting, and who, at the same time, were parties to the adulteration of food that killed each year more babies than even red-handed Herod had killed.

I talked in hotels and clubs and homes and Pullmans and steamer-chairs with captains of industry, and marveled at how little traveled they were in the realm of intellect. On the other hand, I discovered that their intellect, in the business sense, was abnormally developed. Also, I discovered that their morality, where business was concerned, was nil.

This delicate, aristocratic-featured gentleman, was a dummy director and a tool of corporations that secretly robbed widows and orphans. This gentleman, who collected fine editions and was an especial patron of literature, paid blackmail to a heavy-jowled, black-browed boss of a municipal machine. This editor, who published patent medicine advertisements and did not dare print the truth in his paper about said patent medicines for fear of losing the advertising, called me a scoundrelly demagogue because I told him that his political economy was antiquated and that his biology was contemporaneous with Pliny.

This senator was the tool and the slave, the little puppet of a gross, uneducated machine boss; so was this governor and this Supreme Court judge; and all three rode on railroad passes. This man, talking soberly and earnestly about the beauties of idealism and the goodness of God, had just betrayed his comrades in a business deal. This man, a pillar of the church and heavy contributor to foreign missions, worked his shop girls ten hours a day on a starvation wage and thereby directly encouraged prostitution. This man, who endowed chairs in universities, perjured himself in courts of law over a matter of dollars and cents. And this railroad magnate broke his word as a gentleman and a Christian when he granted a secret rebate to one of two captains of industry locked together in a struggle to the death.

It was the same everywhere, crime and betrayal, betrayal and crime — men who were alive, but who were neither clean nor noble, men who were clean and noble but who were not alive. Then there was a great, hopeless mass, neither noble nor alive, but merely clean. It did not sin positively nor deliberately; but it did sin passively and ignorantly by acquiescing in the current immorality and profiting by it. Had it been noble and alive it would not have been ignorant, and it would have refused to share in the profits of betrayal and crime.

I discovered that I did not like to live on the parlor floor of society. Intellectually I was bored. Morally and spiritually I was sickened. I remembered my intellectuals and idealists, my unfrocked preachers, broken professors, and clean-minded, class-conscious workingmen. I remembered my days and nights of sunshine and star shine, where life was all a wild sweet wonder, a spiritual paradise of unselfish adventure and ethical romance. And I saw before me, ever blazing and burning, the Holy Grail.

So I went back to the working-class, in which I had been born and where I belonged. I care no longer to climb. The imposing edifice of society above my head holds no delights for me. It is the foundation of the edifice that interests me. There I am content to labor, crowbar in hand, shoulder to shoulder with intellectuals, idealists, and class-conscious workingmen, getting a solid pry now and again and setting the whole edifice rocking. Someday, when we get a few more hands and crowbars to work, we will topple it over, along with all its rotten life and unburied dead, its monstrous selfishness and sodden materialism. Then we will cleanse the cellar and build a new habitation for mankind, in which there will be no parlor floor, in which all the rooms will be bright and airy, and where the air that is breathed will be clean, noble, and alive.

Such is my outlook. I look forward to a time when man shall progress upon something worthier and higher than his stomach, when there will be a finer incentive to impel men to action than the incentive of to-day, which is the incentive of the stomach. I retain my belief in the nobility and excellence of the human. I believe that spiritual sweetness and unselfishness will conquer the gross gluttony of to-day. And last of all, my faith is in the working-class. As some Frenchman has said, "The stairway of time is ever echoing with the wooden shoe going up, the polished boot descending."

3. The Country I Would Like to Live in

There is no place like home, as they say. As a person who has never lived anywhere besides their home country, I cannot either support or deny this claim. Also, due to this reason, I can sometimes imagine myself living in different countries. Among varying corners of the world I would like to spend at least a couple of years, I think most of all I would like to live in Japan, which is not surprising, considering my deep and long-lasting interest in this country.

The most obvious reason for such craving is my love of the Japanese language and Japanese culture, which comes from my early childhood; I still have notepads filled with fake "Chinese-looking" characters that I wrote in my early childhood. I remember Chinese fairy tales that my Asian friends told me when we were children, and Japanese legends and pictures (now I know it was ukiyo-e) in encyclopedias. This interest has not faded; when I grew up, I studied the Japanese language, I delved into its culture, history, and incredible etiquette. I appreciate the Japanese language for its phonetics, for the variety of artistic techniques, which are not far-fetched but inherent and natural. I like Japanese traditional culture for its simple minimalistic elegance, and for its unique feature of making art almost from anything. Hence, I would appreciate a possibility to live in this country for at least a year to witness it from the inside.

Another significant reason (at least for me) is safety. Known as a country with one of the lowest number of policemen in the world, Japan is a surprisingly safe country; people tell stories that children there can freely roam dark downtown municipal parks at night without any threat to their safety (of course, if children would want to stride among dark trees at night). I cannot say this about my hometown, where it is sometimes dangerous to walk in the center, not to mention suburbs and downtown.

The next reason can seem naive, but I would like to see those wonderful skyscrapers combined with super-narrow, crooked streets shining with neon with my own eyes. This is not the main reason, but if you ask me about my associations with Tokyo, the description above is my answer. Ginza, Shibuya, Roppongi–I believe these names are familiar to every tourist who has visited Japan. I would like to experience life in one of the most overpopulated, futuristic megalopolises in the world, where technological wonders (like vending machines selling almost everything) go hand in hand with customs and traditions that count thousands of years. More precisely, I like how Japanese people take the best from other cultures and adapt it to their mentality and reality.

Along with this, I am aware of the shortcomings. Japan consists of Japanese people at about 98%, and the other two percent is divided between other Asian nations, and a tiny amount of Caucasian people; hence, it is impossible to become one of the lads for the Japanese. Even if you make close friends with some of them, you will still remain "that foreign guy" with all their respective conclusions about your personality. Japan is expensive, sometimes eccentric, and possesses its own unique complicated mentality, which is difficult to understand even if you spend 20 years living there. And still, I would like to live there for some time.

Considering my deep interest in Japanese culture, history, and language, it is obvious why I would like to live in this country. The opportunity to witness all that I have read about and to apply my language and etiquette skills in practice is my main reason to move there. Safety and comfort of living, as well as a strange mix of futurism and tradition also make up my mind, even though I am aware of the shortcomings of living in Japan.

4. If I Could Change One Thing About Myself

One of the most unpleasant feelings one can experience in life is being discontent with oneself. Whereas we are prone to notice negative features in other people, we rarely turn our eyes on ourselves to critically evaluate our behavior or personal qualities. But if we do, we can notice many traits within ourselves we would not like to be there. I try to stay tolerant towards the majority of my personality features. Though, simultaneously with my positive qualities, I can be a lazy, irresponsible, apathetic downer. I learned to live with these and other drawbacks; but the trait that I would enjoy getting rid of is my tendency to doubt my decisions.

It is human nature to doubt ourselves from time to time. Imagine the situation when the five best universities in the United States are willing to have you as their student. This is one chance in a million, and you know this decision could define your entire life. Most likely, you will not randomly point your finger at one of them and say: "I will study here" (well, not immediately, at least). Instead you will conduct serious research, figuring out the advantages and drawbacks of being a student of each particular university; you will sketch out your future career perspectives as a graduate of each of these universities, and check a number of other parameters. And after intense doubts and worries, you would choose your favored institution.

This is the most reasonable approach. But in my case, I am sometimes prone to doubt even after I made a decision. Most likely, I would choose a university carefully, make a final decision, and then doubt the decision for a while, even though I would be already studying there. In real life, such a peculiarity manifests in more everyday situations. To stay at home or to hang out with friends? Whatever I choose, I will spend some time thinking about the opposite variant. To buy chocolate milk or beer? To go to the cinema or to the theater? To spend vacations in the mountains or at the sea? Not always, but more often that I would like, I start to reflect about trivial decisions.

Would I like to completely quit doubting? I think not. Doubts are a natural mechanism that helps us make the best possible decision in each particular case; without this ability, we would most likely make random, uninformed decisions regardless of their possible consequences. But at the same time, when the decision is made, you must start working to actualize it without hesitation, and this is the moment when doubts become troublesome. The more you think over a certain action of yours, the more likely you will delay the realization of what is on your mind.

Wise people teach us to be tolerant towards themselves, and accept both their negative and positive traits. I agree with this thesis, but with one small specification: this acceptance must not be an excuse for not working towards personal development and growth. This is my approach towards my proneness to doubtfulness: I can live with it, I know it is mine, but I am persistently working on getting rid of this quality.

5. Something Nobody Knows About Me

"Be yourself" is perhaps one of the most popular and well-known slogans. It is also a common piece of advice given in cases when one does not know how to behave, or how to get out of a difficult situation. In other instances, individuals say, "be yourself," not knowing how to achieve the same for themselves. The reason for this, in my opinion, is that playing roles in public has become a necessary part of modern life. Due to many factors—a feeling of insecurity, humbleness, forced necessity—we often have to behave not as we would like to. Some of us slightly correct our usual behavior to match the current situation and environment; others develop brand new social roles, pretending to be personalities they never were before in reality. This leads to situations in which people, due to personal reasons, hide their original habits or behaviors; and thus, everybody has something that nobody else knows about.

I am no exception to the supposed majority of people who rarely show what they have in their hearts. It is interesting to watch how my friends, family, and coworkers perceive me, and at the same time to know at some points they are rather far from the truth. An example: some of my friends tend to see me as a constantly merry, optimistic person who can always find an exit from any situation. They are right to a significant extent; however, what they most likely do not know about me is that sometimes my optimism and humorous attitude can be a facade hiding stress and unsolved problems, or my inability to make a decision.

What other people also do not know about me is that it can be extremely difficult for me to listen to what other people say in earnest, especially when I already have my own opinion on a particular subject, or when a person says something nonsensical (in my opinion). In such cases, I do my best not to insult those whom I talk to, but in my mind, I want them either to be silent, or to express my own opposing opinion.

Luckily, these are perhaps the most serious misconceptions other people have about me—I do my best to remain myself, as I believe this is the only way one can be happy. But, of course, I have other lesser habits and oddities that I keep in secret. For instance, men are usually not supposed to be prone to shed tears; however, sometimes I feel that I am about to cry—mostly due to the solemnity or sadness of the moment. This happens rather often when watch films or read books. Every time Boromir dies or Rohirrims charge the armies of Mordor (I love "The Lord of the Rings" trilogy) I feel my eyes becoming wet. Every time I see news about a man or a woman who risked their lives to save somebody, I quickly check if nobody saw my tears. A return of a panda family to a forest can cause me to shed a tear of happiness as well. I have no idea why it happens, but it is one of my reactions to some beautiful and inspiring moments.

By the way, my wife just loves watching sad movies with me—I think because of the aforementioned reason. It is not so bad, but I would be embarrassed if somebody else learned about this peculiarity of mine.

This is what usually comes to my mind when I think about those sides of my personality that I usually do not show to other people. Maybe I have missed something important—but let secrets remain secrets.

6. My First Day at Work

It is a well-known fact people have different temperaments, which is taken for granted in psychology, interpersonal relationships, and even in capitalistic economies. Respectively, each person responds to external stimuli in their own unique manner. Someone self-confidently solve problems, organize work, and take responsibility; others stay behind and act in a less straightforward way. There is no preferred model of behavior; any approach to life is reasonable as long as it is natural for a particular person. But, despite their temperaments, all people get nervous in certain situations. One of the most typical cases when even the most self-confident individuals may feel like a fish out of water is the first day at a new workplace.

Personally, I assess my temperament as a cross between being an extrovert and introvert. Sometimes I am active, communicative, and feel like the center of any company; another day, I am self-absorbed, thoughtful, and unwilling to talk to people. Unfortunately, when I suddenly find myself in a large company of new people, I usually act in the second way. This happened on my first day at work; even more, I behaved like that for the first three months of my employment. I was hired by a news agency right after my graduation; working in media was my dream, and I gladly accepted the offer from the agency's HR manager, though the salary was not satisfactory.

My new workplace was an open office for about 50 journalists, each hunting for new material, interviewing public persons via phones, making business calls, and rushing in all directions. My chief editor briefly explained my tasks to me for the first day and vanished in the surrounding chaos. I was left alone with my computer and a list of newsmakers to work with. The chief editor did not even provide me with phone numbers of people whom I needed to call to verify certain information before publishing it on a website. Besides, everybody around me seemed to be too busy to be willing to help a newcomer like me. To put it short, all I felt in the first couple of hours of my employment was anxiety.

In my opinion (and based on my personal experience), the first day at a new job is difficult for many individuals due to several reasons. The initial reason for feeling unease is a natural embarrassment that is accompanied with being in a completely new surroundings. Each office, each company is a kind of an ecosystem with its own micro-climate, communication and survival laws, already formed groups and relationships. A new person usually is unfamiliar with the local customs of the new company he or she starts to work at, so the first period of time he or she has to spend as aliens. Next, new work—especially if it is one's first workplace—often implies that the newcomer is being tested and watched with special attention; this adds responsibilities and stress. Finally, the newcomer if often extremely critical of themselves because of being alert of even the smallest flaws or mistakes; they have to learn vast volumes of new information and obtain numerous skills.

The first day at work is often similar to initiation tests in distant, primeval tribes. A person is thrown into a collective of completely new and unfamiliar people, who already have their own working micro-climate established; the newcomer is almost inevitably seen as an alien in it. A new workplace also means increased responsibilities and expectations from the fresh employee, both from the employer and from the newcomer themselves. Also, on the first day of a new job, people seem to realize the amounts of new knowledge and skills they need to master, and this may be rather discouraging for them. All this makes the first day at a new job a serious and highly stressful test.

CHAPTER ELEVEN

ANALYTICAL ESSAYS

What is an analytical essay?

An analytical essay takes a look at the components of a story and how the author's deeper meaning is apparent. It is your writing to analyze a novel in terms of literary style, tone, or characters. You use specific quotes from the story to support your thesis. You may be asked to analyze a book in terms of application to modern life, in terms of a continuing theme you are studying in class, or uses of literary terms and styles. The key to understanding its nature is in the word "analyze." To "analyze" the content of a poem, for example, one must break it into its components or parts in order to get a full understanding of its meaning.

This may mean investigating the poem's structure, its language, its symbolism, and even its historical context. All this will help you as the writer and your reader understand what the poet was trying to say. Your analysis may not be identical to someone else's idea of the poem, but, if your investigation is logical, believable, and well-defended, it will be well received. That is an analytical essay is helpful when a more full understanding of an examined object is needed.

General Guidelines:

Anything can become an object of your investigation: an event, a piece of art, or a literary work. Whatever it is, preparation for writing is important.
- when an object is chosen, take it apart, and examine each single part of it thoroughly;
- examine your object in its historical context (if it is a painting, how is it connected to its epoch and artistic requirements?);

- discover the message of the object (what did the author want to say in an evaluated book, for example);

Our tips on an analytical essay writing:

- When analyzing, write down all your ideas. Not all of them will appear in your custom analytical essay writing, but it's always good to have a choice. Plus, you never know what you can come up with, and it can be something really outstanding.
- Don't hesitate to write something new and unordinary.
- It might sound crazy, but try to fall in love with your topic. If you get inspired, your essay writing will be a depiction of your inspiration; therefore, you'll get a positive feedback.

2. How to Write an Analytical Essay. The Introduction

Definition:

The Essay Introduction gives a brief explanation of your topic to the readers. The main item of the Introduction (and an essay paper as a whole) is a thesis statement; therefore, everything has to be built around it:

- an abstract – key information about the evaluated object;
- your claim, or a thesis statement – an answer to this information, and your reaction on it;
- direction sentences - explain how your thesis will be supported or developed in the body of your essay;
- an introduction has to be at least eight sentences long.

Our tips on an analytical essay writing:

Any thesis statement has to give a reply to a topic, and not just restate it.

3. How to Write an Analytical Essay. The Main Body

Definition:

The Body argues the case you have laid out in your Introduction

General Guidelines:

All your evidence and facts have to be stated here. A certain structure of body paragraph is required. It consists of:

- the topic sentence, or the main idea, that tells the reader briefly what the paragraph is about;
- supporting points (from four to five);
- a concluding sentence that ends a discussion on this topic.

What an Analytical Essay Is—And What It Isn't

Stuck on Your Analytical Essay? Check Out These Example Analytical Essays. Before we get to the good stuff, you should know exactly what an analytical essay is. Your middle school and high school teachers probably told you something like, "An analytical essay is writing that analyzes a text."

Helpful, right? Um, not so much.

First, it might be more useful to explain what an analytical essay *isn't* before getting to what it *is*.

An analytical essay isn't a summary. Though this may seem obvious in theory, it's more difficult in practice. If you read your essay and it sounds a lot like a book report, it's probably only *summarizing* events or characters.

One way to figure out if you're summarizing instead of analyzing is to look at your support. Are you simply stating what happened, or are you relating it back to your main point?

Okay, so what is an analytical essay, *exactly*?

Usually, it's writing that has a more narrowed focus than a summary. Analytical essays usually concentrate on *how* the book or poem was written—for example, how certain themes present themselves in the story, or how the use of metaphor brings a certain meaning to a poem.

In short, this type of essay requires you to look at the smaller parts of the work to help shed light on the larger picture.

An example of a prompt—and *the* example I'm going to use for the rest of this post—could be something like: Analyze the theme of sacrifice in the Harry Potter series. (Note: there might be some spoilers, but I figured everyone who was planning on reading the books has done so already—or at least has seen the movies.)

Importance of Analytical Essay

The aim of analytical essay to start is not to present a story but to analyze and it to make readers understand what the writer intends to accomplish with the essay. Some students who are asked to write an analytical essay tend to tell the readers the next scenario of the story instead of analyzing it. Remember that it is not a narrative essay, rather an essay which is aimed at analyzing the subject.

The importance of analytical essay is to provide readers a more comprehensible understanding of a story or a book by assessing all its important elements. It is a good way of practicing critical thinking by looking at a story from different angles.

How to Conclude an Analytical Essay

The conclusion of any essay, like in an expository essay, is to recap the main point in order for the readers to get a gist of the essay. This process of making a conclusion can also be applied to an analytical essay, except the writer should be able to present two important factors: the *analysis* and the *argument*.

- The *analysis* is the study of the main issue that is presented with its supporting elements, like the plot of the story and the characters.
- The *argument* is your personal response to the subject and line of reasoning based on the analysis.

You need to highlight the connection of these two as well as their relation to your conclusion.

Analytical Essay Prompt

You have 45 minutes to write on the following topic.

Please read and think about the following two quotations:

1. "Organized charity is doing good for good-for-nothing people."
2. "Charity is a helping hand stretched out to save some from the inferno of their present life."

Write an essay on the above two statements in three parts as follows:

1. Compare the statements. Explain what the two statements have in common and how they overlap.
2. Contrast the statements. Explain how the two statements differ.
3. Take a position with regard to the two statements by choosing one or mediating between them, and support your view with an example from your own observation or experience.

Sample Essay Score: 6

The two statements address an identical topic. That is, they address charity, which might be defined as--the act of giving something of value, without the expectation of something in return. Further, the two statements address the receiver, the person or persons to whom the charity is directed.

That the two statements both give equal weight to the meaning of charity is evidenced by the descriptions "doing good," and "hand stretched out to save." These descriptions both illustrate the beneficence of the act of charity, that it is in one act, both a recognition of need, and an attempt to fulfill that need. They both paint a picture of goodness, honor and sharing on the part of the charity giver.

Contrary to these similarities, the two statements are in stark opposition to the beneficiary's status in society. The first, calling the receivers "good for nothing people," depicts vagrants, bums, and worthless flies, fouling the smooth-flowing surface of society. The second, seeing the receivers as involved in an "inferno," brings to mind visions of lost souls, wandering homeless and possesionless in the

Dante-esque hell of a society which measures a person's worth by his wealth.

Another contrast between the two statements, more subtle yet intuitively strong, is that the benefactor, the charity-giver, attains an even higher degree of honor when he gives to one in true need, than when his sharing is enforced, by taxes, social pressure or inherited response. The first statement speaks to the latter of these, the second to the former. Thus, the second statement not only attributes a higher character to the beneficiary, but also to the benefactor whose actions are performed from the heart.

Although the truth, as always, lies in the middle ground, between these two extremes, I am more inclined to the second statement. I have felt some degree of sympathy to almost every destitute, penniless or homeless person that I have met. Hobos, bums on trains and the road, are there usually as a result of a fallen thread in the Fates' tapestry or a falling out with society. Some would not accept a handout if offered, demanding to perform work in exchange, while others are every way deserving of a handout, refusing formal governmental welfare.

The poor of the urban slums are, the vast majority of the time, victims of a society which has entrenched them in a lifestyle from which it is virtually to lift themselves out. These are the ones which are most aptly described as falling to an "inferno" in their present life. That society is obligated to providing charity to these victims of its own hand is just.

I have observed examples or persons receiving charity who simply in the act of accepting it, belie a certain "good-for- nothingness." These are usually persons who would be affluent other than for a desire to catch a free ride on societies' back. A part-time employed student, relaxing for the summer at the taxpayers' expense is one example which stands out in my personal experience.

Still those in the category of good for nothing are a minute proportion of those receiving charity. With an optimistic view of the situation of mankind, one cannot deny the value of charity not only to those receiving it, but to the world in general.

Comment: Keeping in mind that this essay was written in 45 minutes, this is a superior response. Although it has some flaws, it is well developed and organized. There are indications ("the Dante-esqe hell of society") of considerable sophistication in language and sentence structure.

Sample Essay Score: 5

Charity has been practiced for thousands of years by human beings. The story of the good Samaritan, found in the bible, is an ancient example of charity that is familiar to many people. The following two quotes are both written about charity: "Organized charity is doing good for good-for- nothing people," and, "Charity is a helping hand stretching out to save some from the inferno of their present life." Both of these two quotes imply that charity involves helping, with acts of kindness, people who are in need or people who are destitute.

However, the two quotes express widely divergent views on the value of employing charity to help destitute people. The first quote suggests that charity is useless. It implies that the people that charity is directed toward are not worthy of such help and that charity does not help them improve their lives. In contrast, the second quote suggests that the recipients of charity are worthy of the assistance afforded. It implies that the lives of the people receiving the charity will be better because of it.

I agree with the latter quote. The first quote shows a lack of belief in the good side of human nature and a disregard to trying to help other people. The second quote supports a belief that all human beings deserve a decent lifestyle. I believe that charity is not a "cure-all", a person must want to work toward helping himself or herself. But sometimes people in need of charity don't have the material means or positive attitudes necessary to help themselves better their lives. Charity can provide both.

One summer my mother and three sisters, and I had to go on welfare. We did not have enough money for the basic necessities of life despite the fact that my mother was working. The food stamps and help from our church that we were awarded were greatly appreciated by us. Unfortunately, there is an attitude held by many in our society that receiving charity is degrading and thus I didn't tell many of my friends about our financial situation. The charity given to us that summer enabled us to eat. It provided us with the means to survive until the fall when my mother worked additional hours teaching. I believe charity is helpful and a necessary act of concern for human beings in need. There are some people who abuse the charity given by others but there are always abusers in society. It is not justified to deny people in need because of the unethical actions of a few.

Comment: This paper handles the question quite well. It is clearly organized and, although it does not explore all of the possibilities of the comparison/contrast, it is strong in its use of supporting example. Its sentence structure, syntax and diction are generally free from major problems.

Sample Essay Score: 4

It is argued that "organized charity provides good for the good-for-nothing" and that charity is a true benefit to those in need. These statements, although quite opposite also have some aspects in common. The difference is largely in the perspective of the individual directly affected.

To say that charity is doing good for the good-for-nothing suggests that those who accept charity are useless and unproductive. In fact it is likely that the receivers of charity are in fact unproductive, ie out of work. In that they represent a potential for production indicates they are not useless however. By accepting charity one may however feel useless. This is due to the pervasive attitude that people must be productive to be good- for-something.

Because people are often thrust out of the work force without any forewarning and because it is common that new work is difficult to find, the acceptance of charity doesn't always cause distress. Workers know that their aid is only temporary until they are matched with a new job.

In either case, when people are in the position where charity is being offered and is needed, it is likely that they will feel both unproductive and grateful. Because they are in trouble economically their lives can indeed be an inferno.

The difference between the gratitude for needed charity and the feeling of "freeloading" is great when the feeling acts singularly. Being grateful for help often induces people to organize and give more of themselves to others. Those who have been helped often feel motivated to help others.

On the other hand, those who feel unproductive and useless are ashamed and bitter. They are too ridden with guilt and self-consciousness to motivate and help others. They are likely to feel anger toward the society that offers them charity rather than gratitude.

The feeling that is probably pervasive among the unfortunate lies somewhere in between guilt & gratitude. The gratitude side of the scale is likely to be more productive in general and therefore is the preferred state. By gratefully accepting aid, a lot of immediate problems are solved for the unfortunate and they can then attempt to reorganize their lives.

The little bit of guilt from the other side of the scale helps those with aid recognize the needs of unfortunate people. Then, they can both work together to rebuild their lives and get back on their feet. For example, a story found in the S. F. Chronicle recently described two people who were out of work who became friends and started a firewood business. They were both previously on public assistance and now are off. They both indicated that had the aid not been available they would not have made it.

Because of the motivation induced by the acceptance of aid the helping hand view is accepted.

Comment: Although competent, this paper is less successful than the previous two. The large number of short paragraphs indicates some difficulties with development of ideas. The overuse of the passive voice ("It is argued," etc.), some diction problems ("the feeling acts singularly," "unfortunate"), along with the sketchiness of the example, sometimes interfere with the writer's meaning.

Sample Essay Score: 3

The two quotes state that charity does good for a part of society. To some people both statements might indicate that "good-for-nothing people" and people in "the inferno of their present life" are one in the same. To other people, the parts of the two quotes dealing with people who recive charity might mean that the type of people mentioned in quote "A" are not the same as those mentioned in quote "B."

Comparison

For many people life is a living hell, and they are thus in need of charity. There are people in society however, that believe that these people create their own hell. While they might maintain that charity is good for these people, they still think of them as "good-for-nothing." They probably think that charity cases could climb out of their "inferno" if they tried, but they will not and are therefore a burden on society.

Contrast

To many people in society there is a distinction between the "good for nothing people" receiving charity and those for whom life is hell also receiving charity. Furthermore, they think that organized charity might tend to do good for those who do not really deserve it (the "good for nothing people"). Whereas, charity in general tends to help out both the good for nothings and the people who really need it.

Pt.3

Statement "B," is the best because takes a more positive view to people in need. Statement "A" takes a less positive, less cynical view.

I know of a person who receives charity that someone who might make statement "A" would refuse to give charity to. This person is to proud to tell anyone of his affliction.

Sample Essay Score: 2

These two statements contain very strong personal biases toward the economically disadvantaged, and the people involved in their welfare. Both quotations seem to contain an element of sarcasm or negativity. The inevitable plight of the financially unfortunate person appears to be the attitude represented in these quotations. Charity is thought to be an ineffective means to this problem.

Quotation A is making a judgment about the people that charity effects. The "...good-for- nothing people, implies that these people don't deserve the aid of the organization." In contrast quotation "B" is speaking more of the hopelessness of charity, and its minute effect on the masses of disadvantaged.

I feel that even though organizations concerned in charitable contributions have only a very small impact on the world at large, it is a beginning in raising the concerns of others.

Comment: This paper is very thin in content and inadequate in interpreting the quotations. Part 3 is completely unsupported and there are some serious problems with sentence structure and diction ("Charity is thought to be an ineffective means to this problem").

Sample Essay Score: 1

The only thing statements A and B have in common is charity being supportive.

Statement A uses "organized" where statement B uses charity in general. This means statement B can include all of statement A but A can only be a part of statement B.

Charity is supportive to a lot of people. It is helpful but charity can also be abused. People living for what other people will hand out to them won't be living their own life.

Comment: This paper is far too undeveloped for even a minimal answer.

One Way To Form Your Analytical Essay Outline

There are quite a few ways to organize your analytical essay, but no matter how you choose to write it, your essay should always have three main parts:

1. Introduction
2. Body
3. Conclusion

I'll get into the nitty-gritty of this soon, but for all you visual learners, here is a nice representation of all the components that make a great analytical essay outline.

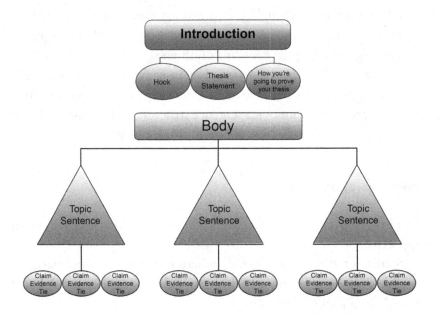

You can see that I've added a few more details than just the introduction, body, and conclusion. But hold your horses—we're getting to those parts right now.

Introduction of Your Analytical Essay Outline

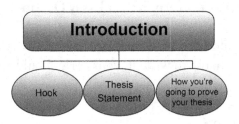

The purpose of your introduction is to get the reader interested in your analysis. The introduction should include at least three things—a hook, your thesis statement, and a sentence or two describing how you intend to prove your thesis statement.

1. You gotta hook 'em from the start. The first part of your introduction should draw the reader in. This is called <u>the hook</u>.

The hook should be interesting or surprising. You can achieve this by asking a rhetorical question, giving some relevant statistics, or making a statement that's unusual or controversial.

For my Harry Potter example, I might say, "Since the publication of the first book in the Harry Potter series, *Harry Potter and the Philosopher's Stone*, some Christian groups have attacked the books for promoting witchcraft. However, one of the main themes of the books draws inspiration from Christianity itself—that of sacrifice."

Okay, so that's two sentences. But it's got a little bit of controversy and relates to what the rest of the essay will discuss.

2. Get to the good stuff—write a killer thesis statement. Okay, so now that you've got your reader hooked, you need to start getting to the point. This is where the thesis statement comes in.

My thesis might be, "The theme of sacrifice is prevalent throughout the series and is embodied as sacrifice for the greater good, sacrifice for an ultimate gain, and sacrifice to keep a promise."

3. It's time to back up your thesis. Let the reader know how you're going to prove your claim.

For my example, I would let the reader know that I intend to analyze the instances of Harry's "death," Voldemort's sacrifice of his soul in exchange for immortality, and how Snape sacrifices in order to honor a promise made to Lily Potter.

These points will be the building blocks of the body paragraphs.

Body of Your Analytical Essay Outline

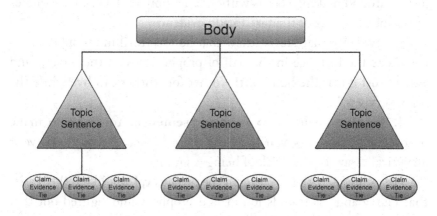

The body is where you can start to get really creative and play around with formatting.

In the flowchart, there are three body paragraphs. But that's because I was trained in the 5-paragraph outline. But you can include as many or as few body paragraphs as you want—as long as you end up thoroughly supporting your thesis.

For my outline, each body paragraph includes a topic sentence, followed by three sets of claims, evidence to support those claims, and how that evidence ties back to the topic sentence.

Again, three is not necessarily a magic number here. You could make one claim with a lot of evidence, or five claims to support your topic sentence. But let's get into it, shall we?

1. Develop a strong topic sentence. Each topic sentence in each body paragraph of your analytical essay outline should tell the reader exactly what that section is going to be about.

My first body paragraph might start with, "Harry Potter is willing to fulfill prophecy and make the ultimate sacrifice—that of his life—in order to save the rest of the wizarding world."

2. Make your claim. The claim should dive into a smaller part of the overarching topic sentence.

The topic sentence I gave can be broken down into several smaller claims—that Harry knew that he was fulfilling prophecy, that he was actually willing to die, and that his death would be of profound significance.

3. Provide evidence from the text to back your claim. You can't just go around making claims without any support. You can use quotes or paraphrase parts of the text to add evidence.

For evidence that Harry knew that he was fulfilling prophecy, you could cite the instance in the hall of prophecies with the quote, "and either must die at the hand of the other for neither can live while the other survives."

4. Tie that evidence to the topic sentence. You have to make it absolutely clear why you included the evidence. If you don't, your analytical essay runs the risk of being a summary.

For example, with the citing of the prophecy, I would tell the reader that Harry and his friends found said prophecy and figured out that it had to be about him (although there are objections that it could've been referring to Neville, but we'll leave that out of this example). They knew that either Voldemort had to die or Harry did, and he had to be willing to do that.

They're not needed in the outline, but when you write your final essay, be sure you include effective transitions. This will help your essay flow.

Conclusion of Your Analytical Essay Outline

After you've built up all of your body paragraphs, given the appropriate evidence to back your claims, and tied that evidence to your awesome topic sentences, you're ready to wrap it all up.

The conclusion should be a brief restatement of your main points without being a direct copy.

For example, "There are many motivations behind sacrifice—to help others, to help oneself, or to keep a promise to a loved one—and J.K. Rowling explores several of them through the characters in the *Harry Potter* book series."

This, of course, does not suffice as a full conclusion. To fill it out and give the reader a sense of closure, you can relate the theme to the real world or end with a final quote from the text or the author.

Tips for Your Analytical Essay

1. **Your essay must address and respond to the assignment description**. Most students fail or get low grades because they fail to read the entire assignment, including the grading criteria.
2. Make sure you develop an argumentative analytical essay (i.e., your essay must include an arguable **THESIS** at the end of your introduction, which you should later develop in the body of your essay through an **ANALYSIS** of the selected work of art and illustrate with **SPECIFIC EVIDENCE**). Consider the

following formula to help you develop a working thesis for your essay: "In [title of art piece], the author challenges/reinforces traditional notions of gender/female sexuality/standards of masculinity/etc. by [doing blah, blah, blah]."

3. Your essay must contain **INTRODUCTION + BODY + CONCLUSION + WORKS CITED**. Forget about the 5-paragraph essay; those only worked in high school, when the essays were shorter and less complex.

4. All your paragraphs should be fully developed and include transitions. The paragraphs in the body of your essay should contain a **topic sentence** introducing the topic to be discussed and relating back to the thesis.

5. Avoid "lab talk" (e.g., "In this paper I will prove…") and phrases like "I believe that" or "In my opinion." Your reader assumes that everything you write that you do not attribute to another author is your opinion. See Dr. Easton's handout for more information.

6. Do not abuse plot summaries and/or unnecessary long descriptions. Remember that your argument is based on an analysis; you're not writing a book report, but an argument. Consider including a <u>brief</u> summary of your work of art (in the case of novels, plays, movies, and the like) or a <u>brief</u> description of it (in the case of paintings and sculptures, for instance) in the introduction. Later, as Celia Easton points out, "Your job is to remind your audience of passages in the text that provide evidence for the argument you want to create about your text, not to describe the plot to someone who has never read the text."

7. Select lines, quotes, passages, or specific details to discuss to make a claim about the whole work.

8. Make sure your essay follows a **logical structure and organization**. It is not necessary to imitate the chronology of the literary work you are analyzing.

9. **Avoid generalizations and oversimplifications**, such as "all men think…" or "since the beginning of times."

10. Remember you need to incorporate at least one academic (nonfictional) source to develop your argument. Check our website for more information about what counts as an academic source.

11. **Don't let your secondary sources dominate your essay.** In order to avoid this problem, use a yellow marker and highlight every sentence in your essay stating ideas that are not your own (quotes, paraphrases, and summaries of other people's works). If you see too much yellow in your paper, chances are your voice and ideas have not been fully develop.

12. **Quote only passages that would lose their effectiveness if they were paraphrased.** Never use a quotation to substitute for your own prose. Always include a tag line on any quotation in order to introduce it (e.g., "According to author X, ..." or "As author Y points out, ...")13. **Cite your sources properly in MLA style.** When in doubt, ask.

13. **Make sure your essay meets the length requirement**: 4-5 pages, including "Works Cited" (at least 4 FULL pages).15. Read Celia Easton's "Conventions of Writing Papers about Literature."

14. Check the links included in the online version of the grading criteria for the assignment.

15. Consider coming to my **office hours** and/or going to the **Writing Center** for help with your writing. Note: I will only address questions about your essays by e-mail only if it takes me a couple of lines to answer. Don't e-mail me your drafts.

Examples of Analytical Essays

1. Just Confessions

Saul Kassin and Gisli Gudjonsson, in their article for Scientific American Mind, "True Crimes, False Confessions," argue that "society should discuss the urgent need to reform practices that contribute to false confessions and to require mandatory videotaping of all interviews and interrogations" (2005, p. 26). After analyzing their argument, I shall argue that, although one might object that Kassin and Gudjonsson focus too heavily on the importance of protecting criminal suspects, they provide a compelling argument that social justice requires such reforms as mandatory video-tapping of police interrogations.

In developing their case for the need to reform interrogation tactics,

Kassin and Gudjonsson survey a number of studies regarding the role of confessions in criminal investigations. For example, they are at pains to provide evidence that interrogations are often influenced by a bias on the part of the interrogator. Further concern is found in the fact that Miranda rights, as found in the American legal system, are insufficient safeguards, given that suspects, especially innocent ones, often waive those rights. Finally, Kassin and Gudjonsson note that aggressive interrogation tactics can often produce false confessions.

What makes these findings most troubling, according to Kassin and Gudjonsson, is the strong correlation between false confession and wrongful conviction. Trial jurors, we are told, are inclined to give disproportionate weight to a confessions, even taking it to outweigh so-called "hard evidence." As a characteristic example, Kassin and Gudjonsson cite the case of Bruce Godschalk. Even when DNA evidence proved Godschalk could not have been the rapist, the District Attorney of the case refused to release him from prison, stating that "...I trust my detective and his tape-recorded evidence" (Kassin and Gudjonsson, 2005, p. 28). Because of this tendency on the part of jurors and prosecutors, together with the facts listed above regarding the potential for unrestricted interrogations to elicit false confessions, Kassin and Gudjonsson argue for the need to reform police interrogation tactics.

Underlying their argument is the implicit moral principle that social justice requires that we do everything we can to minimize the potential to wrongly convict innocent persons. This may seem obvious, but one could reasonably question whether it puts too much emphasis on protecting potentially innocent suspects and not enough on convicting potentially guilty criminals. In a perfectly just system, criminals would always be brought to justice and treated appropriately, and innocent suspects would always be exonerate. However, any system devised and implemented by humans must deal with the reality of imperfection.

The difficult moral question we need to ask is how we are to balance the needs of society to protect itself from criminals while at the same time protecting the rights of innocent persons. We need to ask at what cost we are willing to limit the ability of police and Crown prosecutors to prosecute criminal suspects. Imagine, for example, the following two systems: (1) Almost no innocent persons are ever convicted, but a very high percentage of recidivist offenders are able to escape conviction, (2) A very high percentage of offenders are caught and brought to justice; however, a small but non-negligible percentage (say 3%) of innocent persons are unjustly caught in the system and thus wrongly punished for crimes they never committed. Neither of these is very palatable, but if forced to choose, my intuitions favor result (2). Of course, there are many variables at work here, and I do not have the space to delve into a detailed discussion of all the relevant trade-offs. My basic point is that social justice requires not only that we protect innocent individuals from prosecution, but that we hold guilty persons accountable for their actions.

While I think that this is a reasonable worry to raise given the tenor of Kassin and Gudjonsson's article, I do not think it ultimately undermines their argument. That is, I think one might reasonably object that they are overly focused on the possibility of false confessions without saying much about the utility of true confessions. However, their specific proposal that interrogations be video-taped does not seem to diminish the ability of police to effectively interrogate suspects and, when possible, to elicit a confession. Indeed, they conclude their essay by citing a study showing that police largely found the practice of video-taping to be quite useful and not to inhibit criminal investigations.

So, even if one thinks that Kassin and Gudjonsson are a bit one-side in focusing on false confessions, ultimately I think these authors provide a compelling argument for the need for such reforms as mandatory video-taping of police interrogations.

References

1. Kassin, Saul and Gudjonsson, Gisli (2005). "True Crimes, False Confessions," *Scientific American Mind*, July, pp. 24-31.
2. Games and Violence Essay

Introduction: Computer games have seriously caught the attention of Mass Media and nowadays every channel considers its duty to remind people how much damage these games cause to children and adults.

The increasing amount of games with violent scenes sock the society and makes it very aware of them. It is already common knowledge that violent games cause violence in people. This fact is not even doubted by the majority of people. Every other person says that the reason lies in games being too close to reality. The opinion that games make violent actions normal for the player and therefore make the player pitiless can be often heard. In this case the game is the cause of violence and the act of violence by itself is a consequence. And can real-life violence exist in the reality of a game? Is the transfer of the definition of "violence" with all its peculiarities from one world to another justified only according to the external similarity of these two worlds?

Games originally are entertainment. Contemporary games are very realistic and for this reason they are a source of great experience for the player and develop the imagination. Games are entertainment and even more then that. In addition, the statistics of the New York University lead by Green and Bavelier claim that the player preferring active games get an improvement of some types of brain activity, related to processing of visual information. In particular, game players cope with problems of simultaneously tracking several moving objects at the average level of 30% better then people who do not play active computer video games. The "gaming" violent experience may not be the cause of violent behavior in reality. None of the playing experience will become the priority in making important decisions concerning problems in real life. A game is an abstraction. A player gets abstract tasks and acts according to abstract rules. Games are also the possibility to be however a person wants to be and to rest from the outside world for some time. But what if a person gets so much excited with the game scenes that he becomes violent in reality? Then, it proves that the games cause people to become violent. Let us stop for a moment right at this point. Those who do not participate in this type of activity usually make the conclusion of presence of violence in the game-world.

Conclusion: Nobody will ever hear this kind of statement from those who play, from those who know the rules of the game and understand that it is just a virtual world. A psychologically healthy person will never confuse or connect these two different worlds. A game is a virtual world with visual images very similar to human. These images represent by themselves nothing but simple playing obstacles. A game may potentially give the opportunity to "destroy the obstacles" that may not be destroyed according to the rules but it is more about personal choice whether to do it or not. This leads us to the conclusion that violence is not a consequence but the cause. People who are originally prone to violence may get irritated by games and perform violence in the "real world". But in this case violence in games is a simple justification of the violent nature of the player.

3. A Short History of Celebrity

By Patrick West

When you read tirades about today's cult of celebrity, you can invariably expect two axioms to present themselves. One is that this development is lamentable and ghastly, symptomatic of an inane, dumbed-down culture. A celebrity now is someone famed not for necessarily having done something interesting or useful, but for merely having grabbed the public's attention sufficiently. Secondly, it is invariably a given that the cult of celebrity is a relatively new phenomenon, an unintended consequence of modern technology such as mass print, television, and the internet, all of which have made it possible to imagine a stranger to be your friend.

Fred Inglis broadly agrees that our cult of celebrity is dismal, nurturing vacuous, vicarious, and malicious sensations. 'Celebrity,' he writes 'is always an ambivalent designation, the feelings it engenders at once bilious and rapt, envious and dismissive' (p157). The Janus-faced sentiments it cultivates are the logical result of its inauthentic nature, in that it leads us to confuse non-intimates with people we actually know. 'The parallel orgy is one of sanctimonious fascination and distate' (p253). His materialist explanation is that this parallel capacity to worship and detest celebrities satisfies a timeless human vice: envy. Modern technology has made it easier to be jealous of the riches of others.

Inglis disagrees, however, that the cult of celebrity is new. The author argues that as celebrity can only exist in an truly urban society, which, unlike a rural one, facilitates familiarity, we can trace it in some form back to the birth of the Modern itself—namely, the late-18th century.

Joshua Reynolds, he writes, was the first true celebrity, who reinvented the concept of a painter not as an industrious figure reliant on a patron, but who achieved notoriety as much for his sexual licence, gluttony, drunkenness, and gambling. Byron attained comparable infamy for his licentiousness, while Admiral Nelson's dalliances with Lady Hamilton aroused as much prurient interest as did his naval triumphs. George IV's fecklessness and disastrous marriage to Caroline of Brunswick were the source of much tittle-tattle and public disapproval. Long before Twitter made it possible to feign outrage about a public figure's conduct or pronouncements, etchings by the likes of caricaturist and printmaker James Gillray permitted the public to pass collective judgment on the Prince Regent's libertine behavior.

In many respects, the 20th century saw an extension, not a revolution, in the way public figures were regarded. The likes of Jackson Pollock and Tracey Emin continued where Reynolds left off. After Byron has come a multitude of stars, from James Dean to Pete Doherty, whose embrace of the Dionysian has enthralled and appalled. Out of the lives of statesmen and politicians, narratives are still weaved and mythical figures created. The tragedy of John F Kennedy, and the Kennedy clan itself, is an obvious example. Nelson Mandela's continued sainted status is another. Although 'an inadequate economist and an ineffective policy maker', the figure of Mandela, through his suffering, meekness, displays of forgiveness and reconciliation, has become, 'as figureheads must, allegorical. His benign smile, his Hawaiian shirts, his informal readiness to cut a caper, take a turn on the drums, drink tea in the townships and entertain any and every passing dignitary come to pay homage, each aspect of the man captured and made real the celebrity peacemaker, gregarious and good-humored' (p274).

It could be argued, however, that the cult of celebrity predates Modernity (the epoch which the Enlightenment and the Industrial Revolution brought into being). For instance, the 1st century BC Roman orator Quintus Hortensius achieved not just recognition but celebrity on account of his talent as a wit and mime artist. Cicero was likewise renowned for his oratory skills. In Rubicon: The Triumph and Tragedy of the Roman Republic (2003), Tom Holland writes: 'Like actors, orators were celebrities, gawped at and gossiped about. Hortensius himself was nicknamed "Dionysia", after a famous dancing girl'. You don't require an urbanised society for 'celebrity' to exist, and not even the technological mediums of print and screen. You just need a city that contains enough strangers to produce at least one figure everyone can talk about. 'Celebrity' is a requisite and consequence of large, non-intimate, imagined community.

Still, we may grumble, at least the likes Hortensius and Joshua Reynolds had palpable talent. Inglis echoes the familiar lament that today's celebrities often do not. They are famous for being famous, as the cliché goes. The concept of fame has always been with us, but 'celebrity has largely replaced the archaic concept of renown' (p4). Fame used to be the reward of social achievement in the public field or the tribute paid to power, wealth, and privilege. 'Celebrity, by contrast, is either won or conferred by the mere fact of a person being's popularly acknowledge, familiarly recognised, attended to, selected as a topic of gossip, speculation, emulation, envy, groundless affection, or dislike' (p57).

Fred Inglis, in blaming television, glossy magazines, and capitalism for leading us to this pitiful state of affairs, sounds like an old-fashioned socialist—the type who a few generations ago would have exhorted the working class to better themselves by reading classics from Everyman's Library as opposed to penny dreadfuls. Indeed, he is, by his own admission, an unreconstructed Old Labourite. Not that there is anything wrong with this. Today's widespread (and quintessentially New Labour) assumption that difficult literature or art is 'elitist', and therefore beyond the comprehension of the working class (who should stick to watching football and the telly), is a disgrace, and an unwitting form of inverted snobbery.

Yet, a failing of the Old Labour mentality was its distrust of aesthetics and its puritanical suspicion that art can serve as a social opiate. One of his main objections to celebrity magazines and reality television shows such as Big Brother is that they lead us to comprehend our emotions through the actions of others. But has not vicarious emotion always been intrinsic to the arts, and indeed the human condition? Would he similarly denounce those who shed a tear at the end of Casablanca (1942) or The Sound of Music (1965) for being 'vacuous'? I suspect that had he lived in early-17th century England, Inglis would have bemoaned those transfixed by Shakespeare's plays for being all silly. It is not real life, you know. It is only a play.

Of course I exaggerate, and for all its lapses into verbosity, modish po-mo italicizations and episodes of peculiar rhetorical flourishes ('[Marilyn Monroe] served as a sex object... and therefore, to tens of thousands helpless wankers, as the magazine cover they kept handily to hand'), A Short History of Celebrity is a wonderfully curmudgeon work. Inglis' reading—and viewing—is deep and wide, his prose rich and erudite without being forbiddingly esoteric. And unlike so many who excoriate our 'dumbed down' culture, at least he has examined it before doing so. Just as there is nothing wrong with the working class bettering themselves culturally, there is nothing wrong with hideously middle class people like myself reading OK! or watching The Jeremy Kyle Show. Indeed, if you seek to fully understand Western society today, I would say it is imperative.

Source:

Written under a Creative Commons License, with edits: https://creativecommons.org/licenses/by/1.0/

3. Better Schools for All?

By Anwar Oduro-Kwarteng

Introduction

In the midst of the government's 'reform' agenda in which the NHS, higher education, welfare, and schools are to be radically remodelled, it would appear the government is in a hurry to change the way we experience public services. State education is not immune from this, as evidenced by the Education White Paper and the wide-ranging reforms proposed in it. From the expansion of the academies program, to the introduction of the 'English Baccalaureate', it is clear the government is anxious to reform an education system it feels is failing and falling behind international competitors by all accepted measures.

The education white paper, 'The Importance of Teaching', ambitiously sets out to halt this decline by altering the system completely, and learning from other countries, such as Finland, whose education systems fare better. It aims to de-centralize the system, streamline the curriculum, and empower the teaching profession to act on its own initiative. Freedom and autonomy are the key concepts in the paper, and the government claims that in tandem, they will produce educational excellence, and allow schools to provide the most stimulating educational experience that they possibly can.

Shamefully, many students in this country leave school without the most basic knowledge of maths, English, and science; the UK continues to slip alarmingly down the OECD PISA rankings, with the overwhelming majority of these poorly-achieving students being from low-income and deprived backgrounds. And so it is imperative that the government's proposals address the existing problems, and find a way of ensuring a higher general level of educational engagement and attainment for all within the state system.

Central to the government's proposals is addressing the disparity between rich and poor in the education system. For many years, it has been apparent that the outcome of one's education has been closely linked to socio-economic circumstances. Those from better off backgrounds overwhelmingly outperform their poorer contemporaries at every level, leading to a number of other inequalities in job prospects, income, and access to higher education.

Attainment is the main criteria the government uses to measure educational inequality, and so I too will use the potential effect on attainment as the criterion by which to judge the policies. And although it is problematic and perhaps simplistic to understand inequality purely through the prism of attainment, it is clear that there is a definite disparity in achievement between rich and poor within the state system. And so whilst this approach has its limits, it does give us the opportunity to compare empirical data which is both measurable and observable and offers insight into this complex issue.

Thus, in order to discern whether or not the Education Bill is equipped to narrow the attainment gap, this paper will look at three key areas of reform and assess how far they deal with this vital problem:

1) The change of curriculum—the implementation of the new 'English Baccalaureate' as the gold standard of educational achievement.
2) Widening the Academies program—the extension of the existing program, this enables any 'outstanding' school to achieve academy status and freedom from local education authority (LEA) control. Together with this, the government aim to include primary and special schools for the first time.
3) Extension of Teach First and reform to teacher training and development.

1) Curriculum Reform

Within the Education White Paper, the streamlining of the syllabus and the introduction of the 'English Baccalaureate' are key components in the government's drive to improve standards in schools. Concern has been growing for a number of years over the perceived diminishing of standards within the curriculum. Evidence of this erosion is said to be shown in the way that more students are achieving A grades at GCSE and A-level, ultimately resulting in the recent introduction of the A* grade at A-Level so that universities can distinguish between the very best students and the rest. Whether the curriculum has been 'dumbed down' or not is difficult to ascertain, but the government claims that too much 'unnecessary' knowledge is been taught in schools. And as part of their proposals, there will be more of an onus on teachers to concentrate on core subjects, and in making sure that pupils have a better grasp of 'essential' knowledge.

By introducing the 'English Baccalaureate', which will be obtained if a student attains a grade A*-C in maths, English, science, a language, and a humanity, the government is hoping to focus teaching on these core academic subjects. The logic for this is clear: attainment in these subjects is poor in the state system, with fewer than 15% of pupils achieving A*-C grades in these subjects at GCSE, and just 4% of students eligible for free school meals doing so. Obviously this is not good enough, and is a cause for concern which urgently needs to be addressed. However, the problem is not that all state school pupils are attaining poorly. Rather, the problem is the glaring disparity between those that perform well, and those who do not. And the majority of those achieving poorly are from the most disadvantaged backgrounds, whereas those performing well are from more affluent ones. This gap is simply too large.

That said, it is questionable whether prescribing which subjects are preferable to study is the way to go about achieving better results, if this is indeed the aim. The most likely outcome of this policy in its current form is that it will encourage schools to focus on those students who are most likely to attain the Baccalaureate, as this will reflect positively on the school in league tables. An alternative way to deal with poor attainment in the state system would be to learn from the model used in Alberta Canada, which is the highest-ranked English speaking region in the PISA assessment.

Here, instead of stipulating which combination of subjects is preferable, they have a holistic approach to the curriculum. Obviously, students have to take the traditional subjects and pass them, but students of all abilities are encouraged to take a host of other subjects, including vocational and technical ones, which allows the schools to engage all of the students by holding all subjects in the same esteem.

The success of this approach, however, is predicated on the insistence that all subjects are taught to the highest possible standard, regardless of whether they are vocational or academic. In this way, schools and parents can be sure that whatever choices the students make, the quality of teaching, and the academic demands are as high as they can be. This also relies on teachers having the in-depth, specific knowledge of their subject, as well as the rigorous curriculum content that allows them to use this knowledge in the most effective way possible.

Nevertheless, the danger of implementing the English Baccalaureate is that certain subjects will be prioritized over others, meaning that a situation could arise where student X attains A*-C grades in English, maths, science, languages, and either history or geography, but does poorly in all of their other subjects. In this scenario, the poor attainment in the other subjects is irrelevant, because the Baccalaureate subjects are the priority. And as a result, this student will get the extra qualification that the Baccalaureate provides—whilst student Y gets A*-C grades in 3 Baccalaureate subjects as well as 5 others, and does not get this extra qualification because theirs is not deemed to be as worthy an achievement as that of student X.

A more equitable way to drive up standards for all and proactively tackle the attainment gap would be if league tables reflected the number of students that a school lifted from below a C grade to a C or above in their 5 traditional GCSEs. This would be a more thorough evaluation of the performance of the system, because a school that helps a whole host of students go from D to B grades should be more praiseworthy than a school that just concentrates on ensuring that B grade students attain B grades for example.

But more importantly, this would ensure that the league tables acknowledge the contribution that schools make towards improving the attainment for all of its pupils. As simply stating in the league tables the number of Baccalaureate awards that a school attains, and then using that as a measure of success, does not necessarily provide an accurate snapshot of a school's overall performance with regards to its entire student population, or press forward the governments stated aim of creating a more equitable system.

Moving on, another area of concern is the confused message delivered by the government on vocational education. The White Paper, on the one hand, notes with disparaging alarm that the number of vocational courses has risen 3,800% in 6 years, from 15,000 in 2004, to 575,000 in 2010, whilst simultaneously stating that they are immensely important and play a key role in the education system.

The danger is that the government risks undermining vocational or technical subjects through a negative attitude, which suggests that those students that may wish to take a more vocational route are having an easier time of it than their peers following a more traditional path. This is a very practical problem, because these perceptions have the potential to feed into the mindset of teachers and students, and if the culture in the system reflects these thoughts, then the esteem in which vocational subjects and those that wish to study them would always be in question.

To be fair however, this government is treading a familiar path. As the previous government was just as impotent, presiding over a system in which vocational subjects were seen by many schools as an easy way to boost performance in league tables, rather than a genuinely rigorous alternative and addition to traditional subjects. This attitude must change, and so if it is the case that these subjects are not taught to the same standard as the rest of the curriculum as the government suggests, then the upcoming review on vocational education will hopefully offer some guidance on this issue, and its recommendations will be key to any further and much-needed improvement in this area.

2) Academies

The academies program has perhaps been the most contentious issue within the White Paper. It proposes that all 'outstanding' schools should be able to gain fast track academy status, and thus remove themselves from the control of LEAs. The government cite Sweden and Finland as countries in which freedom and choice have meant an improvement in standards, and as such see this autonomy and freedom as the medicine to cure all the ills of our education system. Thus far, academies, which were first introduced by Labour in 2002 to address the issue of failing schools, have been on the whole successful in improving attainment in many instances, with OFSTED stating that 26% of academies were 'outstanding', compared to just 18% of maintained schools in 2010.

Nevertheless, the modification of this policy risks further widening the achievement gap between rich and poor, and not closing it. This is because originally, the academies program was explicitly aimed at the improvement of standards and attainment in some of the most poorly performing schools in the country, and has been largely successful in doing so. But the government have reversed this policy, and now only the top comprehensives will be able to convert initially. And as a result, one struggles to understand how this re-prioritising of academy status to already successful schools will help the most disadvantaged.

As well as this, the government claims that the extension of academies and Free Schools will provide more choice in the system, but they fail to acknowledge that the ability to exercise choice is not equally shared. And to reinforce this point, research commissioned by The Sutton Trust suggests that the majority of the best comprehensives already have a disproportionately-large middle class demographic, regardless of the socio-economic makeup of the areas that the schools are in. This suggests that currently, some parents are better able to exercise their choices in the state system than others.

Two main reasons can be given for this; the first of which being that these parents have the financial resources that enable them to buy into the catchment areas where the most desirable schools are found. And secondly, and perhaps more importantly, as a recent RSA report observes, they have the cultural capital to navigate the admissions process with confidence and effectiveness, as well as being able to draw on their educational experiences and professional networks to help them. This is not the case with lower-income families, who according to research by Simon Burgess et al, are far less likely to gain a place for their children at their 1st choice school than their middle class peers.

But worryingly for the government in their pursuit of educational equality through the expansion of the academies program, social attainment disparities within academies are already rife. Evidence from the National Audit Offices 2010 report on the academies opened by the Labor government states that, 'On average, the gap in attainment between more disadvantaged pupils and others has grown wider in academies than in comparable maintained schools'. They go on to propose that this may be caused by the fact that pupils from better off backgrounds benefit faster from the improved standards than the more disadvantaged, and conclude that, 'This suggests that it is the substantial improvements by the less disadvantaged pupils that are driving the academies improved performance overall'. Thus, taken at face value, this questions how far academies help improve standards for all students, and whether their proliferation will do anything to seriously change the trend of class inequality and attainment within the school system.

We must however be even handed; offering more choice within the system is not a bad thing in itself. The problems arise when there are not the checks and balances as well as incentives to make sure that these choices are open to everyone and not just those with enough nous to navigate the system. And this must be done through fair and transparent admissions procedures, and overseen by local LEAs, which have been disempowered to a large extent in this Bill, but must still play a crucial supervisory role within the system if it is to be truly equitable. Angus McBeath, the former Superintendent for Edmonton Schools in Canada, highlights the care that needs to be taken when introducing more choice into the system when he notes; 'You can make choice schools that benefit only the middle classes and above, or you can design a choice system that benefits all students.' and this is something that the government needs to be mindful of in its proposals.

On the issue of autonomy, the government claims that it is a prerequisite for a successful schools system. They cite Finland, Sweden, and the existing academies program in England as examples of the impact that it can have on the attainment of pupils in these schools. And the available evidence does indeed suggest that the ability of a school to set its own destiny, free from arbitrary control does help raise attainment to some degree over time. But we must however be cautious not to overestimate its effect on narrowing the gap between rich and poor. As in Alberta, where all state schools have the freedom to choose their curriculum, and manage their own budgets, autonomy in itself, although beneficial, is not seen as the educational panacea that it is here. This is exemplified by Edgar Schmidt, the Superintendent for Edmonton Schools, when he notes that, 'Autonomy is simply a management process, and has very little impact on achievement and results'.

Instead, they place far more emphasis on collaboration between schools and teachers, so that there is a sense of collective accountability for the system, rather than one of competition within it. This allows the system to improve as a whole, to the benefit of everyone, as opposed to a climate in which one school may prosper to the detriment of a neighboring one. It is this pervading sense of collaboration rather than pure competition that brings success, and so we must welcome with caution the government's attempt to go some way towards encouraging collaboration in the system through federations of schools, but more needs to be done if this ethos is to successfully permeate throughout the system.

Teaching Reform

Evidence suggests that the subject knowledge of teachers has a huge impact on the eventual level of attainment in the student body. And so, the government must be praised for extending the successful Teach First program, which aims to attract top graduates into the profession. Together with this, they will no longer fund teacher training for those students who do not attain at least a 2:2 in their degree, which is part of the attempt to ensure that teaching is seen as a prestigious profession, thus attracting the most able graduates. This is a step in the right direction, because if we look to other countries that achieve highly in the PISA rankings such as South Korea, they recruit from the top 5% of their graduates, whilst Finland recruits from the top 10%, and research suggests that the educational attainment and academic ability of a candidate has a significant bearing on their potential as a teacher, together with other traits such as communication skills and resilience.

Crucially, the proposal to create a national network of Teaching Schools is one that has the potential to have a positive impact with regards to the standard of teaching. Taken from the model of Teaching Hospitals, these schools will be rated as outstanding, and will adopt the role of creating an atmosphere of professional excellence throughout the system as a whole. This should continue the progress that has been made over recent years, in which much more of the initial training has been conducted within the school environment, allowing teachers to gain more confidence and practical experience. As well as this, the steps to increase the level of professional development throughout the course of a teaching career are also to be welcomed.

As mentioned in the introduction, one of the main themes running through this White Paper is freedom. And the freedom for teachers to find innovative and practical ways to impart knowledge is one of the government's main priorities. They claim that teachers have been unduly stifled by targets and prescription both in terms of the requirements made of them, and more fundamentally in terms of how they are meant to teach the curriculum. Thus, they aim to free teachers from central target setting, and allow them to plan for their lessons in their own way, which seems eminently reasonable, and should allow teachers to engage with their students in more creative ways. This is also to be welcomed.

The quality of teaching within schools is the key component of any attempt to raise standards. With poor teaching will come poor results, regardless of whether it is a Free School, academy, or otherwise. And as such, any attempt to strengthen the recruitment processes and training, as well as professional development, are important, and the government has made some positive moves in this regard.

Conclusion

The government has made some important proposals, such as refocusing on teacher quality as the key determinant of educational attainment. And the attempt to streamline processes and cut out unneeded bureaucracy is also to be welcomed. But this good work is in danger of being undone by the overly prescriptive and quixotic nature of the curriculum changes, and the proliferation of market forces into the state schools system. The aim should not merely be to have good schools, but instead, a good schools system, so that all pupils regardless of their background and where they live have the chance to progress in a stimulating and challenging environment.

And by reserving special praise for those who achieve well in Baccalaureate subjects, rather than concentrating on engaging all students with a wide and challenging set of curriculum choices that are taught to a high standard and held in equal esteem, the government risks alienating a section of pupils through its reforms. In this way, there is little point in speaking about choice within the system, as the government has made it clear through the Baccalaureate, that some academic choices are held in higher regard than others.

This is a concern, as education and the acquisition of knowledge are ends in themselves. And the state education system should reflect this by ensuring that all subjects are taught to the highest possible standard, in order to accommodate and engage the differing talents and aspirations of all its students. Instead of attempting to distinguish between what constitutes essential knowledge and what is unessential, the government should concentrate on ensuring that all knowledge taught in school is to a higher standard than it currently is.

Insisting on higher standards with regards to subject knowledge is not a bad thing in itself. Indeed it is to be welcomed. But it should apply to all subjects, not a select few. It is this kind of disjointed thinking that has created a system in which non-traditional subjects are not held to the same standard as the rest of the curriculum. Resulting in them being seen as lesser, easier options—thus discrediting them entirely from an academic point of view. With this in mind, one hopes that the government is serious about reforming the way in which vocational subjects are administered, as this would really make a difference in the quality and breadth of the curriculum as it stands.

Furthermore, the widening of the academies program will do little to address the attainment gap, because new academies are now likely to be already highly achieving schools, and so it is unclear how this will improve attainment for the poorest students, in poorly-attaining schools in deprived areas. And the National Audit Office make clear that extending the program beyond its intended remit will not necessarily yield the improvements that it does in its current form. As such, the academies program needs to be redefined: if its primary aim is still to improve standards in the most deprived schools, then the government must explain why it is that the best schools will take priority in the new arrangement, and not the poorest. This development is incoherent, and the contribution that it will make towards its stated aim of narrowing the attainment gap between rich and poor is certainly in question.

As well as this, the Pupil Premium, which is the government's flagship measure to address inequality in the system, has serious flaws. It is undoubtedly an important proposal, but the fact that schools can use the extra funding in any way that they see fit means there is no guarantee that it will filter down to those for whom it is meant. But, if implemented correctly, by funding more one to one teaching and catch up lessons for example, the Pupil Premium has the potential to make a real difference to the most deprived students in the schools system, and go some way towards the government's aim of narrowing the attainment gap.

Source:

4. Wasted: Why Education Isn't Educating, by Frank Furedi

By Michele Ledda

Asked about the persistence of historical determinism in the 20th century in an interview given two years before her death, Hannah Arendt replies that the main reason is the overwhelming attraction of reality. We act into the future, she explains, but cannot predict the result of our actions. Since we are not alone in the world and our actions provoke other people's reactions, our actions, unlike our behaviour, cannot have predictable consequences. There is an almost infinite number of variables involved. Contingency is the biggest factor in history. And yet, when we look back, we are able to explain events, to tell a coherent story. How is it possible that in retrospect it looks as if events could not have happened any other way? It is the pull reality exerts over us. All the variables have suddenly disappeared and reality has such an overwhelming impact upon us that it looks as if what has happened was bound to happen, as if there were logic to history.

The same is true for the reality of our present. We are so used to the practices that shape our professional lives, day after day, that, although we can fantasize about an infinite number of changes, it is difficult to believe that these could work in practice and that things could be done in an altogether different way. The world of education has been drifting for so many decades in one particular direction that it has become one area where it is difficult to obtain the necessary critical distance. Yet, if you were educated in a completely different system, at a different time, or in a different country, that critical distance is easier to achieve. Of course, critical distance can also be achieved by thinking and reading books (ie, by travelling virtually through space and time) or by visiting other countries. Then one realizes that what is considered impossible or inappropriate in Britain today was actually achieved or greatly valued in another country or historical time.

For instance, the Italian curriculum in the 1970s still made it compulsory for all middle school children (aged 12-14) to study Latin grammar. Everyone, no matter their socio-economic background or intellectual ability, was deemed capable of learning Latin. Of course, this is before the curriculum was 'modernized' and Latin remained compulsory only in the last five years of a handful of secondary courses, though it is still available to all state pupils who choose those particular schools. Compare this with today's Britain, where it is exceptionally rare for a state school to offer Latin. We can say that usually no state pupil is allowed to choose Latin as a subject, whereas it is usually compulsory in independent schools, which is a shining example of New Labor's belief in both equality and education.

To illustrate the point further, when a group of parents led by journalist Toby Young decided to set up a school where Latin is compulsory until the age of 16, they were accused of elitism, not by the *Socialist Worker*, but by a columnist of that venerable institution, *The Times*. The author of what is an otherwise sensible article on consumerism and education does not for a moment think that Latin is an essential part of universal culture or that children from a deprived socio-economic background could benefit from it. Such is the contempt in which 'old-fashioned' knowledge is held by many in mainstream British society, particularly numerous among the elite. And, as Frank Furedi has recently pointed out, while in the UK the serious study of classical music is considered too difficult for most children, it has flourished in Venezuela among a much poorer population.

It is also interesting that there are quite a few foreigners among the more incisive critics of Anglo-American educational practices. One is certainly Hannah Arendt, whose essay *The Crisis in Education*, first published in 1954, to this day remains the most insightful analysis of the problems faced by modern western education systems, problems that are more advanced in Britain and the US, but which are similar in the other western countries, which are catching up fast. Another is Austrian-born educationalist, Rudolph Fleisch, the author of *Why Johnny Can't Read*, the book that started the reading wars in the US in the 1950s by criticizing child-centered reading methods and advocating phonics instead.

Influenced by Arendt's *The Crisis in Education*, Hungarian-born British sociologist Frank Furedi's latest book, *Wasted*, certainly displays a lot of critical distance from the current British education system. One myth after another is systematically demolished. Theories that in our schools have the status of unassailable truths are shown to be nothing more than snake oil. Respected professors of education look like the modern equivalent of Mark Twain's characters The Duke and The King in The Adventures of Huckleberry Finn. The politicians and bureaucrats who manage our education system are shown either to be incompetent or to have little interest in knowledge and education.

For instance, Furedi points out that the widely discussed discipline problem includes children so young that the problem must reside with the adults' difficulty in exercising authority, rather than in our children. In 2007, he points out, 1,540 infants were suspended from nursery schools, many for attacking their teachers. How can so much money, time, and energy be spent on our education system, and no one seems to realize that something is seriously wrong with the adults, including those who devise education policies, when even children under 5 are suspended for violent, sexist, or racist behavior?

Education as a conservative enterprise

What Furedi takes from Arendt, and which is crucial in enabling him to see through the smokescreen of the ossified left and right positions in the education debate, is the understanding that conservatism is the essence of educational activity, through which the older generation transmits the knowledge accumulated by humanity in thousands of years to the 'new ones', as the Greeks used to call the young, or the 'newcomers to the world', in Arendt's words.

Far from having a conservative outcome, in the sense of indoctrinating the young into unquestioning respect for authority, the formal knowledge transmitted through the teaching of the various school subjects is essential for the young to understand the modern world and to be able to question it. The transmission of knowledge helps children to develop as intellectually and morally autonomous individuals who are capable of contributing in their turn to the making of the human world.

Once we understand education as the transmission of knowledge, it is clear that the most elitist and old-fashioned kind of education is positively revolutionary compared with what passes for progressive education today: a series of educational theories, practices, and policies that see the exercise of adult authority and the transmission of knowledge to the next generation as activities fraught with great dangers, not least because of an exaggerated sense of children's vulnerability.

The suspicion, if not outright rejection, of subject knowledge at the heart of our child-centered system is well expressed by the Plowden Report (1967):

'at the heart of the educational process lies the child. No advances in policy, no acquisitions of new equipment have their desired effect unless they are in harmony with the nature of the child, unless they are fundamentally acceptable to him. [...] Knowledge of the manner in which children develop, therefore, is of prime importance, both in avoiding educationally harmful practices and in introducing effective ones.'

Unfortunately, humanity has accumulated its knowledge, through millennia of struggles and discoveries, with no regard whatsoever for the nature of the child. On the contrary, education is the process whereby the child acquires a culture that is by definition heterogeneous to his nature. There is nothing natural in learning the multiplication tables, the alphabet, musical notation, or the correct movements of tennis. Even if the way in which these are learnt can be more or less humane to children, the acquisition of knowledge is a cultural, as opposed to natural process. On the other hand, learning is part of human nature. Unlike animal nature, human nature is extremely malleable. In the modern world, it would be 'unnatural' for a child to acquire no culture. The Plowden Report's notion that there is a correct, 'natural' way in which children should learn is therefore a fashionable myth. Children can learn in many different ways, and what they learn is more important than how they get there.

The ossified positions in the educational debate often leads one to identify child-centered practices with left wing, progressive education and subject-centered ones based on the transmission of knowledge as right-wing and elitist.

This was not always the case. Furedi shows that in the past, both left and right, despite their political differences, saw education as the transmission of knowledge to the next generation. He quotes very similar statements from such different thinkers as the Italian Marxist Antonio Gramsci, the literary critic Matthew Arnold, Lenin, and conservative philosopher Michael Oakeshott. All understand education as the new generation's rightful inheritance of the 'store of human knowledge', in Lenin's words.

In the 1930s, Gramsci understood that what was elitist about liberal education was not its content or its teaching methods, but that it was the preserve of the few. 'Grammar schools for all' would have been his slogan.

How is it possible that teaching methods and education policies that represent an attack on the very precondition for progress, the transmission of knowledge to the next generation, can now be called progressive? And how did teaching methods become so central in defining one's political identity?

The changing meaning of change

For Furedi, this is due to what he calls the 'fetishisation of change' by educationalists and policy makers. Having accepted Arendt's point that conservatism, in the sense of preserving human knowledge, is the essence of education, Furedi is in a position to question 'progressives'' claims that a modern education system should reject old-fashioned and academically-oriented curricula and teaching methods in favor of child-centered pedagogies and future-oriented curricula, more in tune with the lives of modern children and with the realities of the world of work in a global economy.

The way Furedi deals with the question of change is crucial to understand both the effectiveness and the limitations of his critique. On the one hand, Furedi convincingly argues that 'progressive' pedagogues invert the old meaning of change as a political category, from one associated with human agency, as in 'humans changing the world', to one that posits humans as the passive recipients of change, as in a social Darwinist (in my opinion) 'There Is No Alternative but to adapt to a changing world'. While the modernizers' rhetoric of change and their corresponding attack on tradition sound progressive, they convey an extremely limited idea of people's autonomy. So far, so good.

But change is such a fundamental category to Furedi's own political tradition (revolutionary communism) and above all to his theoretical principles (materialist dialectics) that he cannot bring himself to perform a thorough critique. Instead, his use of the term 'fetishisation' of change serves two functions. Firstly, it conveys the reassuring impression that Marxism, at least in its fundamental categories, is still relevant to understand modern developments, and untouched by said fetishisation. Secondly, it implies that modernizers favor a merely rhetorical version of change or that they only favor change in the world of education, while they are conservatives in politics: 'too often, conservatism becomes the hallmark of public life, while the school is turned into the location for social experimentation'.

In fact, New Labor has actively experimented with wider society just as much as with schools. Extraordinary security measures, ASBOs, smoking bans, the war on obesity, the overregulation of pubs, the vetting of adults who have contact with children and a myriad other initiatives (all criticized by Furedi himself) have greatly contributed to changing British society—an attack on the British way of life compared to which demographic changes and Islamic extremism pale into insignificance. The fact that they might have changed it for the worse is no argument for calling it conservatism, except that the words 'conservative' or 'reactionary' have lost their significance as political categories and have come to mean pretty much anything that we do not like while 'progressive' means little more than 'good'.

Furedi, like other social critics coming from the left, tends to portray developments he dislikes as conservative or reactionary, and to counterpose them to progress. For many thinkers, modern developments are still to be judged according to two fundamental principles of left and right: conservatives are hostile to change, while progressives embrace change. Despite having realized long ago that we need to go 'beyond left and right' in Furedi's words, even more critical thinkers from a left-wing tradition seem unable to do so comprehensively. They interpret most of the problems faced by modern society, not as a fulfilment of modern trends, but as a deviation from modernity and progress.

New conditions mean that both left and right have been cut off from their past, argues Furedi. But no one has been cut off from their past, and from their utopian future, so thoroughly as the revolutionary left. In the absence of a political vision, Furedi himself seems to depend on the rhetoric of change just as much as, if not more than, social critics from other political traditions.

But if we live in conservative times, prey to an exaggerated fear of change, as Furedi often argues, why do modern politicians of all political persuasions, including the Conservative Party, feel the need to show their embrace of change so conspicuously? Why do not politicians reassure their constituencies by saying that they are against change? Instead, even right-wing modernizers such as French Prime Minister Sarkozy and his cabinet sing about changer le monde.

If we consider how arguments for change are used by politicians bereft of political vision in order to implement the most illiberal legislation and how people's resistance, when it manifests itself, is easily portrayed as 'reactionary' and as favoring an unsustainable status quo, it seems clear to me that in today's conditions, the category of change is a much more subtle and more effective tool for the exercise of power and the denial of human subjectivity than old-fashioned respect for authority. Today, embracing change means accepting the chains of a powerless status for humanity, and the failure to rethink this category from scratch leads to serious theoretical shortcomings and, ultimately, to the consolidation of a political impotence that affects those in power as much as the population.

'Give me a place to stand on, and I will move the Earth,' Archimedes is said to have stated. In order to effect change, you need a fixed point. This is particularly true in our times, when anyone with a vision can be easily accused of dogmatism, essentialism, and conservatism and invited to embrace change instead. It is precisely the absence of a fixed place where to stand that prevents the formation of a potentially world-changing subject. Nothing is more anti-revolutionary today than the call to 'embrace change'.

The trap of modern instrumentalism

The dominance of change is strictly related to modern instrumentalism, which is the inability to pursue ultimate ends, such as education for its own sake, and is at the heart of the crisis of authority and of political vision. The Oxford English Dictionary provides this definition of instrumentalism:

A pragmatic philosophical approach which regards an activity (such as science, law or education) chiefly as an instrument or tool for some practical purpose, rather than in more absolute or ideal terms, in particular:

The pragmatic philosophy of John Dewey which supposes that thought is an instrument for solving practical problems, and that truth is not fixed but changes as the problems change.

Although Furedi is a critic of instrumentalism, and of the educational theories of John Dewey, his critique is tempered by the fact that he comes from a tradition that is itself instrumentalist and theoretically dependent on the idea of change. This appears clearly in his inability to see the importance of a common school curriculum and in his willingness to adopt the pragmatism of modernizers with regard to this question.

Ultimately, a critique of modern instrumentalism and the category of change can only be achieved through a critique of modernity, but Furedi and similar thinkers have long understood their work as a defense of modernity, science, and progress against the rejection of modernity by self-hating western elites that have lost confidence in themselves.

Although it is true that there are many contemporary trends towards the rejection of modernity, such as many forms of environmentalism, a critique of modernity need not be a rejection of the huge improvements to our lives that modern science and technological and economic progress have made possible. It only means considering the possibility that the problems of modernity have been created by trends inherent in modernity itself and that perhaps through understanding its impasses, we may start to envisage the possibility of a different, better modernity.

The inability to decide on a school curriculum

In education, the single most important area for debate, and the one where the crisis of authority highlighted by Furedi presents itself most starkly, is the content of the school curriculum. Yet, this is a topic that no one seems willing to tackle, not even Furedi.

The myth that the National Curriculum, introduced in 1989 by the Thatcher government, restored a traditional kind of education and stifled teachers' autonomy is very widespread, but it is just that—a myth. The Conservative government did increase regulation through the creation of Ofsted and school league tables, but the National Curriculum is a very vague document that is built around skills rather than content.

The Thatcher government had the intention of restoring a traditional education, but it lost the battle against its own educational establishment, because it had underestimated the task at hand, namely the difficulty that a government of modernizers would have in arguing for a traditional curriculum. Brian Cox, the educationalist that the Conservatives had chosen to chair the working group on the English curriculum, because of his reputation as a critic of progressive pedagogies, pointed out that 'the desire for a national culture is seen as damagingly conservative, often 'racist' and almost inevitably unsympathetic to the rights of women … Conservatives desire a common curriculum—any common curriculum—because this would have a unifying effect upon [an excessively pluralist society].'

Therefore, the English Working Group decided that no judgment should be made on which texts children would study, as 'the number of suitable authors would make any list quite impracticable'. It devolved this responsibility to examination boards and individual schools and teachers, after setting general parameters such as 'syllabuses must consist of both male and female authors'.

According to educational publisher Philip Walters, exam boards have now a combined turnover of £200 million, Edexcel is owned by a FTSE 100 company, and schools spend on average four times as much on examinations as on teaching material, including electronic equipment. The government has created a phoney market whereby examination boards now compete for customers by suggesting to schools that their examination is likely to enhance the school's position in the league tables, which means that if a syllabus is considered too demanding, it is unlikely to be successful. This has created an enormous pressure towards the dumbing down of exams, but it is also a way for the government to wash its hands of responsibility for the curriculum.

Yet anyone who runs a school, whether public or private, has the responsibility to provide a good curriculum, made up of the best possible subjects and the best possible content that each discipline has to offer. The government has the duty to provide a good curriculum, by drawing on the knowledge of the best minds in the country for each discipline—a decision that individual teachers cannot make. Teachers should of course be free to use whatever teaching methods they prefer, provided they are effective.

The debate over the curriculum is first and foremost an ideological and not a technical matter. The content of the curriculum depends on what kind of educated citizens we would like to have. Should children receive 'the store of human knowledge' and become educated citizens, morally autonomous subjects who contribute to shaping the world, or should they learn workplace skills and transferable skills such as learning to learn, and become lifelong learners, ready to be guided by experts and re-skill themselves in order to adapt to a changing world and to the needs of the global economy?

If we prefer the first option, then we have a duty to decide what children should study in the 21st century. We must answer the question, what is the best knowledge humanity has produced so far that we can enthusiastically pass on to the next generation? If we prefer the second, then we opt for an empty curriculum, where the content must change all the time in order to adapt to a changing world (or the fashions and policies of the moment). Moreover, we opt for a personalized curriculum, where the part of the modern world that is deemed relevant to the socio-economic background and the life prospects of each particular child will be considered important, while the rest will be deemed irrelevant.

The inability to determine the content of the school curriculum, the most important problem in education and one that no party seems willing or able to handle, goes right at the heart of the government's crisis of authority and lack of vision. Although some timid hints have come from the Conservatives that they might just look into this problem, it remains to be seen if a party of modernizers can find the conviction to argue for a common curriculum as representing the best that has been thought and said—something that the Iron Lady herself was unable to do.

It is therefore disappointing to see that Furedi, having analyzed so well some aspects of the crisis of adult authority and other failings of the education system, has nothing to say about the biggest elephant in the room.

On this matter, Furedi's position is not very different from the Conservatives' hope that a good curriculum will emerge through the invisible hand of the market or New Labor's agenda of the personalization of public services, both representing an outsourcing of responsibility to individual schools, teachers and parents (or public service users). Furedi is similarly confident that education should 'discover its future direction for itself'. His conclusion that, beyond a very basic common curriculum, we should let schools experiment to decide 'what works', seems not that different from conventional thinking in education policy today.

'One solution, devolution' seems to be the all-too-familiar slogan. But it should be clear by now that the discourse of devolution and empowerment at a local level on the one hand and increasing regulation of the 'empowered' on the other, who, precisely because they have been set free must be guided and regulated through a 'system of accountability', are part and parcel of the same process—a process that anyone interested in understanding the contemporary crisis of authority cannot afford to ignore.

Furedi suggests that anyone with a vision for the content of the curriculum can only be someone 'wedded to a dogma'. But anyone with a vision these days can be easily accused of dogmatism, or essentialism— often by those who are wedded to the dogma of change, which has the advantage of appearing as the quintessentially non-dogmatic position but can be used, just like any other received idea, in a dogmatic way.

Source:

CHAPTER TWELVE

PERSONAL ESSAYS

What is a Personal Essay?

A personal essay is a piece of writing that addresses a given topic from the writer's own perspective, usually including some examples from the person's life to support the main ideas. It allows readers to get a sense of someone's abilities and personality, so some people see it as a type of interview. Although it is similar to other formal papers in that it usually needs at least five paragraphs, the use of "I" language and acceptance of bias make it distinct. Many people have trouble constructing one, but most of the problems authors encounter are either avoidable or can be fixed.

Common Uses

Many college admissions boards ask prospective students to write a personal essay as part of their general application process. Scholarship, internship and contest committees also often request them. Reviewers use them not only to get a general sense of a writer's history and philosophies, but also to analyze whether he is educated, creative or experienced enough to stand out from other applicants.

Parts

Opinions on how to best write a personal essay vary, but typically, one has an introductory paragraph that ends with a main thesis. Most use at least three supporting points and paragraphs, and a conclusion that wraps everything up is also fairly standard. It isn't necessary to write these parts in the order they will appear in the final draft, but when everything is put together, the work as a whole needs to flow well, transitioning logically from one idea to the next.

"For more than four hundred years, the personal essay has been one of the richest and most vibrant of all literary forms." (The Art of the Personal Essay by Phillip Lopate.) The personal essay is also one of the most popular forms of creative nonfiction. A personal essay can be based on a personal experience that results in a lesson that you learn. A personal essay can also be a personal opinion about a topic or issue that is important to you. This article defines the personal essay.

A personal essay is therefore either a personal narrative in which the author writes about a personal incident or experience that provided significant personal meaning or a lesson learned, or it is a personal opinion about some topic or issue that is important to the writer.

Personal Essay versus a Formal Essay

The personal essay is different from a formal essay. In the personal essay, the writer writes about experience without having to prove the point. The author needs only to introduce the subject and theme. It is based on feeling, emotion, personal opinion, and personal experience. It is autobiographical. On the other hand, in the formal essay, the writer states the thesis, and then attempts to prove or support his point with facts—to provide proof. To do this, the author must do research.

The Personal Essay as a Personal Narrative

A personal narrative has the following elements:

- It is based on a personal experience in which you have gained significant meaning, insight, or learned a lesson. It can also be based on a milestone or life-altering event.
- It is personal narrative. The writer tells the story by including dialogue, imagery, characterization, conflict, plot, and setting.
- It is written in the first person. ("I" point-of-view)

- It is an autobiographical story in which the writer describes an incident that resulted in some personal growth or development.
- A personal essay is a glimpse of the writer's life. The writer describes the personal experience using the scene-building technique, weaves a theme throughout the narrative, and makes an important point. There must be a lesson or meaning. The writer cannot just write an interesting story.
- It does not have to be objective. However, the writer must express his/her feelings, thoughts, and emotions.
- The writer uses self-disclosure and is honest with his/her readers.
- The writer writes about a real life experience. The incident or experience must have occurred. The writer must use fact and truth.
- The writer must dramatize the story by using the scene building technique. A scene includes setting/location, intimate details, concrete and specific descriptions, action, and often dialogue.

The Personal Essay as a Personal Opinion

A personal essay can also be an opinion piece, an opinion that is based on a particular political or social concern or topic of interest. In this type of personal essay, the writer can states the problem, provide solutions, and then write a conclusion—which must state an important point. Whatever the writer discusses, the topic is of interest to the writer. The writer frequently seeks to explain the truth or reality has he/she views it. Sometimes the writer ponders a question. Other times the writer explores a topic from his own perspective. The writer must not lecture, sermonize, or moralize. In other words, the writer must present his/her opinion in such a way that allows the readers decide for themselves.

In Writing Life Stories, author Bill Roorbach provides an excellent definition of the personal essay, one that is based on a personal opinion. He states that the personal essay that is based on a personal opinion has these attributes:

- A personal essay is a conversation with your readers.
- The personal essay is an informed mixture of storytelling, facts, wisdom, and personality.
- The personal essay examines a subject outside of yourself, but through the lens of self.
- The subject of the personal essay may be the self, but the self is treated as evidence for the argument.
- Passages of narrative often appear but generally get used as evidence in the inductive argument.
- The personal essay strives to say what is evident, and to come to a conclusion that the reader may agree or disagree.
- A personal essay can wonder through its subject, circle around it, get the long view and the short, always providing experience, knowledge, book learning, and personal history.

It should also be noted that a personal essay doesn't need to be objective. It can be purely subjective. You don't have to prove a point or show both sides of the argument. But you must express your own personal feelings, thoughts, and opinions on a topic or issue in a logical manner.

Subjects for the Personal Essay

Your subject can be about anything that you are passionate about. You can write about a "turning point" in your life, or a milestone, or adversity, such as death, illness, divorce. The subject you choose must have provided you with significant personal meaning or a lesson that you have learned. But, keep in mind, you are not just reflecting or remembering, you are going to make a point, some universal truth that your readers can appreciate. Otherwise, your story is just a story. So, write about the following:

- Personal experience
- Incident
- Anecdote
- Topic

- Issue
- A memory

The easiest way to write a personal essay is to use the standard form taught in Composition 101: an introductory paragraph followed by three paragraphs outlining three main points and a final summary paragraph. But instead of just blathering about yourself, describe vivid scenes and what they mean to you, such as when your 2-year-old son, Jordan, solemnly declares from the bathtub "I can't swim—my penis is hard" and you tell him it's OK, it's normal, knowing it'll subside and he'll be able to swim soon, but you don't tell him that teeny little weenie he's holding will be the source of the most intense worries, sorrows, and pleasures he'll ever experience, and you wonder if you'll ever be able to tell him the truth. You could follow this thought with the trials and tribulations of your own penis, unless you're a woman— but of course females are involved with love, sex, and life built around their own body parts, which can provide many interesting topics. The key to maintaining reader interest is to be open and honest, displaying your concerns and fears through specific, true-life examples rather than abstract concepts about how you think sex education is important because you learned the hard way on your own and you doubt you'll explain things any better than your own father did. Follow this format and, while you may not become a world-renowned author, you will be able to complete a personal essay.

Use five sentences in each paragraph. Some authors, like Faulkner, write immensely long sentences that drift into nooks and crannies of life, enlightening the reader about how, at age 16, you were tricked by a girl into trying on ring sets from her mom's jewelry-making equipment to find your ring size and later presented with a black onyx and silver ring you were too scared to wear because it implied going steady, which leads to sex, and Dad had just given you and your brother a box of Trojans the week before when Mom and Brooke had gone shopping at Sears for dresses and you were as uncomfortable as Dad when he grunted out his heart-to-heart "Use these to be safe," especially since you'd recently calculated and realized he'd knocked Mom up with you when she was 16 and he was out of the army after a four-year hitch and you figured it must have happened by accident since their meeting was accidental, him picking her and her sisters up at a railroad crossing in the rain on Halloween and giving them a ride home, coming later to visit, finally getting down in April without a condom or maybe with one that broke and there you are in December but at least they'd gotten married over the summer and you realize it's April now and you stare at the ring and finally throw it away and tell her later you don't wear jewelry. Tough guys like Hemingway write short, straightforward sentences, such as: "The author stopped typing. His thick fingers lay bare on the keyboard. Although he's been married for eight years, his ring finger is naked. His wife knows he doesn't wear jewelry. Ever." Yet other writers like to mix up the lengths of their sentences, using long, compound run-ons that begin with one thought then drive on to others but eventually circle back for completion, then follow with a short, crisp, prissy sentence that would satisfy an eighth-grade grammar teacher. Not me.

The Personal Essay Writing Steps

Intro

The valedictorian at my school can play the trombone. She's a black belt in jiu-jitsu, and she invented a new way to keep bread fresh. She's pretty amazing, but I don't think she's that unusual. In the stack of essays being considered for admission, I would guess she's the rule more than the exception.

I haven't invented anything. I can only play the kazoo, and the only belt I own came free with the suit. What I have to offer isn't as obvious as most applicants, but what I represent is important. My generation is one raised by pop culture, and while denigrating it, scions of elder generations ignore one simple fact: today's pop culture manufactures tomorrow's legends.

How can an encyclopedic knowledge of pop culture contribute to a better way of life? Partly because this is the language of the future. I already speak it fluently, and any other ideas will be layered on top. The other reason is that although things like popular movies, books, and video games get dismissed, they actually have a lot to say.

Body

While teachers might struggle to bring the story of *Oedipus* to modern students, I got what was going on quickly…because I watch *Game of Thrones*. The plotlines of incest and revenge, as well as defying the gods, are explored in great detail on the show. So when it came time to understand, I was able to map the characters onto one another, facilitating both my understanding and that of my friends, whom I could help with the reading.

Additionally, when I learned about the Wars of the Roses, it didn't take long for me to understand the importance of the Yorks and the Lancasters. I already had a window into both art and history from a television show, and my knowledge of it helped me understand both incarnations better.

It's not just facts and art that pop culture helps illuminate; most of my moral leaders have been fictional. Katniss Everdeen and Tony Stark both taught me about the importance of perseverance. Spider-Man's motto is "with great power comes great responsibility." The *Terminator* movies pressed the importance of preparing for the future while pointing out that the future is not set. While the teachers of these lessons might be unorthodox, they are the cornerstones of many religions and philosophies.

These stories are often rooted, consciously or not, in religion and folklore. When Captain America chooses not to fight his friend, instead literally turning the other cheek in the face of violence, not only do I understand the significance, but I am also able to point to a concrete place in space and time where this was the correct response.

Many people will agree that books, movies, and even television can contain lessons, but they still say to throw video games away. They call them a waste of time at best. This falls apart under a similar examination of the form.

The *Assassin's Creed* series, for example, taught me a bit about history. While I understand the Assassins and the Templar are not really secret societies fighting a millennia-old war, the people they run into are real. During the Revolution section in American History, I was the only one who knew minor players like Charles Lee and understood his significance. I also know names like Rodrigo Borgia, Robespierre, and Duleep Singh thanks to these games.

Conclusion

We all embrace what we love, and I have done that with the culture that has raised me. While I appreciate it on the surface level, as entertainment, I understand there is more to it. It has caused me to learn more than I would have in school. When I fight a new enemy in a historical game, I look him up.

Many of your applicants will run away from their time appreciating the mass art of their generation. Not me. I am fluent in the language of my time. I am uniquely suited to understanding and applying these concepts to higher learning. What you're getting with me is someone who will be able to bridge the gap between past and present, and apply their education to the future.

Why This Essay Works

This essay acknowledges the applicant's weaknesses from the beginning. By adopting a funny, self-deprecating attitude, the essay instantly stands out from the others around it. Although humor is there and is an integral part of the essay, it never takes over the narrative. It's used in the very beginning to separate itself from the pack, then moves into a more traditional inventory as it develops.

After humorously deconstructing the candidate's weaknesses, it moves into strengths. Many applicants don't know what their strengths are, and the purpose here is to show that even what you might regard as a weakness can be recast as a strength if you know how. Essentially, the writer declares a paradox in their thesis statement: all that time people say they wasted watching movie and playing video games is actually a strength.

The most important part is in the body, where the writer then backs up what they're saying. Making unfounded claims is good for attracting attention, but not so good for getting into college. The key is understanding what you've learned from your time enjoying culture.

The writer then hits it, point by point, showing where movies, television, and video games have all made them a more ideal candidate for entry.

The conclusion dramatically restates the thesis, and includes the most stirring line at the end. This applicant is fluent in the language of today, and uses a rhythmic three-part statement on the end to drive the point home. This student knows they are not the traditional over-achiever that colleges are said to want; instead, they show that they're bold and innovative, two qualities that are irresistible.

How to Write a Personal Essay with examples

A good personal essay can move and inspire readers. It can also leave the reader unsettled, uncertain, and full of more questions than answers. To write an effective personal essay, you will need to first understand the structure of a personal essay. You will then need to brainstorm ideas for the personal essay so you are ready when it is time to sit down and craft your essay.

Part 1

Starting Your Personal Essay

Find an angle for your essay. Your life may not be littered with exciting stories or intense drama, but that's okay. Your personal essay can still be engaging for your reader if you focus on finding an angle for your essay. You should try to find a unique or interesting take on an experience or moment in your life. Looking at an experience from a particular angle can turn it into deep, meaningful subject matter for your essay.

> o   For example, maybe you want to write about an experience where you learned about failure. You may think the time you failed a pop quiz in class. Though the quiz may have seemed insignificant to you at the time, you realized later that failing the pop quiz forced you to reassess your goals and motivated you to get a passing

grade. Seen from a certain angle, your small failure became a gateway to perseverance and determination.

Write about a significant moment. A good personal essay will explore a specific experience that created a sense of conflict in your life. The personal essay can be a way to explore how and why you were disturbed, bothered, or hurt by the experience. Think of it as a space where you can discuss a significant moment and reflect on its impact on your life.

o This could be a seemingly small moment that ended up having a profound influence on you later, such the first time you experienced disgust as a child or the look on your mother's face when you told her you were gay. Try to really dig into why you were bothered, hurt, or disturbed by this moment in your essay.

o Remember that moments charged with strong emotion will often be more engaging to readers. Having a strong reaction to a specific moment will allow you to write passionately about it and keep your reader interested in your essay.

Discuss a specific event that triggered an emotional response. You may also explore a specific event in your life that left a lasting impression on you. Often, personal essays act as reflections on an event that occurred in your life and shifted it in some way. Think of a specific event that is unique and personal to you. The stranger the event, the more likely the essay will be engaging to read.

o For example, you may focus on the day you found out your father cheated on your mother or the week you mourned the death of a loved one. Think about a heavy experience in your life that shaped who you are today.

o You may also decide to write about a seemingly light topic or event, such as your first ride on a roller coaster, or the first time you went on a cruise with your partner.

No matter what event you choose, make sure it is an event that triggered a strong emotional response, ranging from anger to confusion to unabashed joy.

Think of a person in your life that you have difficulty with in some way. You may want to explore a tenuous relationship with a person in your life in your personal essay. Think about a person you have grown apart from or feel estranged from. You may also choose a person that you have always had a difficult or complicated relationship with and explore why this is in your essay.

- o For example, you may think about why you and your mother stopped speaking years ago or why you are no longer close to a childhood friend. You may also look at past romantic relationships that failed and consider why they did not succeed or a relationship with a mentor that went sour.

Respond to a current event. Good personal essays consider the specific, such as your experiences, as well as the general, such as a current event or larger issue. You may focus on a current event or topic that you feel passionate about, such as abortion or refugee camps, and consider it from a personal perspective.

- o Ask yourself questions about the current event, such as: How does the current event intersect with your own experiences? How can you explore a current social issue or event using your personal thoughts, experiences, and emotions?
- o For example, you may have an interest in writing about Syrian refugee camps in Europe. You may then focus your personal essay on your own status as a refugee in America and how your experiences a refugee have shaped the person you are now. This will allow you to explore a current event from a personal perspective,

rather than simply talk about the current event from a distant, journalistic perspective.

Create an outline. Personal essays are usually formatted in sections, with an introductory section, a body section, and a concluding section. These sections are broken down as follows:

o   The introductory section should include "the hook", opening lines where you catch the reader's attention. It should also have some sort of narrative thesis, which is often the beginning of an important event in the piece or a theme that connects your experience to a universal idea.

o   The body sections should include supporting evidence for your narrative thesis and/or the key themes in your piece. Often, this is in the form of your experiences and your reflections on your experiences. You should also note the passage of time in your body sections so the reader is aware of when and how certain events occurred.

o   The concluding section should include a conclusion to the events and experiences discussed in the essay. You should also have a moral of the story moment, where you reflect on what you learned from your experiences or how your experiences changed your life.

o   In the past, it was advised to have five paragraphs total, one paragraph for the introductory section, two paragraphs for the body section, and one paragraph for the concluding section. But you do not need to be limited to five paragraphs only for your personal essay as long as you have all three sections.

Part 2

Writing the Personal Essay

Begin with an engaging opening scene. You should open your personal essay with an introductory section that is engaging and interesting for your reader. The opening section should introduce the key characters of the essay as well as the central theme or themes of the essay. It should also present the central question or concern in the essay.

    o   Don't begin with a line that explains exactly what is going to be discussed in, such as, "In this essay, I will be discussing my fraught relationship with my mother." Instead, draw your reader into your piece and still provide all the information needed in your opening line.

    o   Start instead with a specific scene that contains the key characters of the essay and allows you discuss the central question or theme. Doing this will allow you to introduce the reader to the characters and the central conflict right away.

    o   For example, if you are writing about your fraught relationship with your mother, you may focus on a specific memory where you both disagreed or clashed. This could be the time you and your mother fought over a seemingly insignificant item, or the time you argued about a family secret.

Write from your unique voice or perspective. Though you are writing a personal essay, you still have the freedom to use a unique writing voice or point of view. Like other writing genres, personal essays are often more successful when the writer uses a writing voice that entertains and informs the reader. This means using word choice, syntax, and tone to create an engaging narrative voice in the essay.

    o   This writing voice may be conversational, much like how you might speak to a good friend or a family member. Or, the writing voice may be more reflective and internal, where you question your own assumptions and thoughts about the subject of the essay.

    o   Many personal essays are written in the first person, using "I". You may decide to write in the present tense to make the story feel immediate, or past tense, which will allow you to reflect more on specific events or moments.

Develop the characters so they are well-rounded and detailed. Be sure to describe your characters with sensory detail and physical detail. Even though you are pulling from your real life experiences in your essay, you should still consider storytelling elements like plot and character. Using these elements in your essay will keep your reader engaged and help your essay to flow smoothly.

o   You can also include lines of dialogue spoken by your characters, based on your memory of the event. However, you should limit dialogue to only a few lines a page, as too much dialogue can start to veer away from personal essay and more toward fiction.

Include plot in your essay. You should also have a sense of plot in your essay, where a sequence of events or moments add up to a realization or moment of conflict at the end of the piece.

o   You may use a plot outline to organize your essay. The plot points should act as supporting evidence for the central question or issue of the essay.

Focus on uncovering a deeper truth. This means thinking about the deeper meanings that are at the core of your personal experiences. Try to discuss your experiences with honesty and curiosity, where you are trying to uncover a hidden truth or a truth you did not know was there at the time. Often, the best personal essays will try to expose a truth that is uncomfortable or difficult for the writer to discuss.

o   It's important to remember that though an experience may appear to have all the drama necessary to make a good personal essay, it may be a drama that is too familiar to the reader already. Be wary of experiences that are familiar and filled with pathos that a reader may have experienced before.

o   If you are writing about the sudden death of a loved one, for example, it may feel important and deep to you. But the reader will likely know what to expect of an essay about a dead loved one, and may not relate to your essay because they did not know the loved one like you did.

o   Instead, you may try to uncover a truth that is deeper than "I am sad my loved one died." Think about what the loved one meant to you and how the loved one affected your life, in positive and negative ways. This could lead to the uncovering of a deeper truth and a stronger personal essay.

Part 3

Polishing Your Essay

Try out different literary techniques and forms. You can add richness to your writing by experimenting with different literary techniques and forms, such as metaphor, repetition, and personification. Your personal essay may be that much stronger once you add in literary techniques that show how well you can tell your story.

o   For example, you may use metaphor to describe the experience of telling your mother you are gay. You may describe your mother's face as "impenetrable, a sudden wall". Or you may use a simile, such as "my mother's reaction was silent and stunned, as if she had been struck by lightning."

Read the essay out loud. Once you have written a first draft of your personal essay, you should read through it and listen to how it sounds. You may read it out loud to yourself or to a sympathetic audience.

o   As you read it out loud, you should highlight any sentences that are confusing or unclear as well as sentences that do not appear as strong as the rest of the draft. You should also make sure your characters are well developed and your essay follows some kind of structure or sense of plot. Consider if you are hitting a deeper truth in your draft and what you can do to get there if it is not yet on the page. Revising your essay will only make it that much stronger.

Revise the essay. Once you have a strong draft of the essay, you should sit down and revise it. You can take into account the notes you made on the draft as you read it out loud as well as feedback you receive from trusted readers.

- o When you are revising, you should consider if your content is really worth writing about, if you are writing about a topic or subject you are passionate about, and if your reader will understand your writing. You want to avoid confusing your reader, as this can turn her off from reading to the end of your essay.
- o You should also make sure the focus and themes of the essay are clear. Your experiences should center around a central question, issue, or theme. This will ensure your personal essay is well written and concise.

Examples of Personal Essays

1. Personal Essay for Medical Course

When I was a child, my cousin, who was of the same age, died of a particularly vicious flu. This case, however trivial it may sound, impressed me so greatly that I decided to connect my life with medicine when I grow up, so that I would be able to study the disease, understand how it functions and, probably, will be able to save somebody else from undergoing the same experience. By the time I reached high school, this resolution became rather lukewarm, but still I tried to apply it to several biology and medical clubs; and, surprisingly, it turned out that my early decision was completely correct, for biology and medicine became the subjects that I enjoyed particularly throughout my high school years.

Since then, I tried to further develop my interests and, throughout my undergraduate years, took three public health courses in order to familiarize myself with the system of health care in this country and understand how it works and, in perspective, how it can be improved. At the present time, I study biology with specific concentration on microbiology and infectious diseases. I have experience of work in a medical laboratory in Oldcreek, Kansas, where I had an opportunity to see how real research in epidemiology is being done.

I am most interested in the reputation and facilities the Northern University of Alabama provides, and heard a lot of most praising opinions of the people working there. I believe that I may become a valuable member of this scientific community in future, and learn a lot from renowned scientists who work there now. I am most interested in Doctor Bauman's proposed method of working on pathogenic bacteria and hope to make contribution in the research done there.

After receiving the Bachelor's degree in epidemiology, I intend to go on and further deepen my knowledge of the subject. Master's and Doctoral degrees seem to be natural continuation of my way, and I intend to go it up to the end.

In my research work I plan to go along the lines I have defined for myself from the very beginning and try to find new, more effective ways of fighting contagious diseases that still plague people all over the world.

2. Failure and Success

The Prompt

The lessons we take from obstacles we encounter can be fundamental to later success. Recount a time when you faced a challenge, setback, or failure. How did it affect you, and what did you learn from the experience?

The Essay

Intro

I've never been comfortable bragging. In fact, I was raised to be modest about my achievements, whatever they might be. Applying for college is nothing but bragging, and it makes me uncomfortable. In addition, every other essay you're likely to see is nothing but a litany of impressive accomplishments from top to bottom. That's not me.

At least, that's not me yet. Those applicants who have already tasted far-reaching success are pretty well-formed as people. They already know what works and see no reason to change. Why should they? They already invented a new form of pizza. They have life figured out, or sincerely believe they do. They are wrong. There is no better teacher than failure.

Think about it for a second. Wisdom is what you get from experience. Experience is what you get from failure. The transitive property works out from there. I know this because I failed and it turned me around in a way that modest or even spectacular success could not have. It all started with a D.

Body

Getting a D probably isn't the worst thing in the world, but it's not something anyone wants to see, let alone put, on a college application. It came back to me, scrawled in red, on the first big history test of the year. The one the teacher had assured us was a third of our grade. I could already see my chances of a four-year college going up in smoke and my school year hadn't even started yet.

What happened? I'm not a D student. I'll get the occasional C as well as the occasional A. D's are out of character for me, and enough of a stomach punch to really get my attention. The short version is, I didn't study, and I don't remember precisely why. There is always a reason not to study, isn't there? I didn't study and I went into a test woefully unprepared and got beaten up.

I had two options here. I could accept that I was in fact a D student despite what I had thought. Or I could study hard for the next test and try to bring my grade up by the force of the average. I realized something pretty important: while I had already forgotten the reason I didn't study, I never forgot the grade. Thus, the grade itself was far more important than whatever it was I was doing instead.

Imagine, instead, if I had gotten a C or even a B. It would have taken sheer, blind luck, but it could have happened. If this had happened, if I had succeeded rather than failed, I would have learned nothing. Or, at the very least, I would have learned that I didn't have to study, which is the opposite of what any college-bound senior should learn.

Conclusion

I chose to work harder. By my failure, that D, I had already learned the consequences of not studying. I knew both the problem and the solution. It didn't make it easy. I steadily brought my grade up with subsequent tests and papers.

At the end of the year, I got a better grade than I should have, based on strict averages. The teacher weighted improvement over other concerns. Those who buckled down and worked harder as the year progressed were rewarded.

In essence, my hard work paid off twice over. Had I not failed, I would have learned nothing. I might have done much worse on a later test, since I "knew" studying was not important. Instead, by failing, I was able to right my course. Going into college, I have concrete experience with just how important hard work can be. Okay, I might be bragging a little bit.

Why This Essay Works

This essay is a good example of how to turn an ostensible weakness into a strength. The writer takes a prompt, which explicitly acknowledges a failure of some kind, and shows how it leads to later success. This can be a winning combination, as it shows a certain amount of humility, which can be in short supply amongst students.

The writer also uses humor, but does not let the essay get overpowered by quips and jokey asides. Humor can be a wonderful way to liven up a piece of writing, but allow it to work in the service of the piece rather than the other way around. In addition, never be afraid to cut a joke that just isn't working. It's better to have no humor at all than forced attempts at it.

Good writing is all about using concrete examples. In this case, the writer is able to point to a specific incident that shows the prompt in action. This specific failed test gives the writer a sense of immediacy and allows them to explore the idea. In this way, the reader gets the sense that this is truly wisdom gained.

That last point is vital. To truly answer a prompt like this, you have to be completely honest about your failure, whatever it might be. No matter what it was, chances are you learned something from it. There's nothing like a taste of failure to make sure you never experience it again.

3. Personal Development Essay Sample

I have always been popular since I remember myself. I was trying to do my best so that people like me and that worked. I'm definitely an easy-going person who knows what to expect from life and how to shape the reality that I live in. Many of my friends call me a philosopher for that I am always calm and rational and only I know what it costs to me. I am not complaining no way, but from time to time I just get very much tired.

A few weeks ago I started my classes at photo school. The price was rather high, but it was my dream of past 2 months. The atmosphere of creating images and witness transfer from my frame of reference had always attracted me in the greatest extent. My father is an amateur photographer; however he can afford expensive photo camera and different lenses for himself. He had never studied photography anywhere practicing self-education. He has a big library of journals and magazines on this topic, so a received a large basis for my studying. Moreover, he presented me his old camera Nikon D70 with a kit lens, 18-70 mm, semi-professional, but with very outstanding characteristics. So, I saved money for the purchase of the new one, and was able to start immediately to create my masterpieces.

I must say that I am still very shy photographer, as I cannot just photo reportages on the streets, as I am very anxious what would people think of me, but I just love making portraits and close-ups, working with the model, trying to find the best camera angle, installing studio light. I'm thinking about buying some soft boxes for myself, but this idea refers to long-term goals.

My group at school is very nice. There are four boys and five girls, including me. I communicate predominately with boys, as I am older then all girls are, and it is more interesting to me. We joke and laugh a lot; I like their works and the way they make pictures. It is significant for my photographic experience to communicate with other photographs, to hear their opinion, to listen what they are saying regarding my works and how do they percept them. But the one hidden reason of my school attending is that I have always dreamt about becoming a model or at least used as it from time to time. I would like to have professional shoots and that people admired my beauty. And my dreams come true from lesson to lesson. Our teachers choose me more often to be the model for experiments with studio light and I am just very happy of that. And last Saturday we had the outside class to practice landscape shooting with another professional photographer and he was making pictures of me all the time. Probably he just liked me as a person, but it was very pleasant, even though I haven't received the pictures yet.

After this class I met my friends – Veronique and Mathias. They used to go out about five years ago, and now they are just friends. Mathias is from Austria and came for a week to have fun with us. We walked round the city, making pictures of us altogether and predominantly silent. Mathias is not very keen in English and he got tired very much when he speaks a lot. We decided to go to the nightclub in the evening and to show him how to blow up the stage.

I returned home to sleep a little bit. When I entered the house, recollections about the day before yesterday captured me again. I remembered the face, the music and the atmosphere and began to cry. It was my mother's brother whose funeral that day. I cannot even call him an uncle, as we were never close and never communicated since I remember myself. When I learned about his death, I just said: "This is life. Somebody dies, somebody is born". My heart was not cowering of any emotions, I was calm and accepted this fact as I do when I hear weather forecast. But as he was still our family, I decided to go to the funeral to support my mother and grandmother, who were totally broken of this news. He was 47 years old, lived all his life in another city and had no children. His wife died two weeks before his dead. Doctors discovered a tumor in his brains, but I think that he cannot let her go. We arrived in the morning, my grandmother was already there. When she saw us she started keening just on the street even though she already accepted the fact. For me it was a performance that I accidentally bought tickets at. I know that I am saying, as during the funeral she was calm and didn't cry at all. There was an impression that she already rubbed though his death, as she was with him for a week in the hospital and when he died. When the farewell ceremony began and I entered the hall with eternity box, tears appeared on my eyes, but still I was ok. When I saw him, I started to cry bitterly. It was my first funeral and I have never seen dead people before, but the reason was different. He was so beautiful and such a relief was printed on his face that he looked like a saint person. He was just like my grandfather and grand grandfather, whom I love very much. I didn't know what kind of person was he when he was alive, but I realized that he was very kind and talented. I can't explain why I assumed that, but it was a firm conviction. I was folding my mother in my arms, understanding that love and relatives are the most important things in life and it is sad when death makes you to understand that.

When I came back to the city, my emotional state stabilized already. I just accepted that death and let it pass though my heart and I will never forget it.

Going to the nightclub in the evening in such a situation was not appropriate, but still we gathered in the most fashionable and popular nightclub at about 11 pm. There were eleven of us, a half of our company I barely knew. But then we found out that there were no places at none of the six stores of the entertainment center. Me and Veronique went to talk to the administrator:

Please, we need a table for eleven people for about a half an hour, just to have some drinks till the nightclub will be opened. Can you help us?

No, sorry, all large tables at all floors are reserved or taken. I am sorry, but I can't help you.

But please, we need a table just for a half an hour.

Ok, I will ask about VIP for you, but please do not spill anything at white tablecloth.

In three minutes we were already ordering drinks and feeling ourselves like VIP persons who get everything for free.

I came back home at about 3 AM. I didn't want to sleep at all. I started to think about my future, my family and my friends. I was thinking about role of men in my life and my relationships with them. I felt deep pain when thinking about my relationships. Was it something wrong with me or with him? I was not able to answer that question, but it was the only thing I was definitely sure at: nobody can tell me what to do and can make me feel pain. If the person does so, then he is not for me, he is not real. From time to time I miss that guy, I miss his hugs and kisses, and the way he called when we were together, but I try to be strong, as there is no sense in being with the man, who doesn't want to be with me. As genial Omar Hayam wrote: "Better to fast than eat of every meat, Better to live alone than mate with all."

I realized that we are quarrelling about trifles and got mad at each other, but why are we doing that? Why can't we appreciate what we have? Why do we spoil relationships with blames? We are just people. This is our weakness and strength simultaneously. And I will try to be patient and loving, as life it too short to digress for anger and rancor.

In sum, the first type of personal response essay involves the writer discussing their personal feelings about the text. This is similar to a normal essay, as it includes a thesis highlighting strong emotions, a main body discussing them further and supporting evidence in the form of passages and moments. Readers who do not feel they had a strong emotional reaction to the text can discuss the parts that stand out the most instead. Rather than focusing on emotions, this essay discusses why the reader was attracted to certain elements of the text.

Some individuals may find their life experiences are similar to those of the text's characters. If this is the case, they may want to discuss them. This can include why the text drew out certain emotions and memories. All personal essays should include the text's title and author, how the text inspired their emotions and which elements of the text did this. Writers can use the first person, but their writing should remain consistent throughout.

CHAPTER THIRTEEN

CAUSE AND EFFECT ESSAYS

What is a Cause and Effect Essay?

The Cause and Effect Essay is one that asks you to explain what reactions come from certain actions and why. Normally, you would be given a certain scenario in which an action occurred. From there, using things such as logic and analysis, outcomes (reactions) must be carefully crafted and explained.

With every action comes a certain reaction. To understand how a cause and effect essay works let's break down its definition. A cause and effect essay is a format of writing where the writer describes reasons and actions that lead to certain consequences or results. Even though the essay can have a variety of different structures, the primary goal is to show a logical consequential correlation between Point A (an action, event, etc.) and Point B (a result, outcome, consequence). However, there are a few steps you need to complete before jumping into writing.

Human beings often try to find root causes of things, happenings and phenomena. This research leads to the discovery of effects, too. It is because human beings always desire to understand reasons for things, and why they happen. A composition written to find out reasons and results is called a cause and effect essay. It makes discovery of the causes of something and resultantly finds out effects.

In this kind of essay, the aim is to explain the causes (reasons) or the effects (results) of an event or situation.

e.g. Causes of air pollution (multiple factors leading to air pollution).
e.g. Effects of watching too much TV (many effects of a situation).

Sometimes an event causes something to happen, and that situation leads to another event, and it causes another event to happen. This is called the causal chain or *domino* effect.

e.g. Use of deodorants will bring the end of the world.

There may be several causes or effects of a situation. However, in a student essay, it is advisable to keep the number of major points to 2 or 3, which form separate developmental paragraphs.

Where Do You Begin?

When you receive your assignments, whether it is for college, university or high school, make sure to read the directions to identify the requirements thoroughly. More often you will have to choose your own cause and effect essay topic. Therefore, brainstorming is a must.

In most cases, the information you already have will not be sufficient to write a detailed, captivating paper, that is why you will be required to perform research to acquire as much additional information as you can. If the format of your essay allows you to include visuals, then the following will help you to support provided information:

Cause and Effect Venn Diagram
Cause and Effect Graphic Organizer
Cause and Effect Anchor Chart

If you are sure that you have acquired enough material and selected one of the cause and effect topics, then it's time to build an outline.

Sample Topics

- Pollutions effects on society
- Internet's influence on youth development
- Drugs impact on the human body
- Uber effect on taxi companies
- Causes and Effects of Lying
- Causes and Effects of Natural Disasters

Related: Professional Essay Writers At Your Service

Outline

CAUSE AND EFFECT
ESSAY OUTLINE

The cause and effect essay outline is going to serve you as a guide for the rest of the paper. It will help you to stay on track and include all the ideas you have initially pinned down. This paper is commonly written in a 5 paragraph style, but it allows a variation. Depending on the topic of analysis and the depth of the content, cause and effect essays will vary in length. However, the general format will still stay the same. Just like all papers have an introduction, body and a conclusion, the cause and effect essay is no exception.

Before you begin writing, create a cause and effect chart which has two sections. It should include the main points and details relating to Point A and Point B. It will help you to see the bigger picture and to create logical transitions between the two sides.

Cause (Point A)	Effect (Point B)
Cause 1	Effect 1
Cause 2	Effect 2
Cause 3	Effect 3
Cause 4	Effect 4

Furthermore, you can create a cause and effect graphic organizer. Not only does it make the process smoother, but getting that visual allows for the creation of even more ideas and analysis!

Introduction

The main purpose of the introduction is to inform the reader of the topic of conversation, giving necessary background if needed. The highlight of the introduction is to provide a relevant thesis statement, explaining the cause and its effect.

- **Hook:** The sentence that grabs the reader's attention. Since we are doing cause and effect, this could be some foreshadowing or some rhetorical question. Its main purpose is to serve as an appetizer for the reader to get a sense of what's to come!
- **Background Information**: In this case, background information is *very important*. Not only does it give more insight towards the cause, but sometimes can help explain some of the effects. This is especially true if we are talking about a historical topic such as World War 2 or some Natural Disaster. Another key point is to make sure that this information follows a linear path. State information that helps understand the cause(s), instead of just filling up space. *It should also be applied towards the main point (thesis) of the essay.*
- **Thesis Statement**: The thesis statement is highlighting the main point of the entire argument in one sentence. Along with the setting of the situation, it should state the general point of your entire essay in a few words. The goal of the essay is to prove the thesis statement, so make sure that it flows accordingly with what you plan on writing about in your main body paragraphs.

Learn how to write a killing **THESIS**

Also, it's super important to base your essay around your main bodies rather than your thesis statement. The type of content that you provide depicts what kind of thesis statement you should have. Make sure they match!

Body Paragraphs

All body paragraphs should always have some kind of introductory sentence and an assertive concluding sentence. However, the "meat" of the paragraphs isn't absolute. Great news, this is the part of the essay where variety is in abundance! Unless we are specifically writing a 5-paragraph essay, there are a lot of options in turns of forming the paper. Assuming we are using the 5 paragraph style, there are **3** options to pick from.

- **Cause-Effect-Effect**
- **Cause-Cause-Effect**
- **Cause/Effect-Cause/Effect-Cause/Effect**

Obviously, these should be picked according to the subject of discussion. Sometimes there are situations where *one thing creates mass chaos*, or *many small parts create one big problem*. Depending on the situation, it's important to pick the paragraph style **accordingly.**

If we aren't using the 5 paragraph style, then you are free as a bird when it comes to choosing your approach. The options come from as simple as one cause and one effect body to having multiple paragraphs that each contain a cause-effect style.

Being meticulous for these paragraphs is super important. For example, if you are using the *Cause-Effect-Effect* style, the first paragraph should specifically be focused on the **causes**. It's also incredibly important to make sure that there is an evident correlation between the initial cause and the duel effects. Once again, depending on the content you have to provide, the essay should be organized to suit your information efficiently and neatly.

Concluding Paragraph

Just like the introductory paragraph, this paragraph has 3 parts that practically follow the reverse order of the intro. The highlight of the conclusion is to create an impact upon the reader before fully concluding, emphasizing the strength of your argument!

- **Restatement of Thesis**: Now would be a good time to check if your thesis statement was actually proven by your body paragraphs. After confirming the following, the paraphrased sentence should assertively state that the thesis has been proved.
- **Summarizing Main Argument**: You should use this section to simplify your argument into a couple concise sentences. Explain the general outline of the cause and effect from one to three sentences. The strength of this sentences is incredibly important. The manner in which the main argument is summarized shows the reader the proficiency of the content. Also, make sure these summaries come back to that core thesis statement.
- **Overall Concluding Statement**: Just like your hook gave a thrilling intro to your essay, you must know provide a meaningful conclusion. This argument was developed for a specific purpose, whether an essay for college or a presentation at work. Just like in a court case, it's necessary to provide the importance of your argument. In other words, explain why your argument should be taken seriously and present the consequences if ignored. You wrote this essay for a purpose, not just to get a good grade. (Or at least I hope so....)

Additional Writing Tips

In the preparation stage, it is always a very good idea to read other cause and effect essay examples to understand the structure better. Not only it will allow you learn more about the outline, but help you to distinguish between good and bad papers.

If the project is quite substantial and important, then you will need an in-depth understanding of the topic. One of the things that we always recommend is to involve yourself in extra activities. Cause and effect games will help you understand the concept of action - reaction system and cause and effect worksheets can give you a detailed perception of your topic.

Finally, you have to review the paper on multiple occasions.

- Print out a hard copy and edit it yourself with a red pen. Watch the flow of your transitions. Make sure there is a logical connection between different ideas.
- Send your paper to someone who is more experienced in writing than you are and more aware about your theme. Let them give you professional feedback.
- Send your paper to someone neutral, to receive impersonal, straightforward reader review.

Examples and Observations

- "If you prove the **cause**, you at once prove the **effect**; and conversely nothing can exist without its cause." (Aristotle, *Rhetoric*)
- **Immediate Causes and Ultimate Causes**

   "Determining **causes and effects** is usually thought-provoking and quite complex. One reason for this is that there are two types of causes: *immediate causes*, which are readily apparent because they are closest to the effect, and *ultimate causes*, which, being somewhat removed, are not so apparent and may perhaps even be hidden. Furthermore, ultimate causes may bring about effects which themselves become immediate causes, thus creating a *causal chain*. For example, consider the following causal chain: Sally, a computer salesperson, prepared extensively for a meeting with a client (ultimate cause), impressed the client (immediate cause), and made a very large sale (effect). The chain did not stop there: the large sale caused her to be promoted by her employer (effect)."

   (Alfred Rosa and Paul Eschholz, *Models for Writers*, 6th ed. St. Martin's Press, 1998)
- **Composing a Cause/Effect Essay**

   "For all its conceptual complexity, a cause/effect essay can be organized quite simply. The introduction generally presents the subject(s) and states the purpose of the analysis in a clear thesis. The body of the paper then explores all relevant causes and/or effects, typically progressing from least to most influential or from most to least influential. Finally, the concluding section summarizes the various cause/effect relationships established in the body of the paper and clearly states the conclusions that can be drawn from those relationships."

(Kim Flachmann, Michael Flachmann, Kathryn Benander, and Cheryl Smith, *The Brief Prose Reader*. Prentice Hall, 2003)

- **Causes of Child Obesity**

  "Many of today's kids are engaged in sedentary pursuits made possible by a level of technology unthinkable as recently as 25 to 30 years ago. Computer, video, and other virtual games, the ready availability of feature films and games on DVD, plus high-tech advancements in music-listening technology have come down into the range of affordability for parents and even for the kids themselves. These passive pursuits have produced a downside of reduced physical activity for the kids, often with the explicit or implicit consent of the parents. . . .

  "Other fairly recent developments have also contributed to the alarming rise in child obesity rates. Fast food outlets offering consumables that are both low in price and low in nutritional content have exploded all over the American landscape since the 1960s, especially in suburban areas close to major highway interchanges. Kids on their lunch breaks or after school often congregate in these fast food outlets, consuming food and soft drinks that are high in sugar, carbohydrates, and fat. Many parents, themselves, frequently take their children to these fast food places, thus setting an example the kids can find justification to emulate."

  (MacKie Shilstone, *Mackie Shilstone's Body Plan for Kids*. Basic Health Publications, 2009)

- **Cause and Effect in Jonathan Swift's "A Modest Proposal"**

  "'A Modest Proposal' is a brilliant example of the use of non-argumentative devices of rhetorical persuasion. The whole essay, of course, rests broadly upon the argument of **cause and effect**: these causes have produced this situation in Ireland,

and this proposal will result in these effects in Ireland. But Swift, within the general framework of this argument, does not employ specific argumentative forms in this essay. The projector chooses rather to *assert* his reasons and then to amass them by way of proof."

(Charles A. Beaumont, *Swift's Classical Rhetoric*. Univ. of Georgia Press, 1961)

- **Effects of Automobiles**

"I worry about the private automobile. It is a dirty, noisy, wasteful, and lonely means of travel. It pollutes the air, ruins the safety and sociability of the street, and exercises upon the individual a discipline which takes away far more freedom than it gives him. It causes an enormous amount of land to be unnecessarily abstracted from nature and from plant life and to become devoid of any natural function. It explodes cities, grievously impairs the whole institution of neighborliness, fragmentizes and destroys communities. It has already spelled the end of our cities as real cultural and social communities, and has made impossible the construction of any others in their place. Together with the airplane, it has crowded out other, more civilized and more convenient means of transport, leaving older people, infirm people, poor people and children in a worse situation than they were a hundred years ago."

(George F. Kennan, *Democracy and the Student Left*, 1968)

- **Examples and Effects of Entropy**

"Because of its unnerving irreversibility, entropy has been called the arrow of time. We all understand this instinctively. Children's rooms, left on their own, tend to get messy, not neat. Wood rots, metal rusts, people wrinkle and flowers wither. Even mountains wear down; even the nuclei of atoms decay. In the city we see entropy in the rundown subways and worn-out sidewalks and torn-down buildings, in the increasing disorder of our lives. We know, without asking, what is old. If we were suddenly to see the paint jump back on an old building, we would know that something was wrong. If we saw an egg unscramble itself and jump back into its shell, we would laugh in the same way we laugh as a movie run backward."

(K.C. Cole, "The Arrow of Time." *The New York Times*, March 18, 1982)

Examples of Cause and Effect Essays

1. EFFECTS OF WATCHING TOO MUCH TV

Discoveries and invention of devices are always welcome till we, humans, find a way to abuse its benefits and be adversely affected by it. This was the case when Wilhelm Roentgen discovered x-ray and within five years, the British Army was using a mobile x-ray unit to locate bullets and shrapnel in wounded soldiers in the Sudan. TV was also invented with positive thoughts in mind – there would be no national borders, education and communication would be worldwide, etc. However, we are now trying to overcome its physiological and psychological adverse effects on human beings.

One of the physiological effects of watching TV in excessive amounts is eye-strain. It is true that there are specifications for watching TV; TV should be 5 m. away from the eye, the room should be adequately lit, TV should be placed at the same height with our eyes, etc. However, these do not prevent our eyes from getting tired if we keep watching TV for a long time. Another effect is obesity, which is widely observed in people who like watching TV and eating snacks everyday (there is even a term "TV snacks" to refer to fast food that is suitable for eating in front of the TV). TV is such a powerful machine that people cannot get away from it – it is addictive.

Apart from the physiological effects, TV also causes psychological effects. One is a result of being exposed to violence. After seeing so many violent scenes on TV, people start considering violent actions normal and they lose their sensitivity to their environment. Partly connected to this effect, the interpersonal communication among people decreases. Being insensitive to the suffering of other people causes people to become alienated. Also, after coming home from work people seek to relax in front of the TV, and generally people prefer watching TV to talking to each other. This issue is very important since lack of interpersonal relationships mostly end with divorces.

Shortly, inventions are meant to be beneficial for human beings, if we know how to benefit from them. TV is one of such inventions that need to be used for the right purpose only – being educated and entertained for a reasonable (according to age) period of time. We may, then, be safe from or at least reduce the adverse physiological and psychological effects of watching too much TV.

What were the causes of the American Civil War? the causes of World War I? the causes of the American Great Depression? What caused the AIDS epidemic? the bubonic plague? What are the causes of unrest in Ireland? the Middle East?

What effects can be attributed to phenomena such as El Niño? the hippies of the 1950s and 60s? the Civil Rights movement of the 50s and 60s? Affirmative Action? Apartheid? the uses of DDT? holes in the ozone layer?

Cause and effect papers are among the most common (and among the most fun to write) papers in a Composition course. It is intriguing to explore the causes of some event that you always took for granted or to chronicle the effects of some phenomenon in society or nature. The two strategic points you have to consider are (1) whether you're exploring causes or effects or both and (2) what is the order of the causes or effects you're going to pursue — from least to most important or vice versa.

In the following two paragraphs, Bob Kutter analyzes the effects on American workers of an economy that relies increasingly on technology. In a sense, the paragraphs provide an outline for exploring the various causes and effects which are the substance of the article. (See below for a hyperlink to the entire essay (*Atlantic*, July 1983.) In these paragraphs, what sentences could be listed as major points and what sentences play a supporting role? What is the role of the first sentence in each paragraph?

The erosion of the middle of the labor market is easy to misinterpret, because its roots are multiple. During the 1970s, the entry into the work force of an unprecedented number of women and of young adults born during the baby boom resulted in too many workers for the jobs available, and depressed wages. The decline of the middle also has something to do with the explosive growth in world trade since 1960. As manufacturing technologies have become more mobile, and multinational firms more footloose, production jobs have migrated from the U.S. to countries where wages are low. In addition, technology itself has helped to provoke the shifts in the job market. For example, fewer American workers would have been needed to make steel in 1980 than in 1960 even if the pressures of global competition had not been a factor, because new machines have made many of their tasks redundant. Finally, the high rate of unemployment caused by these trends has tended to drive wages down further, especially at the low end, since it forces unskilled workers to compete for their jobs with unemployed people who are willing to do the work for less.

Although demographic shifts, stepped-up world trade, unemployment, and especially the advance of technology all have had an effect on the shape of the job market, middle-level jobs have been disappearing ultimately as a result of the ways in which technological gains are being distributed. When a machine replaces a production worker, both the firm and consumers as a group benefit. The loss falls mainly on the worker who is displaced. If that loss is generalized to millions of high-paid workers, they suffer as a group, and the economy as a whole suffers a loss of worker purchasing power. Thus the lack of a mechanism to distribute some of the financial gains from technology to the work force comes back to haunt the entire economy.

You will have to determine which causes or effects you're going to write about. For instance, if there are too many causes for you to deal with in the scope of your essay, you'll have to decide what are the main causes, the ones you have to treat, and then suggest to your reader that there are other, relatively minor, causes outside the scope of your essay. Even in an essay as extensive as Kutter's, there are surely things he could have said but chose not to. In an essay on the effects of El Niño, the price you pay for orange juice might not belong in an essay alongside the devastating effects of tornadoes and ice-storms and mudslides and people's fear of uncontrollable weather patterns.

The cause and effect essay can end in a number of ways. It might be enough for your paper to point out causes or effects that people might not have thought of before, or to sort out those causes or effects so that people can grasp them with fresh insight or in a newly organized fashion. On the other hand, your essay might lead to a call for action based on patterns of cause and effect that you have perceived. The essay below, for example, from *Mother Jones* magazine, ends with a plea for Americans to change the way they use antibiotics in situations where the antibiotics won't do any good. The alternative to this over-use of antibiotics — the consequence if this trend is not reversed — is well spelled out in the essay.

The one caution you have to keep in mind is not to become logically simplistic when considering causes. It is nearly cliché to say that the Civil War was fought to free the slaves of the American South, but it is also far from the whole truth. There were monumental economic and political causes behind that war; without those "other" causes there might not have been a war at all. There is an important logical fallacy (see the section on Logic) called *Post hoc, ergo propter hoc* ("After this, therefore because of this"). We can't assume that just because something follows something else chronologically that the earlier event caused the later event. Other causes — intervening causes or causes we might not be aware of — might be at work.

2. Soccer: Why It Can't Make the Big Time in the U.S.A.

Soccer — or football (or foosball or futbol), as it is called by the rest of the world outside the United States — is surely the most popular sport in the world. Every four years, the world championship of soccer, the World Cup, is watched by literally billions all over the world, beating out the United States professional football's Superbowl by far. It is estimated that 1.7 billion television viewers watched the World Cup final between France and Brazil in July of 1998. And it is also a genuine *world* championship, involving teams from 32 countries in the final rounds, unlike the much more parochial and misnamed World

Series in American baseball (that doesn't even involve Japan or Cuba, two baseball hotbeds). But although soccer has become an important sport in the American sports scene, it will never make inroads into the hearts and markets of American sports the way that football, basketball, hockey, baseball, and even tennis and golf have done. There are many reasons for this.

Recently the New England Revolution beat the Tampa Bay Mutiny in a game played during a horrid rainstorm. Nearly 5000 fans showed up, which shows that soccer is, indeed, popular in the United States. However, the story of the game was buried near the back of the newspaper's sports section, and there was certainly no television coverage. In fact, the biggest reason for soccer's failure as a mass appeal sport in the United States is that it doesn't conform easily to the demands of television. Basketball succeeds enormously in America because it regularly schedules what it calls "television time-outs" as well as the time-outs that the teams themselves call to re-group, not to mention half-times and, on the professional level, quarter breaks. Those time-outs in the action are ideally made for television commercials. And television coverage is the lifeblood of American sports. College basketball lives for a game scheduled on CBS or ESPN (highly recruited high school players are more likely to go to a team that regularly gets national television exposure), and we could even say that television coverage has dictated the pace and feel of American football. Anyone who has attended a live football game knows how commercial time-outs slow the game and sometimes, at its most exciting moments, disrupt the flow of events. There is no serious objection, however, because without television, football knows that it simply wouldn't remain in the homes and hearts of Americans. Also, without those advertising dollars, the teams couldn't afford the sky-high salaries of their high-priced superstars.

Soccer, on the other hand, except for its half-time break, has no time-outs; except for half-time, it is constant run, run, run, run, back and forth, back and forth, relentlessly, with only a few seconds of relaxation when a goal is scored, and that can happen seldom, sometimes never. The best that commercial television coverage can hope for is an injury time-out, and in soccer that happens only with decapitation or disembowelment.

Second, Americans love their violence, and soccer doesn't deliver on this score the way that American football and hockey do. There are brief moments, spurts of violence, yes, but fans can't expect the full-time menu of bone-crushing carnage that American football and hockey can deliver minute after minute, game after game. In soccer, players are actually singled out and warned — shamed, with embarrassingly silly "yellow cards," for acts of violence and duplicity that would be smiled at in most American sports other than tennis and golf.

Third, it is just too difficult to score in soccer. America loves its football games with scores like 49 to 35 and a professional basketball game with scores below 100 is regarded as a defensive bore. In soccer, on the other hand, scores like 2 to 1, even 1 to 0, are commonplace and apparently desirable; games scoreless at the end of regulation time happen all the time. (In the 515 games played in the final phase in the history of the World Cup games through 1994, only 1584 goals have been scored. That's three a game!) And if there is no resolution at the end of overtime, the teams resort to a shoot-out that has more to do with luck than with real soccer skills. Worse yet, it is possible for a team to dominate in terms of sheer talent and "shots-on-goal" and still lose the game by virtue of a momentary lapse in defensive attention, a stroke of bad luck, and the opponent's break-away goal. Things like that can happen, too, in baseball, but the problem somehow evens out over baseball's very long season of daily games. In soccer, it just isn't fair. Soccer authorities should consider making the goal smaller and doing away with the goalie to make scoring easier. And the business of starting over after each goal, in the middle of the field, has to be reconsidered. It's too much like the center-jump after each goal in the basketball game of yesteryear.

It seems unlikely that Americans will ever fully comprehend or appreciate a sport in which players are not allowed to use their arms and hands. Although the footwork of soccer players is a magnificent skill to behold, most American fans are perplexed by straitjacketed soccer players' inability and unwillingness to "pick up the darn ball and run with it!" The inability to use substitutes (unless the player to be substituted for is lying dead or maimed on the field of play) is also bewildering to Americans, who glorify the "sixth man" in basketball and a baseball game in which virtually the entire roster (including an otherwise unemployable old man called "the designated hitter") is deployed on the field at one time or another.

Finally, the field in soccer is enormous. Considerably larger than the American football field, the soccer field could contain at least a dozen basketball courts. Americans like their action condensed, in a small field of vision — ten enormous sweaty people bouncing off one another and moving rapidly through a space the size of a medium-sized bedroom, twenty-two even larger people in bulky uniforms converging on a small, oddly shaped ball. In soccer, on the other hand, there is a premium on "spreading out," not infringing upon the force field occupied by a team-mate, so that fancy foot-passing is possible. This spreading out across the vast meadow of the soccer playing field does not lend itself, again, to close get-down-and-dirty television scrutiny.

Soccer is a great sport and it certainly deserves the increased attention and popularity it is getting on all levels. But — primarily, again, because it does not lend itself to television — it will never make it big in the United States the way these other sports have, not until it changes some of its fundamental strategies.

3. Causes of Divorce

Divorce rates point to a world that does not see much success in marriage. For instance, in Maldives, the divorce rate is so high that the UN calculated that the typical Maldivian woman, by the age of 30, has been divorced three times (Marriage Advice). What are the causes of these high divorce rates? There are 10 main causes we can discuss.

Extramarital affairs is the main reason for divorces (Oliver). Infidelity causes anger and resentment among those who are married, and often tears apart the emotional connection couples have. Though one event of infidelity can be tackled through counseling, multiple accounts of extramarital affairs usually result in divorce.

Another main reason why people get divorced is money. Different spending habits, opposite financial goals, and a lack of money can produce great strain on a marriage (Oliver). If the couple has children, money becomes even more vital to the sustainability of the relationship.

Though it may seem minor, a lack of communication is another key reason for divorce. If one or both partners in the marriage feel they cannot express themselves properly, or feel they are not being listened to, resentment can easily settle in (Oliver). Yelling and interrupting are common signs that a couple is not communicating well.

Some people cannot stand the amount of arguments they have with their partners. If couples are bickering constantly, the joy of marriage cannot show through (Oliver). Arguments commonly stem from not being able to understand another person's view, which is essential in a healthy relationship.

Unfortunately, weight gain leads to many divorces. Say if a couple started out as both skinny, and one partner became overweight, the attraction to that partner might be lost. That loss of attraction causes many to turn in divorce papers, as they cannot fathom staying in a relationship with someone they do not feel comfortable with in a romantic way (Oliver).

Another prominent cause of divorce is unreasonable expectations (Oliver). It is good for the partners in marriage to discuss each other's expectations before signing the matrimony papers, as partners often have varying expectations of what the marriage entails, and the positions the partners will hold in it. Sometimes one partner will have lofty expectations for the marriage without his or her partner realizing it.

Though love should be the overriding reason to get married, it seems, a lack of intimacy causes many couples to get divorced. The romantic, maybe even infatuated love that married couples feel in the beginning of their marriages eventually subsides. It is natural, but how the partners deal with this decrease in sexual contact often decides how the future marriage will pan out (Oliver).

Though common sense, equality in marriages is not often achieved. Each partner should feel equal in the marriage, and not dominated. Though it is delicate balance, it can be accomplished. Those who cannot achieve this often ask for a divorce, as they feel they are being shackled by his or her marriage instead of feeling a sense of joy and happiness from the relationship (Oliver).

Alas, some people are not prepared for marriage. Many people rush to get married in a romantic frenzy without taking in the consequences of such an action (Oliver). They could be unprepared in terms of financial stability, emotional stability, and mental stability. Surprisingly, the age group with the highest rate of divorce are people in their 20s (Oliver). So, when getting married, be sure that you feel that everything is set for the occasion.

A sad fact about marriages is that with emotional, physical, and mental strain, abuse can follow. This abuse does not have to refer to only physical abuse, but also emotional and psychological abuse (Oliver). Abuse can come from both men and women, and should not be thought of only as an attack against women, however women are subject to most of the physical abuse that occurs.

As you can see, the cause of divorce is multifaceted. Though one issue might put enough pressure on a marriage for the couple to go for a divorce, commonly a combination of problems arise that lend to the couple pondering the end of their relationship. Through infidelity, money issues, a lack of communication, constant arguing, weight gain, unrealistic expectations, a lack of intimacy, a lack of equality, a lack of preparedness, and abuse, marriages are broken. It is important for couples, therefore, to get counseling when any of these issues arise.

References

Oliver Smith (2017). Mapped: The countries with the highest divorce rate. [online] The Telegraph. Available at: http://www.telegraph.co.uk/travel/maps-and-graphics/mapped-countries-with-highest-divorce-rate/ [Accessed 20 Sep. 2017].

Marriage Advice – Best Marriage Advice & Tips for Couples. (2017). 10 Most Common Reasons for Divorce | Marriage.Com. [online] Available at: https://www.marriage.com/advice/divorce/10-most-common-reasons-for-divorce/ [Accessed 20 Sep. 2017].

4. What Causes Low Self-Esteem?

Throughout the recent decades, psychology has become extremely popular in western countries. Starting from all kinds of coaching programs, personality trainings, and professional psychotherapy sessions, psychology is constantly being at the center of public attention. Terms like "subconsciousness," "psychological resistance," "self-esteem," calls to "love yourself" and "accept your uniqueness" sound from almost everywhere. At the same time, people seem to often simplify and misunderstand the basics of psychology. People talk about how important it is to increase self-esteem and accept oneself—but no one says how exactly this can be done, or what may become an obstacle. Self-esteem, in particular, is the term that is juggled with the most frequently; "increasing self-esteem" is probably the most popular advice people give to each other on every possible occasion. At the same time, as it is often the case in psychology, low self-esteem is not just the way a person thinks about himself or herself, but rather a complex aggregate of behavioral and mental patterns, changing which requires much more patience and effort than simply saying to oneself, "I am awesome." Let us take a closer look at what exactly causes people to underestimate themselves.

Decreased self-esteem, or the inhibited feeling of self-worth is influenced, as it is often the case, by the problems in communication with authoritative others in childhood. This is especially true if a child is raised while being constantly criticized, taught how to do things "right," and not appreciated no matter how hard he or she tries, or shamed and blamed. This causes a child to grow up into an adult that constantly doubts his or her worth, trying to please other people in order to gain acceptance or to avoid critics. At the same time, there is a "passive" way parents can harm their child. Even if they do not criticize their child, inactive, emotionally-cold parents contribute to a child developing low self-esteem in the future; children need to feel love and attention from their parents, and if parents are preoccupied and do not (or cannot) notice their child's behaviors, accomplishments, and manifestations, it can also cause psychological harm. A child in such a family may feel unnoticed, unimportant, and abandoned. This may cause a person to develop a need to "apologize" for their existence—for example, trying to be "useful," or justify the fact of his or her life in some other ways. In addition, when parents or other authoritative figures raising a child are in conflict with each other, it can pose psychological danger as well: feeling overwhelmed and scared by constant conflicts, a child may develop a sense of guilt, considering himself or herself somehow responsible for the fact that adults are fighting with each other. This may result in feeling "tainted," "guilty," and can be carried on into adult life (Psychology Today).

Children, when in groups, can be extremely cruel—this is a well-known fact, although it does not mean that children are bad: because they are in the process of adopting and understanding social norms, since they are only learning empathy and compassion, children often cannot distinguish between what is wrong and what is right. As a result, they can cause physical and psychological pain to each other. Rather often, there is a child who is somehow different from others: poorer, smarter, awkward, and so on; such children usually become objects for bullying and hatred. Negative attitudes from peers and being subjected to bullying decreases self-esteem dramatically. It is an innate need of every person to be a part of some group, to be respected and recognized; even for adults, it can be difficult to stay in a hostile or negligent collective of people. For children, it can be devastating: having to face hostile environments day by day, year by year (for example, because a child has to go to the same school, and is ashamed to tell his or her parents about being bullied and humiliated) may cause an individual to think that something is wrong with them, that they are somehow "bad" or inferior (Good Choices Good Life). Needless to say that such feelings transit to adult life, causing painful doubts in a person's self-worth, obstructing communication and trust with other people, and making such a person to feel ashamed for every small discrepancy in their looks, way of thinking, and so on.

Yet another way to cause a child to develop low self-esteem is abuse: emotional, physical, or sexual—it does not matter. Any case of abuse is a potential psychological trauma, which can remain in a child's psyche for years (sometimes for his or her entire life); abuse in the past may even cause PTSD (post traumatic stress disorder), which only makes a child's condition worse, making him or her constantly feel "damaged" and worthless (self-confidence.co.uk). For many people, the facts of physical or any other abuse cause severe distress, and can lead to depression, addiction, and other forms of negative self-attitude. An abused child requires psychological help—the sooner, the better.

There are many ways in which parents, environments, and peers can cause a child to develop low self-esteem, which later transits to adult life. Negligence, emotional coldness, criticism, a lack of appreciation, bullying, humiliation, as well as abuse (physical, emotional, or sexual) can harm a child's psyche. In order to help a person overcome such traumas, the help of a professional psychotherapist may be needed.

Works Cited

Lachmann, Suzanne. "10 Sources of Low Self-Esteem." Psychology Today. Sussex Publishers, 24 Dec. 2013. Web. 05 July 2017.

"8 Common Causes of Low Self-Esteem." Good Choices Good Life. N.p., n.d. Web. 05 July 2017.

"Top Ten Facts About Low Self Esteem." Self-confidence.co.uk. N.p., n.d. Web. 05 July 2017.

CHAPTER FOURTEEN

CLASSIFICATION ESSAYS

What is a classification Essay?

In rhetoric and composition, *classification* is a method of paragraph or essay development in which a writer arranges people, objects, or ideas with shared characteristics into classes or groups.

A classification essay often includes examples and other supporting details that are organized according to types, kinds, segments, categories, or parts of a whole.

Classification is a method of developing an essay by arranging people, objects, or ideas with shared characteristics into particular classes or groups. Once you have settled on a topic for a classification essay* and explored it through various prewriting strategies, you should be ready to attempt a first draft. This article will show you how to develop and organize a five-paragraph classification essay. In other words, a classification essay, a writer organizes, or sorts, things into categories.

Three Steps to Effective Classification:

1. Sort things into useful categories.
2. Make sure all the categories follow a single organizing principle.
3. Give examples that fit into each category.

Finding Categories

This is a key step in writing a classification essay. To classify, or sort, things in a logical way, find the categories to put them into. For example, say you need to sort the stack of papers on your desk. Before you would put them in random piles, you would decide what useful categories might be: papers that can be thrown away; papers that need

297

immediate action; papers to read; papers to pass on to other coworkers; or papers to file.

Thesis Statement of a Classification Essay

The thesis statement usually includes the topic and how it is classified. Sometimes the categories are named.

(topic)...(how classified)...(category) (category) (category)

Ex: *Tourists in Victoria can enjoy three water sports: snorkeling, surfing, and sailing.*

How to Write an Effective Classification Essay

1. **Determine the categories.** Be thorough; don't leave out a critical category. For example, if you say water sports of Hawaii include snorkeling and sailing, but leave out surfing, your essay would be incomplete because surfing is Hawaii's most famous water sport. On the other hand, don't include too many categories, which will blur your classification. For example, if your topic is sports shoes, and your organizing principle is activity, you wouldn't include high heels with running and bowling shoes.

2. **Classify by a single principle.** Once you have categories, make sure that they fit into the same organizing principle. The organizing principle is how you sort the groups. Do not allow a different principle to pop up unexpectedly. For example, if your unifying principle is "tourist-oriented" water sports, don't use another unifying principle, such as "native water sports," which would have different categories: pearl diving, outrigger, or canoe racing.

3. **Support equally each category with examples.** In general, you should write the same quantity, i.e., give the same number of examples, for each category. The most important category, usually reserved for last, might require more elaboration.

Common Classification Transitions

- The first kind, the second kind, the third kind

- The first type, the second type, the third type
- The first group, the second group, the third group

Remember: In a classification essay, the writer organizes, or sorts, things into categories. There are three steps to remember when writing an effective classification essay: organize things into useful categories, use a single organizing principle, and give examples of things that fit into each category. Below are some sample classification essay topics:

- Classification of historical events in US
- Countries classification (territory, popularity, etc)
- Sport Cars Classification
- Most Popular TV Shows in America
- Classification of Physiological Diseases

Introductory Paragraph

In your introduction, clearly identify your subject—in this case, the group you are classifying. If you have narrowed your subject in any way (for example, types of *bad* drivers, *rock* guitarists, or *annoying* moviegoers), you should make this clear from the start.

In your introduction, you may also want to provide some specific descriptive or informative details to attract the interest of your readers and suggest the purpose of the essay.

Finally, be sure to include a thesis sentence (usually at the end of the introduction) that briefly identifies the main types or approaches that you're about to examine.

Here's an example of a short but effective introductory paragraph to a classification essay:

It's a warm evening in July, and all across the country Americans are gathering to watch a game of professional baseball. Armed with hot dogs and cold drinks, they stroll to their seats, some in grand stadiums, others in cozy minor-league parks. But no matter where the game is played, you will find the same three types of baseball fan: the Party Rooter, the Sunshine Supporter, and the Diehard Fan.

Notice how this introduction creates certain expectations. The specific details provide a setting (a ballpark on "a warm evening in July") in which we expect to see the various fans described. In addition, the labels assigned to these fans (the *Party Rooter*, the *Sunshine Supporter*, and the *Diehard Fan*) lead us to expect descriptions of each type in the order they're given.

A good writer will go on to fulfill these expectations in the body of the essay.

Body Paragraphs

Begin each body paragraph with a topic sentence that identifies a particular type or approach. Then go on to describe or illustrate each type with specific details.

Arrange your body paragraphs in whatever order strikes you as clear and logical—say, from the least effective approach to the most effective, or from the most common type to the least familiar (or the other way around). Just make sure that the order of your body paragraphs matches the arrangement promised in your thesis sentence. Here, in the body of the essay on baseball fans, you can see that the writer has fulfilled the expectations set up in the introduction. (In each body paragraph, the topic sentence is in italics.)

The Party Rooter goes to games for the hot dogs, the gimmicks, the giveaways, and the companionship; he's not really that interested in the ballgame itself. The Party Rooter is the sort of fan who shows up on Buck-a-Brew Night, often with a gang of fellow partiers. He cracks jokes, hurls peanuts at the team mascot, applauds the exploding scoreboard, blasts an electronic horn whenever he pleases—and occasionally nudges a companion and asks, "Hey, who's winning?" The Party Rooter often wanders out of the park in the sixth or seventh inning to continue his celebrations in the car on the way home.

The Sunshine Supporter, usually a more common type than the Party Rooter, goes to the park to cheer on a winning team and bask in its glory. When the home side is on a winning streak and still in contention for a playoff spot, the stadium will be packed with this sort of fan. As long as her team is winning, the Sunshine Supporter will be roaring at every play, waving her pennant and shouting out the names of her heroes.

However, as the name implies, the Sunshine Supporter is a fickle fan, and her cheers quickly turn to boos when a hero strikes out or drops a line drive. She will stay around until the end of the game to celebrate a victory, but should her team fall a few runs behind she's likely to slip out to the parking lot during the seventh inning stretch.

Diehard Fans are also strong supporters of the local team, but they go to the park to watch good baseball, not just to root for a winner. More attentive to the game than other fans, Diehards will study the stance of a power hitter, note the finesse of a quick fielder, and anticipate the strategy of a pitcher who has fallen behind in the count. While the Party Rooter is chugging a beer or dropping wisecracks, Diehards may be filling in a scorecard or commenting on a playe's RBI tally over the past few months. And when a Sunshine Supporter boos an opposing player for tagging out a local hero, Diehards may be quietly applauding the expert moves of this "enemy" infielder. No matter what the score is, Diehard Fans remain in their seats until the last batter is out, and they may still be talking about the game long after it's over.

Notice how the writer uses comparisons to ensure cohesion in the body of the essay. The topic sentence in both the second and third paragraphs refers to the preceding paragraph. Likewise, in the third body paragraph, the writer draws explicit contrasts between the Diehards and the other two types of baseball fans.

Such comparisons not only provide smooth transitions from one paragraph to the next but also reveal the sympathies of the writer. He begins with the type of fan he likes the least and ends with the one he most admires. We now expect the writer to justify his attitudes in the conclusion.

Concluding Paragraph

The concluding paragraph gives you an opportunity to draw together the various types and approaches you have been examining. You may choose to offer a final brief comment on each one, summarizing its value or its limitations.

Or you may want to recommend one approach over the others

and explain why. In any case, make sure that your conclusion clearly emphasizes the purpose of your classification.

In the concluding paragraph to "Baseball Fans," consider whether the author has been successful in his effort to tie his observations together.

Professional baseball would have trouble surviving without all three types of fans. The Party Rooters provide much of the money that owners need to hire talented players. The Sunshine Supporters bring a stadium to life and help boost the morale of the home team. But only the Diehard Fans maintain their support all season long, year in and year out. By late September in most ballparks, enduring chilly winds, rain delays, and sometimes humiliating losses, only the Diehards remain.

Notice how the writer hooks his conclusion back to the introduction by contrasting the chilly night in September with the warm evening in July. Connections such as these help to unify an essay and give it a sense of completeness.

As you develop and organize your draft, experiment with various strategies, but keep this basic format in mind: an introduction that identifies your subject and the different types or approaches; three (or more) body paragraphs that rely on specific details to describe or illustrate the types; and a conclusion that draws your points together and makes the overall purpose of the classification clear.

The Next Step: Revising Your Essay

Writing a classification Essay

Classification is sorting things into groups or categories on a single basis of division. A classification paper says something meaningful about how a whole relates to parts, or parts relate to a whole. Like skimming, scanning, paraphrasing, and summarizing, classification requires the ability to group related words, ideas, and characteristics.

Prewriting and purpose

It is a rare writer, student or otherwise, who can sit down and draft a classification essay without prewriting. A classification paper requires that you create categories, so prewriting for a classification paper involves grouping things in different ways in order to discover what categories make the most sense for the purpose you intend.

An important part of creating useful categories is seeing the different ways that things can be grouped. For example, a list of United States presidents may be grouped in any number of ways, depending on your purpose. They might be classified by political party, age on taking office, or previous occupations, but you could just as well, depending on your purpose, classify them by the pets they keep or how they keep physically fit. If your purpose was to analyze presidential administrations, you would group information focusing on the presidents' more public actions—say, cabinet appointments and judicial nominations. On the other hand, if you intended to write about the private lives of presidents, you might select information about personal relationships or hobbies.

Make sure the categories you create have a *single basis* of classification and that the group fits the categories you propose. You may not, for example, write about twentieth century presidents on the basis of the kinds of pets they kept if some of those presidents did not keep pets. The group does not fit the category. If you intend to talk about all the presidents, you must reinvent the categories so that all the presidents fit into it. In the example below, the group is "all U.S. presidents" and the two categories are "those who kept pets and those who did not":

Some U.S. presidents have indulged their love of pets, keeping menageries of animals around the White House, and others have preferred the White House pet-free.

Alternatively, in the following example, the group is "twentieth century U.S. presidential pet-keepers" and the three categories are "dog lovers, cat lovers, and exotic fish enthusiasts."

Among the twentieth century presidents who kept pets, presidential pet-keepers can be classified as dog-lovers, cat-lovers, or exotic fish enthusiasts (for who can really love a fish?).

Developing a thesis

Once you have decided on your group, purpose, and categories, develop a thesis statement that does the following three things:

- names what group of people or things you intend to classify
- describes the basis of the classification
- labels the categories you have developed

Here is a thesis statement for a classification paper written for a Health and Human Fitness class that includes all three of the above elements, underlined:

Our _last five U.S. presidents_ have practiced physical fitness regimens that varied from the very _formal to the informal_. They have been either _regular private gym-goers, disciplined public joggers, or casual active sports enthusiasts._

Ordering categories

Order is the way you arrange ideas to show how they relate to one another. For example, it is common to arrange facts and discussion points from most- to least-important or from least- to most-important, or from oldest to most recent or longest to shortest. The example thesis statement above is ordered from most- to least-formal physical fitness activities. There is no one right way; use an ordering system that seems best to suit your purpose and the type of information you are working with.

For example, suppose you are writing about the last five U.S. presidents for a psychology class. If you wish to show that these presidents' public decisions spring directly from negative issues in their personal relationships, you might order your information from most private to more public actions to clearly establish this connection. Or, if you wish to give the reader the impression that he is moving into increasingly intimate knowledge of personal presidential foibles, you may choose the reverse, ordering your information from public to private.

Signal words

Signal phrases, or transitions, typically used for classification papers include the following:

- this type of...
- several kinds of...
- in this category...
- can be divided into...
- classified according to...
- is categorized by...

These phrases signal to the reader your intention to divide and sort things. They also contribute to the unity of the essay.

Classification requires that you invent (or discover) abstract categories, impose them on a concrete whole, and derive something new-a tall order that you can, nevertheless, manage if you resist the temptation to skip the brainstorming steps. Remember that clinical dissection is never an aim in itself; the point of classification is to reveal and communicate something meaningful.

Examples of Classification Essays

1. Breakfast Foods

Morning, for me, is the gloomiest part of the day. I always feel that I am missing about three hours of sleep. Still, somewhere in my subconsciousness, I realize that if I don't wake up and get to where I don't want to be, usually my office, my livelihood as I know it would cease to exist! The car would be repossessed, and Fido might have to go back to the pound! What a prospect! Yet, as a cruel joke, I have to face the dilemma of what to make for breakfast as well. Being at the transitional state between dream and reality, it would help me to be more creative if the selection of breakfast foods is less limited and more enticing, but more often than not, the options include cold cereals, hot cereals, and the artery-clotting forms of food.

One of the quickest and most popular breakfast foods is cold cereal. There›s a wide selection and various name brands to choose from. For people with a sweet tooth, the choice is plentiful. For instance, Frosted Corn Flakes, made by Kellogg›s, is a grain cereal that consists of fine corn flour, sugar, sugar, and sugar, plus corn syrup, calcium carbonate, trisodiumphosphate, and topopherol to preserve freshness. For the health conscious, Honey Bunches of Oats is one of many alternatives. Made by Post, it is also a grain cereal which comes with a list of ingredients that doesn't sound like Chemistry 101! It contains corn, whole wheat, rolled oats, and brown sugar instead of processed sugar, almond, rice, and of course, honey. Sure, one can disguise a bowl of cereal with slices of banana or juicy strawberries, but that's where the excitement ends! No matter the camouflage, a bowl of cereal has the potential to become redundant quickly.

Another option that might satisfy one›s palate in the morning is hot cereal. Perhaps not as popular as cold cereal but just as quick to get to the table, this breakfast food does not fall in the «exciting» category. It does, however, command the respect of other health foods; it is wholesome and known to lower cholesterol levels. The only disadvantage is its extremely fixed quantity of assortment. One can only find three or four selections in any given supermarket. One of the most sold is Quaker Oats. Its ingredient is quite simple: one hundred percent rolled oats! Oats can be prepared effortlessly. With just two parts boiling water and one part oats, breakfast is served. Another variety of hot cereal, grits, is equal in taste but very different in texture. It is made of finely ground wheat and salt. It comes in twelve individual packets to a box which makes it convenient. Grits is prepared in the same manner as oats and just as quickly, so quickly that there would still be time to prepare a bowl of corn flakes instead!

The last category of the breakfast dilemma is the greasy food group which includes the likes of bacon, eggs, and their associates. This type of meal is not the quickest to make, but for certain, is the most desirable. After days of corn flakes and grits, this is a criminal›s last meal before the execution! The list of choices is endless. Topping it, of course, is bacon and eggs. Bacon comes not only in different brands but also in different thicknesses, smoked and regular. Some bacon comes with less fat than others, but all comes with much more fat than it should. Eggs come in various sizes and colors: small, medium, large, and extra-large. They're packed in half dozen, one dozen, or a baker's dozen of eighteen to a carton. Their shell's colors range from white, brown to pastel blue and pale yellow. Though there's only one way to prepare bacon, eggs can be cooked in numerous ways. They can be scrambled, hard-boiled, poached, pan fried, or made into omelettes. For those who prefer a "hardier" breakfast, a variety of sausage can be added to the menu. Pork sausage and Kielbasa sausage are the most popular. They can be baked and served sliced with warm bread. Although they're delicious, most sausage contains nitrite, a quantity. However, preferable this group of breakfast food is, it contains too much fat and cholesterol and should be consumed with moderation.

As the most important meal of the day, I wish breakfast would have more alluring choices. While cold cereal has a reasonably good taste, it incorporates too much sugar which has the power to transform a sleepy person into a zombie! Also its redundancy makes the draw of sugar less attractive. Hot cereal, though healthy, does not hold its charm for very long due to the bland taste and curdling texture once it becomes cold. The cholesterol-loaded foods, however, prevail over the rest, but because of the excessive amount of fat in these foods, they're not frequently prepared in most households. Moreover, due to the lack of time in the morning, these laborious meals cannot always be prepared. I now make larger portions for dinner and save the left-overs for breakfast the next morning. This is a healthier alternative, and it also gives me more time to sleep!

2. Types of Computers

There are a lot of terms used to describe computers. Most of these words imply the size, expected use or capability of the computer. While the term "computer" can apply to virtually any device that has a microprocessor in it, most people think of a computer as a device that receives input from the user through a mouse or keyboard, processes it in some fashion and displays the result on a screen. Computers can be divided into five according to the purpose they are used for and their capabilities.

The most familiar type of microprocessor is the personal computer (PC). It designed for general use by a single person. While a Mac is also a PC, most people relate the term with systems that run the Windows operating system. PCs were first known as microcomputers because they were a complete computer but built on a smaller scale than the huge systems in use by most businesses. A PC can come in two types (three if we include the Personal Digital Assistants (PDAs) that differ from PCs not by the working policy but in appearance as well.): Desktop and laptop. The former is not designed for portability. The expectation with desktop systems is that you will set the computer up in a permanent location. Most desktops offer more power, storage and versatility for less cost than their portable brethren. On the other hand, the laptops - also called notebooks - are portable computers that integrate the display, keyboard, a pointing device or trackball, processor, memory and hard drive all in a battery-operated package slightly larger than an average hardcover book.

Another purpose for using a microprocessor is as a workstation. The computers used for this purpose have a more powerful processor, additional memory and enhanced capabilities for performing a special group of task, such as 3D Graphics or game development.

A computer can also be used as a server. For this, it needs to be optimized to provide services to other computers over a network. Servers usually have powerful processors, lots of memory and large hard drives.

A fourth type, a main frame is the heart of a network of computers or terminals which allows hundreds of people to work at the same time on the same data. It is indispensable for the business world.

Sometimes, computers can be used for specialized fields as well. The supercomputer is the top of the heap in power and expense. It is used for jobs that take massive amounts of calculating, like weather forecasting, engineering design and testing, serious decryption, and economic forecasting.

With the increasing demand in different specialties, new adjustments are being made to microprocessors and new types of computers that serve different purposes emerge. In this ongoing process, it would not possible to put a full stop here. What we suggest is that it is better to keep an eye on the development of science in this field and keep updating our knowledge in order not to be out-of-date like the computers of old times that were as big as a room.

3. What Are You Learning In College?

Introduction

Studentship is an important period in every day's life of common people. In fact, becoming a student is a very complicated period in the life of every person. The main difficulty comes as a result of the fact that many students prove to be not prepared for the adult life. Many adult students arrive at the university with the idea that they know everything about this life. Students mistakenly think that the experience they had at school, at home, at work, and at community is enough to help them work successfully within the organization. They pay little attention to the subjects that are traditionally studies at the university. Many of the offers give students the opportunity to earn undergraduate credit for further learning. The other thing students actually lack is the college-level conceptual understanding of what they know. In many cases, problems like this hamper students from achieving positive results during their study period. In this paper I will try to review the main issues that are concerned with the major problems students may encounter in the process of their studying in college.

The issues discussed in this paper will include the following: time management, study and comprehension skills

Time management This is the primary importance issues for a number of students. The problem becomes evident within the first few days of starting college. During this time the students quickly learn the way in which their skills can be managed. In the case described, the presence of strong time management skills can make all the difference. The second recommendation is to write everything. The students are recommended to put down their schedule. Students are recommended to plan all the activities including the mirror activities such as the need to call their parents. The crazier your schedule gets, the more important becomes the issue of proper scheduling.

- *Schedule time to relax* It is strongly recommended not to forget to schedule in time to relax and breathe. This is usually done just because a person's calendar goes from 7:30 a.m. to 10:00 p.m.
- *Keep trying new systems* In the case a person's cell phone calendar is big in size, it is strongly recommended to buy a special paper. In case a person's paper keeps getting torn, it is strongly recommended to buy PDA. If a person has enough things written down each day, it is means that there is enough space for color-coding. Eventually it means that many students are able to accomplish their programs without some kind of calendaring system.

The other important things include the following:

- *making allowance for flexibility*
- *planning events head*

Study and comprehension skills

Reading Comprehension is one important thing to be acquired in the process of work. The strategy can be used to find the main idea in each paragraph of a reading assignment. The use of the strategy is very helpful in comprehending the information that has been contained in your assignment. The reading of the entire paragraph is important while getting the idea of what the paragraph is about. In this case it is rather helpful to whisper the words that once have been pronounced. The knowledge of the above mentioned material can help to examine, decide and put down all the needed information.

College can be regarded as a way to acquire skills that would enable the students to achieve their goals. For the majority of students entering the college can be regarded as a goal in itself. It has been estimated that students need certain time to sit down and figure out what their next goals would be.

Students are projected to achieve a number of short-term and long-term goals. As for a college student, there are a number of short-term goals that can be attained on the basis of a certain GPA that is usually achieved at the end of the semester. That is why I strongly recommend the students to get involved in a club or organization, or to turn in all assignments on time. The goals mentioned above can be classified as long-term goals. These may include gaining an internship, starting a new club or organization. The engagement in the above mentioned activities may help the students grow up as the people who are able to meet their goals.

Conclusion

In this essay I attempted to group and summarize the main problematic issues that might be encountered by the students while entering the university. The discussion of these problems is very important due to the following reasons: (1) the problem is a wide spread one; (2) a good advice may change the things for better. The issues discussed included the need of proper time management schedule. The other issues that are discussed include the issue of study and comprehension and the need to achieve goals.

Bibliography:

Setting and achieving goals in college. http://www.helium.com/items/785558-setting-and-achieving-goals-in-college